THE PHILOSOPHY
OF HUMAN RIGHTS

Contributions in Philosophy

THE PHILOSOPHY
OF HUMAN RIGHTS
International
Perspectives

EDITED BY ALAN S. ROSENBAUM

CONTRIBUTIONS IN PHILOSOPHY, NUMBER 15
GREENWOOD PRESS
WESTPORT, CONNECTICUT

Grateful acknowledgment for permission to reprint is made to:

Librairie Generale de Droit et de Jurisprudence for *Droit, Morale et Philosophie* by Ch. Perelman (Paris: Librairie Generale de Droit et de Jurisprudence, 1976), pp. 67-73.

Library of Congress Cataloging in Publication Data

Main entry under title:

The Philosophy of human rights.

    (Contributions in philosophy ; no. 15
ISSN 0084-926X)
    Includes bibliographical references and index.
    1. Civil rights—Philosophy—Addresses, essays,
lectures. I. Rosenbaum, Alan S.
JC571.P48   323.4 '01   79-6191
ISBN 0-313-20985-5 lib. bdg.

Library of Congress Catalog Card Number: 79-6191
ISBN: 0-313-20985-5
ISBN: 0084-926X

First published in 1980

Greenwood Press
A division of Congressional Information Service, Inc.
88 Post Road West, Westport, Connecticut 06881

Printed in the United States of America

10 9 8 7 6 5 4 3 2 1

81-2152

To Mary, Emily, and Jascha

Contents

Preface

Attention is drawn in this volume to the various philosophical traditions presupposed by some of the inevitable differences of opinion that have characterized the international dialogue on human rights. Whereas the papers were selected in part to represent contrasting viewpoints on the human rights issue, we must view human rights as less an issue than a philosophical idea whose related concepts may be rooted in diverse traditions. Notwithstanding the obvious differences of perspective, each of the philosophers contributing to this volume has directed his inquiry to either the foundation, meaning, or the application of human rights as discussed in Part 1.

Several of the contributors have chosen to discuss the foundation of human rights from a particular religious or cultural frame of reference. In this manner, they have sought to demonstrate the universality of the organizational principles which can function as reference points for a human rights theory. Modern readers expect that a general statement about the philosophy of human rights should include some interpretation of human rights issues from the metaphysical/theological perspective. In the context of the philosophy of religion, Abraham Kaplan explains that Judaism stresses the individual's rights and personal responsibilities. In this respect, it is important to distinguish between individualism and human rights, because the concept of human rights does not always presuppose individualism. Kaplan shows that the vision of social justice as preached by the great prophets is probably the most significant contribution that Judaism has made to Western culture. In acknowledging the strong ethical basis of Jewish philosophy, Kaplan does not assume a purely metaphysical approach. His view of Judaism would hold that rights confer obligations, but also that higher obligations themselves confer rights.

R. J. Henle demonstrates that the concept of human rights as seen from a Catholic point of view has its foundations both in the ancient and medieval doctrines of natural law and in the more recent idea that morality is an expression or natural result of the human love of God. Accordingly, he indicates that a social awareness of human rights and duties evolves from a life that is based upon reason and charity.

In an alternative philosophical view, Henle proposes that human rights are based upon reciprocal relationships between human beings both as individuals and as members of groups. He concludes that the "possessors" of human rights are not isolated, single individuals but rather multiple individuals united in moral social relationships. For example, the right to a certain item of property is, fundamentally, a relationship between persons involving the use of such property. Henle distinguishes between a religious and a nonreligious understanding of human rights, each of which should challenge the critics of a religious basis of human rights. In opposition to the prima facie view of human rights, Henle shows that the reciprocal *relationship* between the metaphysical and ethical levels of human rights can function as a standard for social relations in the human community.

Ch. Perelman addresses the concept of human rights from the perspective of a secular rationalism. The characterization that he presents of a "philosophy of the reasonable" is important because it acknowledges the rights of persons to contribute effectively to the concrete progress of rational thought. In addition, it confronts those critics of human rights who believe that the concept of human rights should be dismissed in the absence of absolute criteria for validation. In its focus on situation-dependent interpretations of human rights, Perelman's theory seems to be related to the newer prima facie position as articulated by Kaufman, whereby potentially overriding considerations can interfere in the application of human rights. Nevertheless, Perelman cannot interpret human rights as arbitrary even though he sees them as derived concepts. Rather, they retain an absolutist quality in that they are derived from rationality, which itself is an *intrinsic* characteristic of human beings. In this respect, Perelman's view is somewhat intermediate between absolutist and relativist positions and can best be classified as a secular (nontheological) metaphysical approach to the human rights concepts.

Seyyed Nasr's outline of the general principles of human freedom underscores the differences between Western and traditional Islamic views of human nature as essential to the concept of human rights. In his chapter he seeks to analyze not only the foundations but also the meaning of human rights. Accordingly, he demonstrates that freedom is taken seriously within Islam even though its meaning is interpreted differently from most Western views. In brief, the various individual freedoms are circumscribed by the well-being of the spiritual community of Islam; these freedoms are ultimately acquired as "rights" through the individual's quest for God. Neither the Islamic view nor the secular human rights doctrine holds that human beings have a right to limitless individual freedom of action (as believed by some early Western liberals). Nevertheless, they do agree that "human nature," culture, and a concept of community are basic to a definition of freedom rights. Nasr's position is the Eastern correlate in ethical terms to the interpretation that higher obligations (for example, to a Divine Being) confer rights, each of which in turn has its own correlative duty.

The historical importance of Nasr's chapter is accentuated by the fact that it was received shortly before the events in Iran in which the Shah was deposed and political power transferred to Iran's Islamic religious leaders. Accordingly, it is referenced to the tensions between political authority and the religious interpreters of Islam which assumes a special significance in this context.

In a similar vein, Ishwar Sharma's chapter approaches the concept of freedom in an alternative metaphysical aspect. Sharma's main thesis in his work is that the freedom of the self is at the core of human nature and the protection of this freedom is, thus, a safeguard for human rights. In his metaphysics of human nature, Sharma identifies the dynamic functions of the human self: the intellectual, the emotional, and the volitional. He asserts that these functions must be integrated in each individual in order to promote and maintain human creativity. By implication, a universal and balanced system of freedoms and restraints on the societal level would provide a framework for respecting the dignity of equal membership in society for all individuals. To offer a contrast to this proposed framework, he draws from leading Western philosophical traditions for examples of incomplete and unbalanced conceptions of the human self. Finally, Sharma explains that, although religious and scientific theories of human rights may carry certain universal traits, they lack (respectively) an appreciation for rational, scientific objectivity, and for effective subjectivity. However, he concludes that a comprehensive humanistic view of human rights can encompass both the objective and subjective elements required by a balanced theory of human nature.

In the last chapter of Part 2, Peter K. Y. Woo rejects the Western individualist basis for human rights as an inappropriate model for a Chinese conception. Woo discusses the ethical concepts of universal harmony, compassion, and duty in Chinese philosophy. In tracing these notions to their roots in Buddhism, Taoism, and Confucianism and to their expressions in the constitution of the modern Chinese Republic, Woo notes that the theory of individualism has no true counterpart in Chinese thought. Instead, the Chinese ethical theories hold that human life is predominantly social, with the family or community as the basic unit of human relations. Professor Woo discusses how differences in the conception of human nature can lead to certain international and crosscultural conflicts about human rights. Professor Woo's approach is uniquely a total cultural approach to the foundation of human rights—metaphysical/theological, ethical, historical, and political. It demonstrates how an alternative to the Western natural law doctrine can also offer a metaphysical foundation for human rights without altering the basic conception of rights and duties as derived from the nature of human life.

In Part 3, some chapters extend their investigation of the foundations of human rights to analyses of their meaning in contemporary philosophical discourse. Philosophical inquiry on the meaning of human rights may be approached from various perspectives. One method seeks to investigate the *general* meaning of human rights through a categorical or contextual analysis of component ethical notions. A related method seeks to investigate the meaning of the categories themselves by means of a comparative or contrastive analysis.

R. S. Downie's argument is an unusual attempt to clarify a problem that all believers in human rights eventually must face, namely, the recognition and reestablishment of general standards for deciding in *particular* cases which phenomena are truly human rights. In Downie's argument, human rights attain a universal character as acts of claiming which do not prejudice the rights claims of others. Socioeconomic rights, therefore, may count as *moral* rights but not as universal (human) rights because, if they involve compulsion, they can be applied only at the expense of the rights of others. Downie asserts that the well-being of society is impoverished when civil and political rights (as the universal type of rights) are denied. Downie's position challenges the human rights taxonomy established through the Universal Declaration of Human Rights, which ascribes both social/economic *and* political/civil rights to the same category.

Andrew Levine assumes that human rights are best understood as claims to conditions for fulfilling human nature. He uses a Hobbesian notion of freedom as a basis for this view of rights because he regards Hobbes as one of the most influential originators of Western liberal theory in which human rights claims have been formulated. However, since rights claims vary with diverse conditions, they are formulated forensically. Thus, Levine assumes that the Hobbesian view of freedom is a presupposition that leads to the arbitrary meaning of human rights in the liberal tradition. Contrary to Downie's view, which restricts the meaning of human rights but does not hold them to be arbitrary, the substance of Levine's chapter is an attack on the view that human rights claims have a fixed meaning. However, he concedes in his work that certain appeals to human rights have positive value in their unique articulation of the claims of liberal theory and politics for human dignity. The substances of human rights, in this view, would be found more in the acts of claiming than in the absolute nature of the claims themselves.

Efraim Shmueli approaches the concept of human rights from a more global perspective, investigating aspects of both foundation and meaning.

Specifically, Shmueli explores the significance of human rights within human affairs and in what context their meaning is revealed. He argues that a full definition of self-realization should include the modern idea of human rights because certain freedoms are essential to self-realization. Since the idea of human freedom is often misunderstood, Shmueli seeks to clarify its role in human rights by refuting two common but erroneous claims to absolute freedom: self-creation and radical self-determination. Moreover, he is concerned that the potential for violence and conflict would be increased by unrestrained self-realization. In his view, a subversion of human rights would be "made most efficient by the achievements of modern science and technology." This theme in Shmueli's chapter points to serious issues of application that must eventually arise in any total philosophy of human rights.

As we have shown, the meanings and foundations of human rights have been diversely interpreted, with respect not only to the political but also to the philosophical forum. Perhaps the most practical contribution that a well-grounded philosophy can make to the general human rights doctrine is to clarify these issues of foundation and meaning. Accordingly, many philosophers have directed their analyses entirely to first principles, since basic agreements must exist in these matters prior to the advancement of any true theory of application. The chapters in Part 4 investigate problems of application of human rights, and thus largely stress matters of context.

However, this need not imply that all the contributing philosophers conceive of human rights as prima facie; rather it suggests that contextual considerations necessarily arise whenever the actualization or enforcement of human rights is approached. The ideal role of context in the application of rights may be conceived in varying ways. Certain philosophers in their categorization of human rights have conceived of them as restricted in category. Notably, R. S. Downie argues for a universal but relatively narrow concept of human rights. D. P. Chattopadhyaya, taking an opposite view, argues for the priority but not the exclusiveness of certain human rights. Not only does he assess three distinct theories of justice and their respective roles in the application of human rights, but he also identifies typical difficulties in the construction of a theory of justice: those that result from concealed and relative sociological postulates. In this vein, Chattopadhyaya criticizes John Rawls' theory of justice for its tendency to universalize human rights without contextual considerations. Of special interest is Chattopadhyaya's discussion of contextual differences in the sociopolitical institutions in India and China: these differences are shown to account for (but not condone) certain failures in respecting human rights.

Leslie Armour's paper treats both the meaning and the application of the rights of the individual and the rights of the group. The first issue addressed by Armour concerns the prevention or resolution of clashes between individual rights and group rights. He offers, for example, the entitlement of the

French-speaking majority in Quebec to be educated in their native language —a "right" which collides in current realities with the corresponding entitlement of minority individuals who prefer to be educated in English. As there appears to be no protocol for applying individual rights in the context of rights claims for groups, Armour addresses whether groups indeed have rights (human rights) in the same basic sense as do individuals. He argues that the notion of personal identity as the primary source of human rights can be applied equally to groups and to individuals. The establishment of certain types of rights for groups actually improves the effectiveness of a system of individual rights.

Of particular interest are Armour's statements about how to define a group and how best to determine its legitimacy. These statements seek to integrate group rights with moral individualism (the conceptual basis of classical human rights) attempting to avoid the ascription of basic moral rights to groups in an arbitrary manner. According to Armour, members of "illegitimate" groups like the Ku Klux Klan or the Nazis possess rights by virtue of their humanity but not by virtue of their membership in these types of groups. On the other hand, membership in "bona fide" groups does confer basic rights. Thus, his criteria for distinguishing between legitimate and illegitimate groups are essential for holding that group rights are also human rights.

Unlike the community-based theory of human rights as expressed by Woo, or the "group rights" theory as expressed by Armour, Tibor Machan's approach to the theory of human rights is based on a thoroughgoing individualism. In his view, human rights are a priori, they are rooted in human nature, and they are fundamental to a free and just society. In many respects, Machan's analysis of human rights is a metaphysical analysis of their foundations. However, Machan expands upon this presupposed human rights construct toward a theory of application. He defines human rights and their correlative duties as consistent social principles that place moral limits on what individuals may do to one another and on what government may do to citizens. It is on the basis of this definition that Machan criticizes the United Nations Universal Declaration of Human Rights and certain features of contemporary "liberation" movements. Machan's chapter offers us an example of how a philosopher can investigate human rights applications while opposing a prima facie interpretation of the fundamentals of those rights.

It has been my aim as editor to provide an international forum for the expression of contemporary philosophical perspectives on the conception of human rights. The contributions to this volume have illuminated certain aspects of human rights theory that many philosophers regard as important in shaping the modern conception of human rights. It is evident that the concept of universal human rights has been changing progressively in order to accommodate the variety of demands for human freedom, equality, and dignity by people from different cultural and philosophical traditions around the world. Indeed, the growing list of human rights reflects the diverse conditions and aspirations of these people. Unless we, as members of a universal human community, are willing to recognize seriously that people from cultures different from ours may have valuable and legitimate things to say about human rights, the "human rights" question can always be side-stepped by ideology and partisan politics. Therefore, it is my hope that this volume will contribute to the necessary exploration and clarification of crucial philosophical ideas behind the international controversies that are being framed in the language of human rights.

Acknowledgments

As editor (and contributor) to this volume, I wish to express my sincere appreciation of the encouragement and help I have received during the various phases of its preparation. It is a very real pleasure to be able to thank the many distinguished contributors for their cooperativeness and promptness and for their belief in the importance of my project from its beginnings.

To Leslie Armour (Ottawa), Melvin Rader (Seattle), and John Mourant (State College, Pennsylvania) I owe a special debt of thanks. Their suggestions and critical readings of my own paper, entitled "Editor's Perspective on the Philosophy of Human Rights," greatly improved its accuracy, organization, clarity, and overall readability. Any shortcomings in the finished work are mine to bear—and only mine.

My thanks are due to Ch. Perelman for his approval of our translation of his paper into English and for his permission (and that of his former publisher's) to publish it. George Leibacher was responsible for this translation and assisted in preparing the index and proofreading the text. His perseverance and cheerfulness under the most difficult personal circumstances make his contribution a very special one for which I am grateful. Also, I acknowledge with many thanks Helen Tien, the translator of Peter K. Y. Woo's paper: her enthusiasm and interest in my project is greatly appreciated.

I am obliged to James T. Sabin, vice-president of the Greenwood Press, and to his editorial staff, for believing in my project and for enduring the countless editorial exchanges essential to its completion. My thanks to both Cindy Bellinger and Mary Persanyi for giving so much of themselves to the typing of my manuscript.

To my wife, Mary, I owe the deepest thanks for the many, many hours she spent in discussing human rights and related philosophical matters, the ins and outs of manuscript preparation, and in helping to correct my more egregious mistakes and to proofread the innumerable drafts, which were often unceremoniously placed before her. And without the ever-present love, understanding, and patience of my two children, Emily Rose and Jascha William, this volume would have yet to appear.

PART 1

Introduction: The
Editor's Perspectives on the
Philosophy of Human Rights

Introduction

The Editor's Perspectives on the Philosophy of Human Rights

In recent years, human rights have received increasing attention in political and intellectual spheres as a basis for international moral policy. International diplomacy is framed in the language of human rights, and the elite press maintains a central role in publicizing human rights dialogue. Not only do politicians appeal to universal standards of justice in their censure of human rights violators, but organizations have been founded to document and assess human rights disputes. Although over three decades ago the United Nations adopted the Universal Declaration of Human Rights as a universal expression of the human rights doctrine, it remains a highly contentious issue in current world politics. We shall examine the philosophical dimensions that may be said to underlie these political controversies.

This volume is a collection of essays on human rights by prominent philosophers from many different regions of the world, intended for readers who are interested in the human rights question primarily from a philosophical perspective. The essays discuss human rights in terms of leading philosophical and cultural traditions, thus offering the general reader a framework for discussing and understanding human rights on an international basis. Each essay has been written specifically for this volume to illuminate a preselected feature of human rights philosophy.[1] Thus, each essay falls into one of the major parts of the book: "The Foundations of Human Rights"; "The Meaning of Human Rights"; or "The Application of Human Rights." Each essay is preceded by a headnote defining its philosophical context and relationship to the other essays.

By bringing together this variety of viewpoints from eminent scholars, I hope to contribute to the process of making crucial facets of human rights theory available to those who believe cultural and philosophical traditions have important things to say about human rights.

This introduction presents an overview for analyzing the philosophy of human rights and outlines three major sections to establish a general framework for subsequent chapters in this volume. The first section of this introduction, "Human Rights Today," gives a broad introductory focus to the topic of human rights as a complex idea; thus the significance of human rights is presented as an idea of (potentially) universal scope but with somewhat controversial interpretation in several fields of inquiry. These divergences and convergences of orientation are summarized in terms of the often complementary roles of politics and philosophy in the forging of the human rights theory.

In the second section, "The Western Historical Foundations of Human Rights" are traced from the cognate concepts in classical Greek and Roman philosophy up to the twentieth century. The customary century markers form the natural subheadings for the evolutionary themes treated in this section. The leading contributors are noted in each century, as is their collective impact on forging what has emerged in the twentieth century as a "human rights" doctrine.

The final section of this survey, "Recent Philosophical Perspectives on Human Rights," points out that the concept of human rights today is an idea of global concern. However, the section presents certain controversies in twentieth-century philosophical analysis over the meaning and universality of human rights, by discussing: the various definitions of "human rights" as a general category; the definitions and identification of particular human rights; and four theoretical principles for the analysis and justification of human rights.

HUMAN RIGHTS TODAY

Human rights can be defined, in a modern sense, as the ultimate legitimate basis for a universal human community. *Human community* then refers to an ideal association of human persons that is conceived for the individual and collective benefit of its members. Furthermore, such an association typically implies that a social and political order with its roots in democracy is most befitting to humanity. First, it is necessary to call attention to at least two factors that make the concept of human rights a complex notion: (1) its philosophical features are interwoven with political considerations, and (2) it combines some terminological distinctions in a confusing manner.

It is commonplace to assume that human rights are nearly synonymous with natural rights, individual rights, social rights, or community rights. Although all are philosophically related concepts, each has a discrete linguistic and historical tradition. Indeed, human rights cannot be understood apart from the evolutionary history of these various concepts; they each conform to different facets of the human rights idea, as a breakdown of human rights categories will demonstrate in the final section of this chapter. Yet, the spirit of human rights is far more universal than its component rights categories; according to most formulations, each and every human individual retains his human rights regardless of the particular society in which he lives or the extent to which such rights are recognized. Caution must be taken to avoid confusing "universal" and "natural" with the related concept of "inalienability," as the province of either nature or society cannot be distinguished in any final way. In spite of its centuries-old lineage, there is something unique about the modern human rights idea. It bridges a gap, conceptually, between individualism and collectivism in its emphasis on humanity. Whereas individualism connotes a kind of personal identity, humanity intimates a basic community of human individuals.

The Significance of Human Rights

The significance of the human rights concept can be demonstrated by its importance in both politics and philosophy. In politics it functions as an attractive concept because it provides an ideal basis on which to conceptualize and organize a human community. In this sense "human rights" is linked to certain interpretations of democracy,[2] and gets to the heart of what it means in these times to be considerate of a human being. On the other hand, when democracy is defined as majority government based on equality, certain implicit dangers may befall human rights. Tocqueville warned that "democratic communities . . . call for equality in freedom; and if they cannot obtain that, they still call for equality in slavery."[3] For these reasons, the concept of human rights should not be identified too closely with democracy, which particularly "in the turbulence of contemporary thought and action can acquire a bewildering variety of meanings."[4] Indeed, the language of democratic thought as seen on a worldwide scale has become somewhat inflated and thereby drained of significance. "Human rights" captures the basic democratic values of the absolute moral worth of being human, particularly with respect to community life, but appears to override the ideological tangle surrounding the diversely interpreted idea of democracy.

Judging from the relative scarcity of human rights discussion in contemporary philosophical literature, the value of human rights for philosophy has yet to be fully recognized. In those cases where it is more systematically and broadly examined, it comes to be valued conceptually as a community-based morality that does not submerge the basic interests of the individual human being in the presumably more important interests of community life. In addition, the human rights concept offers a rational connection between the private and public spheres of life, something that extreme individualism fails to do. Thus one's personal belief in the various human rights compels one to uphold them in all departments of human conduct, ranging from morality and politics to law and economics. The justification and force of human rights stems from the values that reflect the meaning of being human, so that the "human person" becomes a philosophical value term whose normative significance may require further examination.

Debates in the Field of Human Rights

A brief survey of the convergence and divergence of opinions in the general human rights literature should bring to light the significant lacunae in the treatment of human rights and, hopefully, establish an orientation and justification for the approach taken in this volume. To facilitate the discussion, distinctions will be made between dialogue occurring in the literature and in the world political arena.

From a political perspective, the conception of human rights has at least three matrices, each corresponding to one of three major political camps: Western liberalism, Marxist socialism, and Third World "self-determinationism." The ambiguity of the criteria for defining human rights in politics is a function of the relativities of the several political orientations, accounting for certain differences both in interpreting the meaning of human rights and in determining the various species of rights and their normative hierarchy. For example, differences among people(s) in resources and political expectations tend to be mirrored in the way human rights are categorized. The premium that poorer nations place on the development of their resources fosters a strong concern for *enabling* rights (or those that guarantee access to, or form real conditions for exercising, freedom rights). Nevertheless, these rights may be viewed as subordinate to *permissive* rights (those that allow individuals the freedom for certain actions) by those nations that, having developed their resources, hold to the primacy of political and civil liberties. Notwithstanding these obvious variations in perspective, one can demonstrate that important concurrences of opinion do exist vis-à-vis the basic foundations of human rights theory.

Agreements. The global attention that human rights have received may well be based on their promise as a universal framework for overcoming rivalries between peoples of different traditions. The allure is rooted in their consideration of the moral health of individuals in contemporary society. Moreover, the endorsement of the human rights idea by the United Nations and by regional associations demonstrates its meaningfulness and applicability beyond the horizons of Western liberalism.

In both politics and the philosophical literature, human rights and human dignity are considered closely associated concepts. Struggles in the name of human dignity have influenced the evolution of human rights discourse; in turn, this discourse has become the principal vehicle for the expression and valuation of dignity. Human rights advocates generally hold dignity to be an intrinsic quality of human life. Most writers imply that if, in light of their universalistic character, human rights go unrespected, human life itself is vitiated. It is argued that respect for human rights ought to be unconditional because a denial of them anywhere poses a threat against peoples' rights everywhere.

There is a general agreement in the philosophical literature about what sorts of questions should be asked about human rights: What is a human right? Do human rights exist apart from legislative enactments? Are human rights distinguishable from other rights, and on what criteria? Most writers concede, or exemplify in their positions, that intellectual responses to such questions are usually framed in the perspective of Western liberalism.

To summarize the agreements on human rights: Most writers acknowledge that a human rights discourse assumes the character of the perspective from which it is conceived; the divisiveness in the formulation of human rights theory is directly attributable to differences in perspective based on practical circumstances, needs, interests, and conflicts. Yet, in another sense, as a universal phenomenon, human rights principles are held to underscore what all persons have in common in spite of their differences. Finally, human rights are claimed only by persons against other persons (or groups of persons) and never against either a god or nonhuman animals; nevertheless, some do regard human rights as divinely sanctioned or as a humanitarian gesture extensible to other species.

Controversies. In spite of a widespread endorsement of the general principles of human rights, there have been certain divergences of opinion and disagreements over the specific interpretations of issues in both philosophical and political contexts. In international politics, differences of culture, national traditions, and political interests must be counted for their impact on the conception of human rights. In support of this claim, a survey of UN debates and voting patterns on human rights issues indicates that many nations have self-imposed standards for their definitions of human rights. In this context, some conclude that human rights criticism is irrelevant and meddlesome unless it issues from one's own internal (political) criteria. Others believe that a broad interpretation of human rights philosophy shows how to overcome narrow self-interest in the international realm as a concession to world peace and security.

Another area of debate about human rights occurring on the level of international diplomacy concerns the terms in which the topic is advanced. In some instances it is denounced as an instrument of political propaganda and opportunism; an opposing view asserts that, despite the partisan treatments of human rights, outside benefits accrue that ultimately justify the continued usage of human rights ideals as a moral standard in the world political arena. What is generally overlooked in both politics and the literature is that differences in the criteria for defining human rights must be recognized before the concept can be clarified.

As a source of some political debate with correlative discussions in the philosophical literature, questions are raised about whether and under what conditions human rights should be given practical effect; but even given an appropriate codified legal structure for human rights, the criteria for their enforcement remain a matter of dispute. For example, the issue is yet unresolved whether human rights legislation and enforcement should be exclusively matters of national concern, or whether they would best be treated in the international sphere through such mechanisms as the United Nations or the International Court of Human Rights. Discussions in the philosophical literature generally follow the world political trend toward unilateral interpretations of human rights issues, rarely incorporating other than Western liberal formulations.

In response to these omissions, this volume appeals to an international spectrum of scholarly opinion in order to broaden the dimensions of the philosophical dialogue on human rights. It is premised on the belief that the future significance of human rights will be determined in a transcultural, international context. The human rights question today is usually raised in connection with international law and politics; philosophy plays a more tangential role. Nevertheless, in the past, philosophers were often at the center of "natural rights" controversies along with jurists and politicians. The contribution of this volume toward increasing the role of philosophy in current human rights discussion should not only update and extend the "natural rights" lineage but, more important, it should offer the systematic analysis required for an adequate clarification and explanation of the topic.

The close connection between philosophy and politics with respect to the natural law tradition (and more recently, the developing human rights tradition) will be addressed in the remainder of this chapter. Indeed, the significance of the concept of human rights cannot be appreciated without an understanding of its formative influences. Hence, the human rights concept will be explored here, initially from an historical perspective, tracing its parallel and intersecting traditions in philosophy and politics with special emphasis on twentieth-century trends.

THE WESTERN HISTORICAL FOUNDATIONS OF HUMAN RIGHTS

The history of the evolution of human rights is associated with what may be called the natural law tradition. In other words, many writers simply take "human rights" as it is generally regarded today to be merely a reinstatement of a much older but frequently criticized theory about the source of moral value, namely, the doctrine of natural law. The rationale behind its latterday rehabilitation will be explored later.

At present, it is true that human rights are not solely an expression of Western liberalism (with which natural law has come to be associated). Human rights today cuts across boundaries. However, the universality of the idea is separable from the history of how it rose to recognition in the context, politically speaking, of a powerful tradition beginning with the ancient Greeks. Because of the importance of human rights in the twentieth century and the way they evolved, their evolution will be traced through the natural law tradition. We should keep in mind that certain current nonliberal viewpoints are traceable to the concepts from which natural law springs. A discussion will then follow about twentieth-century human rights conflicts and issues, showing the profound influence of natural law on the human rights dialogue but also showing how nonliberal views can still accept human rights. In general, I suggest that any final global perspective on human rights will have to include an assessment of the impact non-Western, nonliberal philosophies have had on their conception. Some of the writings in this volume should contribute toward this assessment.

The doctrine of human rights that predominantly influenced the writings of the Universal Declaration[5] is found in the western European interpretation of human rights as an evolved concept in the natural law tradition. By way of introduction, it is interesting to mention that prior to the use of the term *human rights*, such rights were typically called the *rights of man* or *natural rights*. While the difference is more than terminological, the name change was suggested by Eleanor Roosevelt in 1947 and used in the English text of the Universal Declaration. (Thomas Paine may have been the first to use the term *human* rights, in his English translation of the French *Declaration*.)

The Classical Roots of "Human Rights"

The Western heritage of human rights as a normative ethical concept predates classical Greek philosophy and is likely grounded in ancient religious teachings and myths. Philosophers as a rule trace the human rights idea back to its philosophical inception in classical Athenian democracy and in the Stoical influence on Roman jurisprudence. The classical Greeks viewed nature as the objective standard for the instruction of human social conduct. As such, this view was the first major formulation in the history of human rights. The sophists are known to have distinguished between convention (*nomos*) and nature (*phÿsis*), both of which were used to analyze human morality in society. Human behavior and the principles of natural justice were seen as governed by natural law whose ultimate knowledge might be approached through a systematic description of the type of behaviors that ought to occur in society. Conventional morality, on the other hand, was held to be rooted in common social opinion and not to have evolved from knowledge or wisdom, in the *phÿsis* sense. Yet, the classical Greek view recognized that conventional morality and natural law could overlap, but only coincidentally.

Politically, only the citizens of the city-state—less than 50 percent of Athens' population—were the beneficiaries of the natural law. In their general defense of such inequalities, Plato and Aristotle ironically introduced numerous definitions of equality into the philosophical discourse. These various conceptions of equality function as key elements in human rights theory today: equal respect for all citizens (*isotimia*), equality before the law (*isonomia*), equality in political power (*isokratia*) and in suffrage (*isopsephia*), and equality of civil rights (*isopoliteia*). These early natural law principles were believed to be norms for virtuous social relations. They offered an egalitarian framework for the next development of human rights theory and for the later idea that the concept of equality draws its force from nature and is therefore worthy of being preserved in society.

The Roman concept of equality broadened the scope of rights issues in practical affairs to include more beneficiaries than in the Greek tradition but without altering the customary Greek view of nature. The Stoics were the foremost contributors to a natural law theory. In their philosophy, nature was conceived as a universal system of rules both physical, such as the law of gravity, and ethical, such as the obligation of all rational beings to respect one another as equals. Ethical laws could be distinguished by their interpretation of human beings not only as *natural* phenomena but also as moral entities, bound to moral social actions by conscience rather than by physical necessity.[6] Accordingly, a society derived from nature would be governed by a universal system of such laws. Thus, in viewing all rational (human) beings as naturally entitled to equal civic status, the Stoics moved beyond the more limited political standard of the Greeks. Holding that the laws of nature were elements of a "universal" order (embodied in Roman society), the Stoics believed that all persons by virtue of their nature as rational beings ought to be citizens of a single universal (Roman) community.

This original Stoical idea, as presented in the writings of Roman jurists (Ulpian, Gaius) and philosophers (Seneca, Cicero, and others), had implications for both law and philosophy. For instance, in his *Institutes*, Gaius states:

Every human community that is regulated by laws and customs observes a rule of conduct which in part is peculiar to itself, and in part is common to mankind in general. The rule of conduct which a people has settled for its own observance, and which is peculiar to that people, is termed the *jus civile*. Those principles which natural reason has taught to all mankind, are equally observed by all, and collectively are termed the *jus gentium*.[7]

Romanist legal philosophy made a crucial conceptual distinction to be used in criticizing the positive political order. It had interpreted the corpus of Roman law as universal (*jus gentium*), a view that could justify the absorption into the empire of various peoples governed only by local conventional law (*jus civile*). The ethical virtues of goodness and justice were definable by the *jus gentium*, and ultimately the latter is founded on the *jus naturae*. The development of human rights theory during the Roman period reached its peak in the concept of universalistic equality: the Roman doctrine of natural law had imputed to humankind an elemental civic status such that all persons as members of the world community are equal.

Natural Law Theories in the Middle Ages

The human rights tradition received a different impetus in the medieval period as it became rooted in the religious consciousness of humanity. The doctrine of natural law was reinterpreted in a theological tradition. The philosophers of Christianity, particularly Saint Thomas Aquinas, redefined the system of natural law as divinely willed; thus both ethical and physical laws were viewed as objective and good by virtue of the reason and perfection of God. Furthermore, Saint Thomas considered natural laws to be knowable through the faculty of human reason. Natural law theory in the Middle Ages posited an inevitable duality of human existence: persons were seen to be subject to the authority of both God and mankind. This duality was reflected in the pyramidal feudal structure in which the king, although *rex gratia dei*, nevertheless was subject to God's law (that is, King John's concession in the Magna Carta of 1215 meant that English royal authority, like its subjects, was constrained by divine rules). The Christian belief in a "universal brotherhood of humanity" held the person to be an individual apart from his membership in the state. This distinction can be considered the conceptual precursor to the emergence of both individualism as a political theory and the notion of "freedom" rights, each exerting its extensive influence on the formation of the human rights concept.

Natural Rights in the Seventeenth Century

In the modern tradition of human rights, the growth of individualism reinterpreted the person as an individual without regard for his religious or civil status. It was during the seventeenth century in Europe that this development had its greatest impact on the human rights idea.

In an important break with the scholastic tradition, the Dutch jurist Hugo Grotius's *On the Law of War and Peace* (1625) gave further impetus to the secularization of natural law theory. In his effort to prevent the abuse of political power by religious zealots, Grotius developed a nonempirical "scientific" method to justify rationally the provisions of the positive law. Grotius's model conformed to the axiomatic character of geometry in that a set of deducible propositions yielded the self-evident foundations of a universal, immutable order. Thus, natural law, both physical and moral, was held to be "so unalterable that God Himself (could) not change it";[8] yet, by virtue of the axioms, it could be known through the faculty of human reason. This view is somewhat similar to the classical natural law theory in its appeal to reason, and it remained essentially unchanged throughout the tradition of medieval Christianity. However, according to Grotius, the authority and validity of his mathematical model and of the "right rules of reason" could be established independently of the existence of God. Human rights from this secularized perspective would be considered as nonarbitrary, natural, self-evident principles based on the insight of all individual rational beings.

Throughout the seventeenth century and supported by the philosophy of rationalism, natural law came to be understood as protective of the subjective interests and rights of individual persons. This new interpretation, most prominently articulated in the writings of John Locke[9], was a significant departure from earlier theories in which natural law was taken to be merely a natural set of objective norms.

It was Locke who used the theory of natural law as a foundation for a theory of natural rights, and who claimed that the individual possesses, by nature, the rights to life, liberty, and property. These have been called personal freedom rights because respect for them is unthinkable without allowing for each individual a certain range of personal choice and action against public encroachment. Locke argued that the mechanism of a *social contract* (the implicit voluntary social union of all individuals) justifies the role of society as a preserver of the individual's natural rights as well as the institution of government as executor of such rights in society. In Locke's view, natural (human) rights are morally inviolable in a state of nature but enforceable only in a civil society that holds an obligation to protect such rights through the social contract. It was through the innovative contributions of Locke in the seventeenth century that natural rights theory (as a precursor to the human rights doctrine) became recognized as legitimately asserted by all individuals everywhere and obligatorily respected by government as a first condition of its own legitimacy.

Locke used his individualistic theory of rights to justify the supremacy of parliamentary government, that is, the rights of Englishmen against the crown and the Glorious Revolution (1688) in England. The effect of his writings on eighteenth-century political philosophy, particularly Jefferson's and Paine's, is unmistakable. For instance, Jefferson's well-known phrase (in the U.S. Declaration of Independence, 1776) "life, liberty and the pursuit of happiness" was both a modification and expansion of the meaning of Locke's natural rights to "life, liberty and property" (in the second of his "Two Treatises on Government").

In summary, the private sphere of individual life in the seventeenth century was held to embody the natural roots of morality and therefore was considered more important than the public sphere. Thus, the conceptions of universal moral equality and the individual's freedom rights became the main focus of most natural law theories of the day.

The European Enlightenment and Natural Rights

Natural rights theories continued to flourish through the 1700s and for the first time in history became the basis of two national declarations, the American and the French. The American and French revolutions gave social effect to the idea of universal individual "equality before the law." European philosophy in this so-called Age of Reason tended to express the prominent concerns of the day, namely, the liberation of the individual from absolute authority and of human reason from dogma. The effect of the European Enlightenment on natural law theory was to underscore the individual autonomy of reason and morality.

The philosophical views of Immanuel Kant and Jean Jacques Rousseau figured prominently in the development of the human rights lineage in the tradition of the eighteenth-century Enlightenment. Kant's philosophy followed in the same tradition of rationalism as Grotius and Locke in its appeal to a formal, nonempirical system of reason and its support of the free will of the rational individual as upheld through the liberal ideals of the American and French revolutions. Although Kant's ethical absolutism did not contradict the values of his pious Protestant upbringing, neither did it depend upon divine sanction for its validity; as such, it completed the secularization of natural rights begun a century earlier.

Rejecting pragmatism and utilitarian views, Kant sought to establish the validity of his ethical theory through only a priori principles: unconditional, universal, and imperative maxims. Empirical knowledge and hypothetical considerations of consequence he held as relevant to ethics only in the *application* of its unconditional principles. Kant saw the only absolute moral good to be the virtuous will of the rational individual formalized by the *categorical imperative*—a term that Kant used on three levels to specify the moral law governing the actions of this will.[10]

On the first level of analysis, the categorical imperative prescribed the universal nature of specific acts of duty. On the second level, Kant offered rules to define these duties so that human beings, as ends in themselves, ought not to be regarded merely as means. This view underscored Kant's belief in the intrinsic worth of the individual bound by duty to perfect his rational capacities and to "promote happiness in others."[11] On the third level of the categorical imperative, Kant specified the formulas of freedom and responsibility as distinct from the laws of physical necessity; accordingly, persons were regarded as inherently free to choose the moral law.

Although the categorical imperative was predominantly a formula of duty it was implicitly extended to rights as a correlative concept (but not by Kant). In the natural law tradition, rights were seen to be claims justified by the natural law and supported by the related natural duty. But for Kant such a rights claim made by an individual on behalf of himself could be too reflexive, and too dependent upon circumstance, to be capable of being willed as a "universal law of nature" (in its broadest sense). Nevertheless, in distinguishing between the laws of nature (of what is) and the laws of freedom (of what ought to be), Kant placed the study of ethics outside the realm of natural law. The relationship between the Kantian conceptions of freedom and of the individual as an autonomous moral finality had certain impacts on the natural law doctrine.

The will is conceived as a faculty of determining oneself to action in accordance with the conception of certain laws. And such a faculty can be found only in rational beings. Now that which serves the will as the objective ground of its self-determination is the end, and if this is assigned by reason alone it must hold for all rational beings.[12]

If Kant's ideal societal order was a union of rational, self-determining beings ("kingdom of ends"), the moral laws that would bind them could not be based on pragmatism or considerations of pure consequence, but rather would be logical and a priori, as would the moral acts or duties specified by those laws. It was this view that led to the claim that natural (or human) rights are self-evident. Some modern human rights theorists hold a Kantian view in their position that human rights are based on a relationless freedom carrying an unqualified, intrinsic importance. Of course, the extreme abstractness of this view must be somewhat qualified by the coincidental opinion that society functions best when based on morality and justice. In general, self-determination in the Kantian sense gives priority in moral affairs to individual freedom rights. Though basic to some recent Western philosophical views of human rights, this notion is in distinct contrast to the idea of *national* self-determination that is common today among so-called Third World interpretations of human rights.

For Rousseau, on the other hand, the meaning of human rights was ultimately grounded in the "general will" of society, externalized in the sovereign. Rights were considered private and originating in society, not nature. Rousseau contended that individual freedom and equality would predominate if, and only if, people obeyed the laws of society—the issue of the "general will"; only chaos would result from noncompliance to these laws. He considered society to be a natural moral association with a structure and function determined by both reason and conscience. Insofar as Rousseau linked the principle of popular sovereignty with the General Will, he relegated the subjective rights of the individual (in rebuttal to Locke) to a collective general will.[13]

The contrasting positions of Kant and Rousseau exhibit the development of the two primary human rights principles of freedom and equality in the eighteenth-century political forum. Both philosophers construed the notion of the free individual as an independent metaphysical entity. However, to Kant, true individual freedom meant doing one's duty for its own sake and also for individual self-determination, whereas to Rousseau, it implied obedience to the General Will. This dichotomy between the rights of the individual and of society continued into the nineteenth century as a serious dialectical tension; eventually it was reformulated in political terms as individualism (liberalism) versus collectivism (Marxist socialism). For instance, in the writings of John Stuart Mill, but more so in those of the Oxford idealist, Thomas Hill Green, the individualistic conception of human rights was augmented by a social conception of rights. Both attempts to redefine individualism in order to legitimize increasing necessity for "welfare state" legislation represented a further development of traditional liberal theory. In summary, the metaphysical status of the individual was either reinterpreted within a framework of abstract social relationships or else abandoned altogether. Hence, the destiny of natural rights theory came to rest upon the difficulty of holding to a static concept in a changing world.

Natural Rights in the Nineteenth Century

The general breach in nineteenth-century philosophy with the doctrine of self-evident and indestructible individual rights may be attributed to the failure of the French Revolution to institute fully the "rights of man." The Napoleonic era and the tyranny of Robespierre belied any pretensions to the inevitable predomination of natural rights. In France, Auguste Comte's criticism of the rights of man—and of democratic liberalism—was typical of the new spirit:

. . . it was useful in demolishing old feudal-military policy and in exploding the myth of divine right by insisting on the rights of man. But it was totally incapable of projecting any positive conceptions to replace those it had destroyed; every so-called liberal principle was in fact only a "dogma" created by trying to erect some criticism of the theological into a positive doctrine, e.g., the dogma of liberty of conscience—mere abstract expression (like in metaphysics), of the temporary state of unbounded liberty in which the human mind was left by the decay of the theological philosophy.[14]

Early nineteenth-century reactions. The philosophical rection in Germany was expressed in the writings of G. W. F. Hegel, and of his academic predecessor, J. G. Fichte. Both held to the view that the concept of abstract individual rights, far from being the ultimate moral standard for society, was really a characteristic of a more primitive level of morality and politics. For

Fichte, personal individuality must for the sake of national maturity yield to the individuality of peoples or nations.[15] According to Hegel, the dialectical evolution of society would involve the natural supersession of individual rights to achieve some higher ethical synthesis.[16] From another historical perspective, the philosophies of Fichte, Hegel, and Comte represented various aspects of the new social forces of the day which were rapidly transforming the shape of European society: the technological triumphs of science, the growth of industrial capitalism and the increasing conflicts between the working and commercial classes, and the rise of nationalistic politics.

The shift away from the metaphysical, and toward the empirical, interpretation of natural human rights was evident in nineteenth-century England. The utilitarian reformer, Jeremy Bentham, argued that "individual natural rights" had force only if recognized in conventional law; otherwise they would be merely rhetorical. A close reading of his writings shows that he did not reject rights altogether, but only their transcendental conception. The "cosmic evolutionist," Herbert Spencer, in rebuttal to Bentham, contended that moral principles and rights were natural evolutionary emergents necessary for human survival. Each view has at least one feature in common with modern human rights conceptions. In a sense, as Spencer might have argued, human survival today may depend upon an elementary respect for human rights; yet, in the Benthamite vein, human rights principles, unless reinforced by law, may be pointless. Nevertheless, in limiting our understanding about human rights to the domains of science or law, we interpret morals and rights as functions of established authority and thus nullify their formerly conceived critical power over existing political realities. In fact, even in the eighteenth century, David Hume had predicted the conflict that came to plague modern positivism, namely, the inability to separate, conceptually, ethical from nonethical values, or value from fact—the "ought" from the "is." In classical liberal philosophy, responses to this conflict between the metaphysical and the empirical were evident in two basic principles, often extended as both descriptive and prescriptive theories. In the early phase of liberalism the natural condition was portrayed as a fundamental antagonism between the individual and society. The utility, or "greater happiness" principle generally sought to establish and assess the value of social actions and institutions by virtue of the happiness they could produce, both qualitatively and quantitatively. The related principle of natural rights interpreted individuals as naturally free and equally entitled as moral finalities to pursue private satisfactions.[17]

John Stuart Mill and the liberalist view. The philosophical writings of J.S. Mill, following in the larger tradition of nineteenth-century liberalism, show the evolution of the classical utilitarian and natural rights doctrines. Mill's early utilitarianism, rejecting the self-evidence of natural law on empirical grounds, upheld nonconventional formal rights (human rights) as being "in the best interest of human happiness." He believed that individual behavior and social relations were ultimately compatible and governed by "natural law"[18] whose operation, both constant and regular, defied purposeful interference.

In Mill's later works, there was a confluence and modification of the basically conflicting philosophies of utilitarianism and natural rights. Mill departed from the view of traditional political economists in which the laws of nature were seen to govern the social production but not the distribution of wealth. Inasmuch as Mill postulated a "human institutional" basis for the process of distribution, he was offered the challenge of suggesting a suitable mechanism for facilitating such a process. His best response to this query (extrapolated from germane passages in his writings)[19] was to propose that distribution ought to be determined in accordance with the principles of social justice. Accordingly, one of Mill's important contributions to liberal theory was his recognition of the lessening role played by natural laws in the domain of social relations; conceptually, more control over institutions and social affairs was placed in the hands of individuals. Mill used the utility principle rather elastically throughout his work to justify both social change and acceptance of the status quo.

The concept of "right" as an indispensable component of human happiness meant that all persons were naturally entitled to equal moral consideration by others. However, Mill did not translate this idea into an unqualified advocacy of equality for all individuals, the indefensible axiom often linked with implausible types of democratic theory. The democratic idea of a "higher" moral law ultimately sanctioning social, political, and economic arrangements was accepted on utilitarian grounds. Yet Mill's utilitarian position had, by then, received certain modifications such that, as von Humboldt noted, Mill came to stress "the absolute essential importance of human development in the widest diversity."

In principle, democratic liberalism encompassed the "greater human happiness" on the ideal ground of the equal right of *all* individuals to some happiness.[20]

It was his focus on the *individual* that most clearly marked Mill as a liberal. Indeed, the centerpiece of all phases of liberalism is the theory of individualism. Mill's earlier "individual," reminiscent in many respects of some Enlightenment and early nineteenth-century philosophical formulations, was introduced in his various early writings on social science, morals, politics, and economics. In his mature writings, particularly the "Chapters on Socialism," "Thornton on Labor and Its Claims," and in sections of the *Principles of Political Economy*, Mill displayed a transitional attitude toward the individual in society, leading eventually to a reconceived individualism. His view reflected the blurred distinctions between the private and public spheres of life, long recognized in liberalism for their uncertain implications on the concept of the individual. Mill's earliest transition from "atomic" (abstract) to "social" individualism is evident in his reference to a "circle around every individual human being, which no government... ought to be permitted to overstep."[21] The limits of this circle of privacy were viewed to be best determined by concerns affecting the individual only and affecting others only by way of example; for the justification for any interference in the affairs of the individual must rest ultimately on the advocates of interference. Insofar as the circle of self-regarding interests was diminished in Mill's mature view, the notion of interference was reinterpreted to mean "sometimes warranted with qualifications," as when government might be needed to prevent social chaos or promote increased employment. The idea that government should sometimes intervene in the individual's affairs to promote the common good was a position that even in Mill's day could be regarded as socialistic.

Mill's philosophy as it bears on human rights has been treated in greater detail here as it has offered a perspective on some substantive changes that have occurred in the evolution of human rights theory. Moreover, it has raised certain critical questions on some ideas basic to human rights; for example, Are human rights public or private? What is a person, and does a person have basic rights apart from legal recognition? What is the relationship of basic human rights to the common good? and so on. In summary, Mill's concept of individual or human rights is based on a dynamic theory of individualism, holding at first that such rights are best respected when individuals are left alone (laissez-faire or "atomic" individualism), and later postulating a "social welfare" function of government to replace the noninterference function. It is typical for present-day democratic liberals to follow the tradition of Mill by placing public welfare, or equality rights, on the same level of importance as freedom rights in the view that the equalization of opportunities may be as necessary as the freedom to pursue such activities unencumbered by governmental restraint.[22] In this context, Mill's "social" individual was the recipient of these welfare rights and so, in connection with society, attained his greatest freedom.

Recent social liberals such as L. T. Hobhouse and John Dewey recognized Mill as the foremost architect of the liberalist response to the demand of the working class for more, and better, social legislation. Thomas Hill Green may be cited as perhaps a more consistent but less influential social liberal than John Stuart Mill. Certainly, both philosophers encountered similar difficulties regarding basic human rights: how to avoid the conflicts between the rightful powers and immunities of the individual and those of the state. Both philosophies were compelled to reconcile the "will of society" with the "will of the individual," but Green made the "general will" a condition for personal moral excellence. According to Green, human rights should be defined in the context of social life, because human beings (as naturally *social* creatures) pursue moral self-perfection. Since social institutions were thus seen as objective expressions of human moral progress, governmental assistance could only increase the individual's chance for self-perfection. Green believed that the endurance of a free society would require political, social, and economic rights to be safeguarded by the state. From the classical liberal standpoint, this positive libertarian concept effectively complemented the traditional view of negative liberty—the absence of external obstacles and restrictions on the freedom of the individual's actions and choices. Green's philosophy of the ideal society involved a blending of both freedom and equality rights within the tradition of democratic liberalism. Some further discussion about the continued changes in individualism, politics, and philosophy will better convey the nature of certain conceptual conflicts in human rights theories, especially those about "the individual" in whom basic rights are assumed to reside. The ideological disputes between democratic liberalism and socialistic collectivism, both of western European origin, strongly influenced the meaning of individualism and played a leading role in the formulation of contemporary definitions of human rights.

Other nineteenth-century contributions: positivism and socialism. In the nineteenth-century political ideology, two parallel but less important developments occurred in the natural rights tradition that are worthy of mention only because they still retain some surface appeal. Rudolph Stammler, the neo-Kantian idealist, considered that the principles of natural law were essentially moral prescriptions for human behavior. In a general concession to the plurality of individual and social interests, he defended the idea that the application of particular principles of natural law could vary in specific situations, although (in full accord with the traditional Kantian view) he maintained the immutability of natural laws *in se*. Thus, the situation-dependency of natural law application could be understood to shape its practical meaning and the truth-value of specific rights claims; it was a natural law theory with a changing content. In social and legal matters, the formal ethic of individualism remained the standard of the day. Nevertheless, Stammler's interpretation of the Kantian universalization doctrine, the maximization of each individual's freedom consistent with the equal freedom of all other individuals, was implicitly attacked at its foundation by the nineteenth-century positivists Comte, Duguit, and others. They argued that the natural rights theory was an ideology or set of beliefs about reality supporting the self-image of the rising middle classes. As such, the abstract theory of rights that Stammler had depicted was seen by the positivists as having merely use-value without truth-value. The early Marxist socialists dismissed the notion of abstract rights as "outdated bourgeois ideology." They adapted whatever truth-value it might have had to their own programs of socialistic reconstruction, arguing that the "freedom" rights of the individual were meaningless in the absence of a truly egalitarian social system.

In a paper entitled "The Rights of Man in Liberalism, Socialism and Communism" (1949), Sergius Hessen, a Polish philosopher of education, examined the various interpretations of "freedom and equality" within the general philosophies of liberalism and socialism.[23] He sought to establish some common grounds for a higher synthesis and so attempted to reconcile their ostensibly conflicting views of human rights. Despite the undeniable points of convergence and mutual influence among recent conceptions of socialism and liberalism, these philosophies conveyed, particularly in the late nineteenth century, certain irreconcilable differences in their ideological commitments and in their proposals for social change.

The main contributions to human rights theory in the nineteenth century, and particularly to the ideas of freedom and equality, must be appraised with respect to the clash between (liberal) individualism and (socialist) collectivism. Whereas the liberal critique was largely directed toward social change within the capitalist framework, the Marxist critique advocated the abolition of capitalism in favor of economic collectivism.[24] Accordingly, freedom in the 1800s was construed by liberals as the general "right to determine one's own affairs" (Kant's self-determination). The *new* liberalism (of Mill, Hobhouse, and Green) emphasized both negative and positive freedoms in the context of a capitalist society. This composite idea of freedom/liberty took the form of popular, representative government and state constitutional guarantees of individual rights and liberties.

To Western democratic liberals, equality generally meant (1) the equality before the law of all members of society, as individual human beings, and the abolishment of all immoral discrimination (on the basis of sex, race, religion, color, or birthright); and (2) the equality of conditions for individual competition as a fair beginning in life (the state is duty-bound to provide "equal chances for everybody" in labor conditions and in voting power). These meanings are based on the idea of moral equality.

The unit of moral discourse in the Marxist socialist perspective could no longer be the autonomous individual as a free and equal beneficiary of God or nature. Rather, the unit became the "collectivity" whose individual members were creatures of social circumstances, acquiring "social rights" through community affiliation. This "collectivity" did not consist of merely an aggregate of social individuals but represented in its significance a social and economic interdependence with far-reaching implications. Although human interdependence and fraternity were also stressed by some philosophers in the Saint-Simon tradition (Léon Bourgeois and the French solidarists), through a "social debt" arrangement, they basically avoided the "commit-ments of revolutionary socialism." They provided for the "amelioration of glaring social abuses while maintaining untouched the existing bases of capi-talist society in private property and freedom of business enterprise."[25] The true Marxist collectivity (classless society) could be achieved only through a set of different socioeconomic conditions: (a) abolition of private property and of individual competition for a livelihood; (b) collective ownership of the means of production; and (c) centralized socioeconomic planning. Tradi-tional ideals of "freedom" and "equality" would, in such a society, no longer be issues (its defenders believed). They would lose their status as "ideals" by their derivation from unhappy socioeconomic conditions.

In the Marxist view, freedom could only mean the liberation of the working class from capitalist exploitation. All else, save the ultimate goal of classless humanism, was subordinate. Equality in the Marxist view meant *social* (not political) equality. Such a concept could not be conceived apart from the basic institutions of the collectivity and of the classless society that, by its nature, guarantees all members the equal right to satisfy basic needs and to contribute to the collective effort of production. These historical and conceptual differences have a direct bearing upon contemporary human rights politics and philosophy.

In summary, the confluence of many factors in the late nineteenth and early twentieth centuries contributed to the temporary eclipse of natural rights theory. Among the political factors, the most significant were basic ideological disputes, extreme European nationalisms and rival imperialisms for control of nonindustrial countries, the popularity of militant social Darwinist principles (ruthless competition, "survival of the fittest"), and economic competition. In addition, a formidable array of strategies against the natural rights doctrine were being felt in a wide variety of disciplines: law, politics, history, and philosophy. The abstract and formal character, and the formal meaningfulness, of natural rights came under fire in the writ-ings of Western scholars such as John Dewey, Oliver W. Holmes, Jr., and Thorstein Veblen; Wesley Hohfeld's analytic-linguistic approach to the theory of law stressed the language-dependency of the ultimate meaning of natural rights; Rudolph von Jhering conceived rights as secondary by-prod-ucts of historical struggles; Paul Vinogradoff gave a definition of right as a "range of action assigned to a particular will within the social order estab-lished by law," thereby relegating rights to the authority of the existing legal-social order; some contemptuously repudiated the liberal idea of inborn rights of the individual (Heinrich von Treitschke), whereas others attacked the liberal theory of the state, for example, by trying to separate the purpose of the law from ethics (N. M. Korkunov). Philosophically, the revolt against positivism and the excesses of scientism (Freud, Nietzsche, Bergson, Dilthey,

Croce, Weber) sought to contain the reach of the objective scientific mode of thinking. However, the net effect of this revolt was to deprive the natural rights idea of its "rational" underpinnings and, finally, of its universality.

The Twentieth-Century "Revival"

In spite of its passing eclipse, the natural (human) rights doctrine has been revived and popularized in the present century and remains one of the most powerful concepts to motivate juristic, social, political, and philosophical thought. Its regained prominence is apparent in national and international law and politics. Most modern states incorporate into their constitutions some concept of human rights. Human rights declarations have become an increasingly important feature of international relations. Also, the significance of human rights has grown in the international conduct of diplomacy. Other vehicles for expressing human rights have included favorable statements made by world leaders, treaties, conventions, and numerous nongovernmental "watchdog" groups.[26]

The chief technological and ideological influences contributing to the recent revival of the natural rights doctrine as *human* rights occurred largely in the context of an evolving international peace movement. The twentieth century had brought a sophisticated military technology, which caused international concern. To address the increasing threat which this technology posed to civilized society, organizations and alliances were initiated quite early, beginning with the Hague Tribunal in 1899 to arbitrate international conflicts, and followed in 1907 by the fourth Hague Convention to limit armaments and to regulate the conduct of war. These efforts gained impetus after World War I with the founding of the League of Nations (1920), whose intended peacekeeping function became constrained by such practical factors as its limited international membership. The 1929 Geneva Convention continued in the tradition of safeguarding the rights of civilian populations in wartime, but it was the ominous dawn of the nuclear age that gave the world peace movement greater urgency.

Among the political forces that fostered the human rights doctrine were the Nazi holocaust and the allied defeat of Axis powers in World War II. In most Western countries, these events were commonly construed as showing the supremacy of individualism (democratic liberalism) over Fascist collectivism (totalitarianism). Accordingly, there was worldwide moral outrage at Nazi militarism, racism, technologism, and at the image of a society bereft of the ideals of moral universalism and with an astonishing capacity for self-deception and rationalization.[27] By the end of the war, the concerns of the peace movement had dramatically extended in scope. No longer focusing predominantly at the level of wartime technology, "rights" concerns became redirected to the intranational (domestic) level as well, where they were often associated with certain tenets of individualism. When the United Nations was founded in 1945, it became the prime forum for pursuing international peace and cooperation, both in arbitrating issues involving armaments and technology and in expressing serious ideological disagreements about human rights concerns on a broader scale. The Nuremberg trials provided another forum for a human rights dialogue, giving international importance to domestic atrocities under the heading of "crimes against humanity."

Many other catalysts have shaped the evolving human rights tradition since its debut in the 1940s. Among these may be cited: the prospect of nuclear annihilation, coupled with a strong international desire for world peace and security; the international recognition of economic interdependence as overriding major conflicts among existing economic strategies (capitalism, communism, and national self-determination in the Third World); the global impact of terrorism, the stoppage of emigration, preventive detention and torture, racism, and sexism. Human rights have become a fundamental premise for arguments about morality in the international political dialogue. The most apparent political manifestations of the human rights idea on the world scene is the belief that a totalitarian regime may no longer victimize its own people with impunity or in virtual silence. Effective and durable human rights initiatives in the political arena must finally in the future depend on a clear, defensible conception of human rights. Since "human rights" is preeminently a philosophical notion, its intellectual value requires the unique contribution of philosophers.

The widespread appeal of the concept of human rights may now be determining its destiny at the hands of philosophers because the vanguard of human rights thinking in the twentieth century is found mainly in law and politics, not philosophy. In any event, this may be changing as evidenced by the increasing involvement of philosophers in the human rights questions. If philosophy has, in recent years, stood only as an interpreter on the outskirts of human rights discussions, perhaps it is because the overall climate of professional philosophical opinion made it unlikely that the concept of human rights would be pursued as it was traditionally understood. Though no specific philosophy, or group of philosophers, could have been responsible alone for neglecting the idea of human rights, the omission may lie generally in certain biases of the analytic and empiricist traditions, and also in the anti-scientific backlash against them. Although the modern mainstream "scientific" philosophies (naturalism, positivism, and pragmatism)[28] have certainly reflected the prestigious achievements of science, they also have fostered an atmosphere in which there is at least tacit reluctance to explore ideas beyond language, logic, or empirical fact. It had been common to dismiss nonempirical notions such as human or natural rights as being "nonscientific," metaphysical, or speculative nonsense; ethics had been separated from scientific philosophical consideration, unless ethical ideas could be found to have empirical significance, and so on. On the other hand, the reaction against scientific philosophy engendered a spate of either antiscientific philosophies or philosophies with antiscientific elements that tended to favor the "irrational" side of humanity (for example, the works of Kierkegaard, Bergson, Dilthey, Freud); and the effects of these are also still with us, as some philosophers continue to look with suspicion upon the concept of rationality as if it were synonymous with narrow "scientific" reasoning: their restrictive idea leads many in sympathy to abandon "reason" along with science.[29]

Human rights in this setting might not have survived as worthy of philosophical attention if it had not been for the historical events and political forces described above. These factors justify the lengthy treatment given to the historical foundations of human rights. Awareness of these factors is crucial for any understanding of the philosophical problems surrounding the conceptions of human rights. But it is also true that some philosophers from different traditions have attempted to explore the concept of human rights in a variety of ways. Before anyone should attempt to make a final statement about the philosophical conception of human rights as it stands today, a review of what some of these philosophers have had to say about human rights would be necessary.

RECENT PHILOSOPHICAL PERSPECTIVES ON HUMAN RIGHTS

As the preceding sections of this chapter have highlighted, the role of philosophy in the twentieth-century human rights dialogue has been virtually overshadowed by the widely publicized contributions from the realms of diplomacy and politics. Yet, as debates and disputes arise with respect to the general meanings and implications of human rights, many have found it prudent to turn to the philosophical dimension, the matrix within which these rights-related notions have received their most systematic analyses throughout the centuries.

The concomitant increase in human rights literature among philosophers may be considered a virtual reawakening of the natural law tradition to a popular application, offering a clarification of the overall significance of the concept of human rights, beyond the mere acknowledgment of its existence, and from a perspective not restricted to official declarations or political rhetoric. Nevertheless, the backlash of the human rights advocacy has included attempts to keep human rights talk as meaningless as possible. This has been done by reducing rights questions exclusively to the domestic affairs of sovereign nations; to ideological propaganda; to their historical origins; and/or to the apparently insurmountable complexities surrounding the universal application of any set of moral principles; or, finally, to their extreme abstractness and presumed arbitrary practical interpretations.

Although these philosophical perspectives differ to some extent, most philosophers agree on certain issues they consider fundamental to human rights. The advocates of these issues insist that human rights are something that we as persons have, all of us, simply because we are human beings, living among similar others. In general, the possession of a human right is regarded as being beyond the vagaries of fortune, circumstances, accomplishment, or personality; only in their uneven application do human rights become volitional or conditional.

The unbreakable link that is said to exist between human rights and human nature has been poignantly expressed by Gabriel Marcel, the late religious existentialist, as a human right written, as it were, into the very structure of a slave's own nature, for example, the slave can never entirely rid himself of the feeling that his body is his own. Philosophical views that stipulate or presuppose the association of human rights and human nature usually attempt to clarify what is meant by nature and right in order to retain the elemental ethical idea that morality is ultimately voluntary and desirable. The idea is that we can choose to do the "right" thing or act in accord with some preferred rule or standard of conduct, but this itself is a presumption about human nature which requires further philosophical examination.

Definitions of the Human Rights Concept

In basing human rights on human nature or personhood, one must have a defensible concept of the latter; otherwise, human rights will be arbitrarily defined, with no inevitable link having been established between the morality of being human and the facts of existence.[30] In companion with this problem is another equally basic one, originally raised by the eighteenth-century philosopher David Hume, namely, how facts and values are to be related.

The concept of human rights has been defined in a variety of settings by philosophers seeking to clarify its meaning and applications. The nature of the definitions given below reflects the main lines of current philosophical thinking about human rights. Moreover, it accentuates the kind of philosophical difficulties human rights theories must successfully confront. Human rights definitions generally focus upon the idea that human rights includes all, and only, human persons and is linked in a very basic way to being human. In this context, a right is a principle of justification with respect to what is due each person, and which each person must dutifully respect in others, in virtue of being human. This is what upholders of human rights believe distinguishes *human* rights from other special rights, such as legal rights, minority rights, and children's rights.

Broadly speaking, regardless of the specific approach to defining human rights, most philosophical definitions appear to fall under the heading of either "activity" or "commodity," although some more precisely than others. Avoiding the usual denotation of *commodity* as "an article of economic exchange," its usage in the present context is closely related to the term *entitlement*. The connotations of "valuable entity" and "material possession" uniquely carried by *commodity* are distinctively relevant to certain formulations of human rights. The commodity type of theory approaches rights as an abstract construct, not of processes but of moral entities intrinsic to humanity yet, whether by divine, natural, or conventional legacy, *externally* linked to the abstract individual or community. On the other hand, the activity approach has abstractions also, but differs from the commodity approach in that the activity construct begins with a given rights action that is never abstractly divorced from the individual who performs it. Generally, the distinction suffers from the following weakness: once human rights are recognized and enforced, the distinction between "something had" and "something done" seems to collapse, since both are simultaneously suitable as a single human rights description. Nevertheless, the value of proposing the distinction in the first place lies in its overall usefulness in sorting out the numerous preferred definitions of human rights.

As a commodity, Richard Wasserstrom defined human rights as a basic moral entitlement possessed only by persons.[31] Rights are thus seen as entities that are naturally possessed rather than conferred. Morality and personhood become the qualifying factors that constitute this entitlement, furnishing the grounds for making assertions about such "inalienable" human rights as the rights to life, liberty, and the pursuit of happiness. Critics of this view point out its deceptive simplicity, maintaining that actual rights even as species of "natural entitlement" can be defeasible. For example, as everyday conflicts arise between the implications of property rights and freedom rights, ultimate resolutions may require that one right be overruled by another. But the adherents of the "moral entitlement" view counter that the practice of allowing one right to supersede another, or rights in general to be abrogated by such practical considerations as "national interest," would sacrifice the special character of inviolability that the human rights notion consensually conveys. What these human rights advocates wish to avoid is the trading off of human rights for other things or even for each other.

Another definition presented in the rights-as-commodity vein states that the various human rights are universal and irrevocable elements in a scheme of justice.[32] If, on this view, justice is the primary moral virtue within human society, and if all rights are fundamental to justice, exceptions to human rights claims would then be defensible only when some other feature of justice requires it. Therefore, this definition seems to imply that human rights do not always function as *primary* principles of a good human community, since it is conceivable that the human community may suffer if all human rights are treated as absolute or unconditional. Human rights, in this context are "inviolable" only in the sense that their violation is never morally right. In objection to this view, some critics hold that an unconditional regard for human rights could never ultimately harm the human community because by implication human rights are integrally bound up with our self-realization as social beings, which is a primary principle that may itself determine a scheme of justice.

Human rights has been defined in the commodity vein by Joel Feinberg as a valid moral claim based on all primary human needs.[33] Apart from the perennial philosophical debate about what criteria of validity should apply to moral claims, certain considerations about the nature of human needs—that is, what they are, their relative importance, and so on—will inevitably arise whenever morality is based on concepts of human nature. In Feinberg's view, all human rights are presumably possessed equally by all individuals because all persons as such have the same "human" needs, and human rights, or else they could not be regarded as being human. The main difficulty with this position, which its critics recognize, concerns its failure either to distinguish clearly between rights and needs, as Rollo Handy notes,[34] or to explain adequately the enormous variability among human needs[35] and, according to Adam Schaff, their corresponding links to rights; furthermore, apparent conflicts in the human personality itself (noted by Freud[36] and others) raise the question of a basic incompatibility among the various human rights that are linked to conflicting elements in the human personality (due to the intimate association of the former with the latter).

In contrast to these definitions in the rights-as-commodity category are those perspectives (discussed below) that treat human rights as activities performed by persons in relation only to other persons. Martin Golding defines human rights as "acts of claiming" performed on the level of the human community.[37] An act of claiming is an assertion of a rights claim (of whatever kind) that presupposes some activity or behavior in terms of which the claim is made. Golding distinguishes between claims and acts of claiming, holding that the notion of claiming permits the separation in practice of the particular acts of claiming from the claims themselves (the meaning of acts of claiming).[38] Accordingly, a person may possess rights (justifiable claims) never claimed by himself, as long as such rights are predicated upon *someone's* act of claiming. Nevertheless, rights are not seen to exist prior to an act of recognition, although the particular actor remains unspecified. This view anticipates and seeks to avoid a much criticized position that the existence of one's human rights cannot be established independently of one's own recognition of them. The criticism, leveled against certain other theories, has implied that one's occasional withdrawal of recognition of a particular right should not jeopardize the existential status of that right.

Golding's view thus departs from the conventional natural law position that holds rights to be moral norms and values discoverable in (human) nature but existing prior to such a discovery and independently of our knowledge and recognition of them. Moral principles, in the natural law view, are interpreted as applying to persons in a social context per se, specifying which social conditions are good or right for people in view of their humanity.[39]

In another activity-related human rights definition based on a similar philosophy, Henry Aiken proposes that the human rights are merely prescriptions for taking "primary moral responsibility for all other persons."[40] The locus of such prescriptions is fixed, its author suggests, in personal hopes and aspirations for making a moral world. In professional philosophy, Aiken's view can be allied with an ethical noncognitivism, a theory closely related to positivism. The noncognitivist perspective holds that although statements about ethics (and, perhaps, human rights) cannot be classified as knowledge (since they have no truth-value), they fall into the domain of pure ideals for what constitutes the "good life" and, as such, may be worthy of consideration. By classifying Aiken's view in this fashion, it is possible to demonstrate more clearly both its alliance with the activities category and its departure from a natural law theory. His view probably veers farther from conventional natural law than does Golding's view, discussed above, in that Aiken would hold "recognition" to belong to the realm of knowable facts and thus to be inappropriate to an ethical category. Consequently, he would see recognition to precede existence (of human rights), but only if the former is considered as a hope or aspiration and the latter is taken as an ideal.

It is curious but noteworthy that many philosophers today are unwilling to declare outright that human rights exist outside conventional law. Instead, they prefer to conceive of human rights in terms of what such rights would be like, if they were to exist! Various other definitions and characterizations of human rights in the literature, which center on what they are or question whether such rights exist at all, do not always fall neatly into categories of activities or commodities. Good examples of these are the following: Feinberg's view that human rights exist anterior to acts of claiming or to claims[41]; A.I. Melden's idea that the concept of human rights alludes to a basic social role, in essence connected to being a person, and so cannot be included in claims[42]; Wesley Hohfeld's position that human rights are nothing more than certain classes of claims[43]; L.M.G. Clark's view that a human right is a privilege, not a claim[44]; and finally, R.B. Perry's view that a basic right is a moral sphere of individual autonomy.[45]

To further the understanding of human rights from a global perspective, it is necessary to make one particular observation concerning the above views, since it has become a point of contention in the international debate about human rights. In its own manner, each view has been associated with Western liberalism. The abstract character of individualism as a basis for human rights has led many Communist, Third World countries, and politicized intellectuals at various times to reject the idea of human rights altogether. On the other hand, most forms of contemporary liberalism have acknowledged an increasing number of liberty-limiting principles[46], or else have been influenced by severe socialist criticism against such abstractionism.[47] In short, liberal advocates of human rights are becoming mindful of the need for a philosophical rethinking and clarification of the human rights conception.

The Classification of Rights as Human Rights

Human rights might be sorted out from other rights, powers, claims, immunities, and competencies once a preferred philosophical definition can be determined that may provide a basis for distinguishing various categories of human rights. Initially, many philosophers and nonphilosophers are willing to accept the subdivision of human rights into categories that correspond to some principal structures of social relations. The differentiation of human rights into four distinct categories[48] has become a standard feature of human rights in international law ever since the Universal Declaration. These are: civil rights, political rights, social and economic rights, and cultural rights. Each set of rights has a special function in societal structure.

Freedom of speech, press, assembly, and worship are examples of American First Amendment rights that can be interpreted as "civil rights." Civil rights are regarded as human rights arising in the conflict between the citizen and governmental tyranny. These substantive rights are formal assurance for the individual citizen against arbitrary governmental treatment; the "procedural" rights of universal individual equality before the law and of "due process" are the means by which such rights are enforced. Political rights, such as the rights to free elections and representative institutions, are established through constitutional democratic frameworks and provide legitimation, integration, and participation by linking the government to the consent of the governed.

Individual rights to education, to health and medical care, or to the freedom from social want, fear, or terror are called social and economic rights. This rights category, related in history to the growth of industrialism, assumes that the government should act to secure such things for its citizenry. Cultural rights, also emerging within technologically advanced societies, include the freedom of thought, the freedom of communication, and the freedom of aesthetic expression. These freedoms may be claimed as rights in response to a threat of mass manipulation from a monopoly of the public media by certain powerful private interests. To this list may be added a fifth category, the rights of personhood, including the freedom to reside in the country of one's choice, the freedom from torture, medical experimentation, or other physical abuse. These rights are considered to be entailed in virtue of the status of being a person, as an existing, valuing, and meaning-giving being. They are broadly premised on the assumptions that in E.M. Adams's view one has the right to live out one's own life project through the rational exercise of one's own powers,[49] Jacques Maritain's view of the right to a basic personal liberty,[50] and Herbert Kelman's view of the right to a fundamental human dignity.[51]

Philosophers generally agree that civil and political rights must be counted as human rights. However, there is a basic controversy about whether socioeconomic, or, as they are sometimes called, welfare rights, are to count as human rights. To resolve this dispute, the same criteria must be used as a common frame-of-reference for distinguishing between human rights and other sorts of rights. To illustrate, some philosophers, such as M. Cranston, R. S. Downie, and Machan, think that civil and political rights are human rights but are unwilling to include socioeconomic rights.[52] Cranston devised three tests for determining the authenticity of a human right: practicability, paramount importance, and universality. These criteria purportedly offer a clear way of making the desired distinction, such that civil and political rights are considered to be human rights, whereas the other "rights" are not included, at least not in the same sense.

Other philosophers, like W. T. Blackstone and David Watson,[53] hold instead that so-called welfare rights should be included in the list of human rights. They have criticized Cranston's position, using as their conceptual framework such documents as the Universal Declaration, the European Convention on Human Rights, and others that favor a similar interpretation of human rights.

In his revision of Cranston's three tests, Watson criticizes their power to distinguish between socioeconomic rights and civil-political rights in a human rights scheme. In Watson's view, one cannot use the tests to deny status to only one set of rights (as Cranston has claimed) without also proscribing the other set. Watson's preference is to include both sets as human rights.

In support of socioeconomic rights as human rights, Melvin Rader criticizes certain liberals for their failure to interpret freedom in both its negative and positive senses. Rader insists that negative freedom (translated as civil or First Amendment liberties) is often too narrowly construed as the absence of *governmental restraint* on the individual. When power differentials among social classes interfere with the negative freedom of the weaker class, then governmental restraints on the unduly powerful can actually facilitate negative freedom. Rader cautions that although civil liberties are necessary, they are not sufficient for a free society. To guarantee any measure of positive liberty, human beings must have the "instruments" with which to make free choices. For the most part, these instruments are expressed as the basic socio-economic rights satisfying the needs for food, clothing, shelter, health, education, among others. Civil rights cannot be guaranteed if socioeconomic rights are lacking; thus both, in this view, are to be counted as human rights in that both are necessary conditions for freedom. In the present volume, R. S. Downie approaches the issue by arguing that human rights are ultimately compatible with other moral rights. Those rights that are enforceable only at the expense of other rights should not, in his view, be accorded human rights status. These contrasting views illustrate the fact that the choice of criteria for defining specific categories of human rights will largely depend upon the narrower or broader philosophical foundation of a given theory.

Theoretical Orientations of Human Rights Philosophy

Human rights theories have always been framed from the perspective of certain principles of organization that have typically functioned as reference points for interpreting their meaning. In the current philosophical literature, one can witness an overall shift in emphasis from the traditional meta-physical/theological concepts of human rights as God-given and absolute, toward the ethical models of rights as essential to the notions of justice or the ideal human community. Nevertheless, a variety of approaches continues to dominate the literature: ethical, metaphysical/theological, historical, and political theories. Even though one must acknowledge that the practical separation of human rights from law is unthinkable in our time, this essay does not address itself to legal theories. This apparent omission may be justified by the fact that the legal theories are themselves partially understood in terms of these four approaches.

The Ethical Principle

The issue of whether and in what sense human rights can be said to exist is clearly implicit in recent statements in the field of ethics. Certain philosophers may indeed hasten to affirm and qualify the existence of human rights. Others, who are reluctant to declare themselves so straightforwardly, may prefer to speculate about the nature of human rights as if they did exist.

Among the philosophers of ethics who adhere to human rights are those like Gregory Vlastos who regard them as prima facie, and hence applicable to all persons everywhere.[54] However, it can be shown that the meaning of prima facie has changed in recent years with respect to human rights discourse. Formerly, prima facie referred to all actual or valid rights,[55] but more recent interpretations have held this older view to imply that human rights are arbitrary or derivative. Although there are numerous philosophers who believe that human rights are unconditionally valid or actual,[56] as Arnold Kaufman has indicated, the term prima facie now commonly refers only to rights that should be exercised under the condition that better reasons cannot be cited for not exercising them.[57] Indeed, prima facie implies that there may exist some potentially overriding considerations; hence, recognition of this fact would vary with the times, conditions, and other circumstances.

Thus, the modern prima facie argument for human rights becomes strongly relativistic. As such, it becomes sharply criticized by certain philosophers who recognize the danger of selective interpretation and enforcement of an ethical concept they hold to be inalienable and universal. International (human rights) declarations invariably regard rights in this latter tradition. (However, the basic universality of all rights is not considered to be compromised if actual enforcement policies often grant more attention to certain rights than to others.) These critics of the prima facie view maintain that only when basic human rights are superseded by nonmoral considerations is the sense in which these rights are fundamental and inalienable lost. They maintain, moreover, that when conflicts are sanctioned between human rights (*in se* or vis-à-vis other rights), it implies that the highest moral principles are themselves contradictory. The critics of the prima facie view do recognize its allure as a device for circumventing the undesirable implications of morality on human rights but prefer to explain, and dismiss, such conflicts as mistaken interpretations as they arise. They hold that the philosopher must finally recognize that human rights provide a universal and objectively valid standard for social relations in a diverse international "community."

Another closely related and variously interpreted issue concerns the specific character of moral obligations and their correlation to human rights. Since it is one thing to support human rights in the abstract and quite another to enforce them, or oppose any violations of them, a comprehensive philosophy of human rights should establish not only what ought to be done but also how compelling this ethical goal may be. There are at least two main schools of thought about linking rights and obligations. The first of these holds that rights and obligations are correlative because rights confer obligations. Lyons's utilitarianism argues that certain useful rules about the general welfare confer rights which, in turn, entail obligations in view of the same rules.[58] The second school of thought claims that higher obligations themselves confer rights. Pope John XXIII, writing in the natural law tradition, sums up the inseparability of rights and obligations dramatically as follows:

...every fundamental human right draws its indestructible moral force from the natural law, which in granting it imposes a corresponding obligation. Those, therefore, who claim their own rights, yet altogether forget or neglect to carry out their respective duties, are people who build with one hand and destroy with the other.[59]

A minority of philosophers believe that human rights are totally separate from corresponding obligations. For instance, some writers like H. L. A. Hart and Aiken have tried to establish the idea that rights in general, including human rights and moral obligations, belong to a distinct compartment of moral theory. Thus, they conclude that no inescapable bond can be said to connect them.[60] Accordingly, human rights are said to be meaningless apart from successful appeals to our sense of community. This strategy for disconnecting rights from obligations is confronted with a number of conceptual problems on the level of universal human rights: how to obtain universal agreement on the essentials of a community; how it is possible to experience the sense of community when the competing views around the world on the nature of community seem to thwart the development of a unified concept of human rights; how to avoid treating human rights arbitrarily or in a way reminiscent of the earlier prima facie view in which nonrights considerations perpetually outweigh human rights; and how to make respect *for* human rights at least as compelling as a belief *in* human rights. In general, the meaning of a human rights concept, indeed its very fact, hinges on the security of the foundation, moral or otherwise, on which it is developed.

The Metaphysical/Theological Principle

Very few recent philosophers are inclined to found or even discuss human rights at the cosmic or spiritual levels. Most of them prefer to analyze the concept of human rights only within the moral dimension in terms of the status of personhood in the "good society." Some philosophers, nonetheless, do speak of human morality as profoundly as they would of a god, whereas others in this perspective are unable to separate morality from broader religious and metaphysical considerations.

To illustrate, some modern neo-Kantian idealists like Stammler and Emerson have attempted to explain the obvious disparity among human rights concepts as "natural law with a changing content."[61] Accordingly, a "slaveless" democratic society may underscore the principle of "equality before the law" whereas, in times of oppression, its progressive elements may come to regard "freedom from slavery" as being of paramount importance. In other words, the selection of relevant human rights principles may be reflecting differences in social circumstances. The totality of all such principles in this tradition draws its moral force from the (ideal) natural law. Although the neo-Kantian view of natural law may be an attempt to circumvent the modern bias against absolutes, it relies upon a metaphysical, or even theological, conception of a universal order which ultimately authenticates human rights, values, and purposes.

It is in this sense that natural-law metaphysics is closely aligned with religious conceptions of human rights, as has been illustrated by the favorable comparisons of the spirit and purpose of human rights with the basic principles of certain religious traditions in respect of human nature and human destiny.

The Historical Principle

Another popular theory classification scheme for human rights that has frequently appeared in philosophical literature may be called the historical principle. Certain human rights theories, by referring to the evolutionary development of the human conscience or to the growing awareness of the laws of nature, have combined a metaphysical and a historical approach. This overlapping usage must be distinguished from the practical and earthbound sense in which "historical" should be understood here: in application to theories approaching the concept of human rights from the meaning it receives under definite sociohistorical circumstances.

One set of writers, along with J. E. Barnhardt, contends that human rights claims are always relational and contextual[62], in rebuttal to the a priori, absolutist arguments (that human rights exist prior to any recognition or that their meaning is independent of the relativity of time and circumstance). An illustration of a relativist view is the position of Gibson Winter, who holds that the meaning of cultural and socioeconomic rights (such as those described in Articles 22 through 27 of the Universal Declaration) are constrained by current conditions but, nevertheless, have instrumental priority over political rights. The rationale for this differential is twofold: first, that cultural and socioeconomic rights provide the means by which other rights can be realized, and, second, that the absence of cultural and socioeconomic rights renders the other rights ineffectual.[63] Other cases of the historical approach to human rights range from Arthur Nussbaum's idea that their meaning can be discovered by tracing the evolved history of natural law interpretations, either the legal, ethical, or political,[64] to views like that of Wasserstrom, which claim to reinstate the older natural rights doctrine but on grounds other than the absolutist rendition.[65]

Indeed, the recognized relationship between human rights and natural law has been a prominent theme in the related philosophical literature, even among those philosophers who categorize human rights in other than historical ways. Most contemporary human rights philosophers acknowledge that human rights interpretations today are a revival of the natural law traditions dating back to the ancient Greeks and Romans, although non-Western cultures have also had conceptions of entitlements, prerogatives, powers, immunities, obligations, and competencies belonging to special persons or groups. However, the modern human rights dialogue has evolved in a context that has been politically dominated by Western powers and, so, the natural law philosophy has received a perhaps disproportionate emphasis. Yet, in approaching human rights from the perspective of both philosophy and politics, other distinctions in their respective histories are evident. The following has been pointed out in a UNESCO document on "The Grounds of an International Declaration of Human Rights":

The history of the philosophic discussion of human rights, of the dignity and brotherhood of man and of his common citizenship in the great society is long: it extends beyond the narrow limits of the Western tradition and its beginnings in the West as well as in the East coincide with the beginnings of philosophy. The history of declarations, on the other hand, is short and its beginnings are to be found in the West . . . although the right of the people to revolt against political oppression was very early recognized and established in China. The relation of the philosophic considerations to the declarations of human rights is suggested by these two histories.[66]

Both theoretically and practically, a philosophical *or* a political framework may be sought when disputes arise about human rights interpretations. "The utility of a declaration (political framework) depends on the possibility of separating the political from the philosophic question. . . ." An interpretation that is "revolutionary in one set of philosophic assumptions is counterrevolutionary, subversive, or even traditional in another."[67] The framing of the Universal Declaration of Human Rights did take into account both Western and non-Western philosophies. However, the impact of the Western natural law doctrine on the *political* history of declarations themselves in the basic Western tradition of constitutionalism remained profoundly influential.

The Political Principle

The last major foundational principle that may be used to subsume some theories of human rights is the political principle. In treating human rights as a political concept, philosophers almost invariably have in mind a particular political viewpoint from which they believe the human rights concept is to be understood. Despite the variety of partisan political interpretations that the concept of human rights has received, the present discussion concerns only the modes in which political philosophers have dealt with human rights. In general, some prefer to think of human rights only as a political phenomenon, whereas others regard it as an idea whose compass is broader than its political signification.

In the first class belong those theories which postulate that human rights can be understood in a political sense, independently from all other considerations. The majority of these theories treat human rights as belonging to the essentials of modern democracy as well as to traditional liberalism and the natural law doctrine. Although politics is considered by liberal theorists such as Machan to be a branch of ethics,[68] liberalism is, broadly speaking, a political philosophy in which ethics is regarded as supreme. The political principles in this tradition justify or explicate the preferred concept of human rights. For example, the association between human rights and moral obligation found in later phases of liberalism provides a current basis for liberalist analysis of the meaning of human rights.[69] Similarly, the "general utility" principle is redefined in the recent literature by Lyons for the special bearing it is presumed to have on human rights.[70] In the same tradition, the notion of "respect for persons" is explored as a political framework for the concept of freedom and universal equality.

Although various nonliberal political philosophies have challenged the liberal analysis of human rights, most of them are at least willing to acknowledge that modern human rights philosophy has liberalistic origins. For instance, certain Marxist humanists, such as Shibata, Schaff, and Lukacs, have offered their analyses of human rights in the context of democratic theory and thus have not dismissed rights for their links to capitalistic ideology.[71]

The second class of human rights theories founded on the political principle is quite similar to the first class, but it generally considers the political meaning of human rights as derivative from, but *as important* as, one or more of the other foundational principles.

The philosophical issues that develop from the various political perspectives on human rights are closely parallel to those issues arising in the domain of international politics. As noted above, the human rights concept is associated primarily with Western theories of liberalism and democracy. J. S. Mill and L. T. Hobhouse are classic formulators of how these differing political traditions must harmonize in order to benefit community well-being. A recent comprehensive study by Alan Wolfe[72] has adduced abundant evidence of the ultimate incompatibility of these conflicting traditions. Liberalism and democracy are distinguishable by their leading tenets of individual freedom and equality, respectively. As human rights problems are often conceptualized in terms of these tenets, the theoretical tensions between them become evident on the practical level also. Therefore, the different historical motives which engendered these tensions are translated into the new context of contemporary international political disputes. Peter Schneider summarizes this point by stressing that the human rights doctrine today is used by both sides in the political controversy between liberal democracy and communism, but also by the anticolonialist movement in the Third World; Schneider observes that national self-determination or "independence" politics and human rights have become linked.[73]

From this survey of the philosophical issues concerning the concept of human rights, it becomes evident that its interpretation is not univocal and should not be considered so. Consequently, it may appear plausible to argue with Golding and Barnhardt that *human rights* is at least a forensic term[74] (one requiring contextual definition). In the final analysis, however, the clarification of human rights far transcends the level of contextual descriptions. Philosophical treatments of human rights have shown that, very broadly, issues come to be variously interpreted as a priori or prima facie; yet these divisions do not cut evenly across lines of context, national affiliation, or political ideology. Human rights, like democracy, have come to be regarded, at least potentially, as a forensic concept. That so many nations with radically different local conditions and traditions have come to some agreement on their esteem of human rights ideology (as evidenced by their almost unexceptional inclusion of human rights in contemporary national constitutions) attests to the hope that the concept of human rights carries as a universalizing principle.

NOTES

1. Ch. Perelman's chapter is the single exception. With the author's approval, it has been translated into English for the first time here because it was originally published in the French language.

2. Democracy may be defined as a political ideal postulating both the greatest possible participation of all citizens in civic affairs and individual equality before justly based laws. *See* Alan Wolfe, *The Limits of Legitimacy* (New York: The Free Press, 1977), p. 6. In this case, democracy's link to human rights can be disregarded only at the sacrifice of democratic "legitimation" in Jürgen Habermas's term.

3. Alexis de Tocqueville, *Democracy in America* (New York: Oxford University Press, 1947), p. 310.

4. I wish to acknowledge John Mourant who, in our recent correspondence (April 1979), has offered his generous affirmation of my basic point in this passage.

5. *See* Richard McKeon, "The Philosophic Bases and Material Circumstances of the Rights of Man," *Ethics* 58, no. 3 (April 1948): 180-87. This document (Universal Declaration, 1948) reflects this position when, for instance, it refers to human rights as "inalienable," thus incorporating into its structure the traditional distinction between conventional and inalienable rights which is basic to the modern variations of natural law theory. It also vests the final moral authority for human rights in the individual human being, and so considers it to rest beyond legal rights (or positive legal recognition), although the document does maintain that the "rule of law" is indispensable for making human rights socially effective.

6. In our correspondence (April 1979) Melvin Rader drew my attention to this distinction and to his discussion of it in his book. *See* Melvin Rader, *Ethics and the Human Community* (New York: Holt, Rinehart and Winston, 1966), p. 20.

7. L. C. McDonald, *Western Political Theory* (New York: Harcourt, Brace and World, 1968), pp. 98-99.

8. Hugo Grotius, *On the Law of War and Peace,* trans. William Whewell, bk. 1, ch. 1, sec. 5 (Cambridge: Cambridge University Press, 1853), p. 12.

9. The philosophers, Thomas Hobbes and Benedict Spinoza, were well-known natural law theorists, but in a different sense from Locke. For Hobbes, the natural right to self-preservation seems to be a natural necessity, not a moral option. For

Spinoza, natural law was cleansed of morality since he identified it with man's natural behavior. Therefore, the overriding moral value of "human rights" is not for present purposes aptly expressed in their philosophies.

10. *See* Rader, *Ethics and the Human Community*, p. 146.

11. Immanuel Kant, *Fundamental Principles of the Metaphysic of Morals*, trans. T. K. Abbott (Indianapolis: The Library of Liberal Arts, 1975), p. 47.

12. Rader, *Ethics and the Human Community*, p. 44.

13. J. L. Talmon, *The Origins of Totalitarian Democracy* (New York: W. W. Norton and Co., 1970), p. 43.

14. Auguste Comte, *The Positive Philosophy of Auguste Comte*, trans. Harriet Martineau, vol. 2, 2d ed. (London, 1875).

15. J. G. Fichte, *Addresses to the German Nation* (New York: Harper Torchbooks, 1968), pp. 197-98.

16. Georg Wilheim Hegel, *Philosophy of Right*, trans. T.M. Knox (New York: Oxford University Press, 1973),pp. 109-10. For an instructive explanation of Hegel's notion of "supersession" (*Aufheben*), *see:* Melvin Rader, *Marx's Interpretation of History* (New York: Oxford University Press, 1979), pp. 94-95.

17. *See* Wolfe, *The Limits of Legitimacy*, pp. vii, 224-28.

18. John Stuart Mill, *J.S. Mill: A System of Logic*, ed. J.M. Robson, bks. 4-6 —Toronto: University of Toronto Press, 1974), p. 879.

19. John Stuart Mill, *The Principles of Political Economy*, ed. Donald Winch (New York: Penguin Books, 1970), pp. 349, 350.

20. Alan S. Rosenbaum, "The Idea of Liberalism and J.S. Mill," *Philosophy in Context* 5 (May 1976): 57.

21. Mill, *The Principles of Political Economy*, p. 306.
timore, Md.: Penguin Books, 1970), p. 306.

22. David Lyons, "Human Rights and the General Welfare," *Philosophy and Public Affairs* 6, no. 2 (Winter 1977): 113-29.

23. In *Human Rights: A Symposium*, prep. by UNESCO (London: Allan Wingate, 1949), pp. 108-42.

24. Wolfgang Leonhard, *Three Faces of Marxism* (New York: Holt, Rinehart and Winston, 1974), pp. 16-17, 35-36.

25. John A. Scott, *Republican Ideas and the Liberal Tradition in France, 1870-1914* (New York: Columbia University Press, 1951), p. 178.

26. Specifically, I refer to: The European Convention on Human Rights (1950); the American Convention on Human Rights (1969); the Helsinki Final Act (1975) and the follow-up Belgrade Conference (1978); international organizations such as the United Nations, the World Court, and the Inter-American Court of Human Rights (1978); declarations such as the Nuremberg Principles (1947), the Universal Declaration (1948), and other United Nations anticolonialist statements in 1960, 1964, and 1970; and groups like Amnesty International (1961), the International League for Human Rights, the Committee on Human Rights (Russia, 1970), and the Charter '77 group (Czechoslovakia, 1976).

27. *See* Karl Jaspers, *The Question of German Guilt* (New York: Capricorn Books, 1961).

28. A brief description of the social circumstances and of some of the philosophers who contributed to this atmosphere is found in J. D. Bernal, *Science in History*, vol. 4 (Cambridge, Mass.: The M.I.T. Press, 1971), pp. 1091-92, 1157-61.

29. The "new irrationalism" in some recent antinaturalistic philosophies of human existence has been examined in Marvin Farber, *Naturalism and Subjectivism* (Springfield, Ill.: Charles C. Thomas, 1959), pp. 297-372. On the other hand, some conceptions of rationality have been dismissed as being too limited and ideological (Karl Popper's neopositivism), whereas other's have been criticized for being too broad and "irrational" (Paul Feyerabend's antimethodology viewpoint). For a discussion of these controversies, *see The Positivist Dispute in German Sociology*, trans. Glyn Adey and David Frisby (New York: Harper Torchbooks, 1976), pp. xli-xlii, passim.

30. Tibor Machan, "Are There Any Human Rights?" *The Personalist* 59 (April 1978): pp. 165-70.

31. Richard Wasserstrom, "Rights, Human Rights, and Racial Discrimination," in A. I. Melden, ed., *Human Rights* (Belmont, Calif.: Wadsworth Publishers, 1970), pp. 96-101.

32. Tibor Machan, "Prima Facie Vs. Natural (Human) Rights," *The Journal of Value Inquiry* 10, no. 2 (Summer 1976): 119-31.

33. Joel Feinberg, "The Nature and Value of Rights," *The Journal of Value Inquiry* 4 (1970): 247-57.

34. Rollo Handy, *The Measurement of Values* (St. Louis: Warren H. Green, 1970), passim.

35. Adam Schaff, *Marxism and the Human Individual* (New York: McGraw-Hill Book Co., 1970), p. 66.

36. For a clear statement of Freud's view of the conflictual character of mental reality, *see* Thomas Villilamthadam, *Tomorrow's Society* (Kerala, India: Oriental Institute of Religious Studies, 1978), pp. 45, 47, 49.

37. Martin Golding, "Towards a Theory of Human Rights," *The Monist* 52, no. 4 (October 1968): 548-49.

38. The jurist Hans Kelsen makes a similar conceptual distinction in his theory of norms seen not as acts of will but rather as the meaning of such acts. *See* "Kelsen, Pure Theory of Law," in *Cohen and Cohen's Readings in Jurisprudence and Legal Philosophy*, ed. Philip Shuchman (Boston: Little, Brown and Co., 1979), pp. 174-78.

39. Tibor Machan, *Human Rights and Human Liberties* (Chicago: Nelson-Hall Publishers, 1975), p. 107.

40. Henry D. Aiken, "Rights, Human and Otherwise," *The Monist* 52, no. 4 (October 1968): 515.

41. Joel Feinberg, "Duties, Rights and Claims," in *Law and Philosophy*, ed. E.A. Kent (New York: Appleton, Century, Crofts, 1970), pp. 151-53.

42. A. I. Melden, *Rights and Right Conduct* (Oxford: Basil Blackwell, 1959), pp. 13-15, especially p. 84.

43. Wesley Hohfeld, *Fundamental Legal Conceptions* (New Haven: Yale University Press, 1919).

44. Lorenne M. G. Clark, "Privacy, Property, Freedom, and the Family," in *Philosophical Law*, ed. Richard Bronaugh (Westport, Conn.: Greenwood Press, 1978), p. 169.

45. Ralph Barton Perry, *Puritanism and Democracy* (New York: Harper Torchbooks, 1944), pp. 446-47.

46. Joel Feinberg, *Social Philosophy* (Englewood Cliffs, N.J.: Prentice-Hall, 1973), p. 33.

47. Irving Howe, "Socialism and Liberalism: Articles of Conciliation," *Dissent* 24 (Winter 1977): 29-32.

48. McKeon, "The Philosophic Bases," pp. 185-87.

49. E. M. Adams, "Personhood and Human Rights," *Man and World* 8, no. 1 (February 1975): 36-46.

50. Jacques Maritain, *Les Droits de l'homme et la loi naturelle* (Paris: Paul Hartmann, 1975), pp. 110-13.

51. Herbert Kelman, "The Conditions, Criteria, and Dialectics of Human Dignity," *International Studies Quarterly* 21, no. 3 (September 1977).

52. Maurice Cranston, "Human Rights, Real and Supposed," in *Political Theory and the Rights of Man*, ed. R. R. Raphael (Bloomington: Indiana University Press, 1967), p. 43; R. S. Downie, *Roles and Values* (London: Methuen), p. 49; and Machan, *Human Rights and Human Liberties*, pp. 40-41.

53. W. T. Blackstone, "Equality and Human Rights, " *The Monist* 52, no. 4 (October 1968): 636-38; and David Watson, "Welfare Rights and Human Rights," *Journal of Social Policy* 6, pt. 1 (1977): 31-46.

54. Gregory Vlastos, "Justice and Equality," in *Human Rights*, ed. Melden, pp. 82-83.

55. W. D. Ross, *The Right and the Good* (New York: Oxford University Press, 1939), p. 20.

56. Arnold Kaufman, "A Sketch of a Liberal Theory of Human Rights," *The Monist* 52, no. 4 (October 1968): 605-09.

57. Kai Nielsen, "Scepticism and Human Rights," *The Monist* 52, no. 4 (October 1968): 573.

58. Lyons, "Human Rights and the General Welfare," pp. 115-16, 123-25, 127-28.

59. Pope John XXIII, *Pacem in Terris*, English translation (Boston: St. Paul Editions, 1963).

60. H.L.A. Hart, "Are There Any Natural Rights?" in *Human Rights*, ed. Melden, pp. 65-67; Aiken, "Rights, Human and Otherwise," p. 505ff.

61. Rudolf Stammler, *The Theory of Justice*, trans. Isaac Husik (New York: Macmillan Co., 1925); Rupert Emerson, "The New Higher Law of Anti-Colonialism," in *The Relevance of International Law*, ed. K. Deutsch and S. Hoffman (New York: Anchor Books, 1971), p. 203; Rupert Emerson, "The Fate of Human Rights in the Third World," *World Politics* 27, no. 2 (January 1975): 201-26.

62. J. E. Barnhardt, "Human Rights as Absolute Claims and Reasonable Expectations," *American Philosophical Quarterly* 6, no. 4 (October 1969): 335.

63. Gibson Winter, *Being Free: Reflections on America's Cultural Revolution* (New York: Macmillan and Co., 1970), chapt. 1.

64. Arthur Nussbaum, *Concise History of the Law of Nations* (New York: Macmillan and Co., 1954), passim; Melden, ed., *Human Rights*, introduction; Richard Claude, *Comparative Human Rights* (Baltimore, Md.: The Johns Hopkins Press, 1977), introduction.

65. Wasserstrom, "Rights, Human Rights, and Racial Discrimination," passim.

66. *Human Rights: A Symposium*, p. 260.

67. McKeon, "The Philosophic Bases," p. 183.

68. Machan, *Human Rights and Human Liberties*, pp. 52-53, 105-6, 113.

69. Arnold Kaufman, "A Sketch of a Liberal Theory of Human Rights," passim; and D. D. Raphael, "Human Rights, Old and New," in *Political Theory and the*

Rights of Man, pp. 65-66; and D. D. Raphael, "The Rights of Man and the Rights of the Citizen," pp. 106-17.

70. Lyons, "Human Rights and the General Welfare," passim.

71. We may infer this position from the following references: Shingo Shibata, "Fundamental Human Rights and Problems of Freedom," *Social Praxis* 3/4 (1975): 157-85; Schaff, *Marxism and the Human Individual,* pp. 146-49, 160-61, 200-1, and 222-23; Georg Lukacs, *Marxism and Human Liberation* (New York: Delta Books, 1973), pp. 9-12.

72. Wolfe, *The Limits of Legitimacy,* pp. 1-10.

73. Peter Schneider, "Social Rights and the Concept of Human Rights," in *Political Theory and the Rights of Man,* ed. Raphael (1967), p. 81.

74. Golding, "Towards a Theory of Human Rights," pp. 548-49; Barnhardt, "Human Rights as Absolute Claims and Reasonable Expectations," pp. 335-39.

PART 2

The Foundations of Human Rights

CH. PERELMAN —— 1 ⌐

Can the Rights of
Man Be Founded?*

Professor Ch. Perelman seeks to establish a sufficient grounding for a theory of human rights by linking it to both a concept of the reasonable and the theory of man. He thinks that human rights can be founded upon the reasonable exchange between general moral rules and particular moral experiences.

Any search for a foundation presupposes the need for solid grounding. However, if this need should manifest itself regarding just anything, the problem of grounding would never receive a satisfactory solution because the search would lead to infinite regression. For the search to be a sound undertaking, one must admit the existence of realities or principles that serve as foundation for other things and are, themselves, incontestable or, at least, uncontested. On the other hand, what one proposes to ground would either be contestable by right or contested in fact.

I stress the distinction between the incontestable and the uncontested, the contestable and the contested. The failure to recognize this distinction is the source of confusions that make philosophy oscillate between absolutism and skepticism, two extreme positions that both seem contrary to effective thinking, which normally falls between them.

The search for a foundation (or a proof that guarantees it) presupposes a doubt, a disagreement, or an argument, sometimes as to the existence, the truth, or the necessary character of a reality, proposition, or norm; sometimes as to the nature of that which exists, the meaning of the proposition, or the range of the norm. Everyone admits that doubts, disagreements, and disputes can arise regarding one or another of these points, and that it is then necessary to clear them up or sidestep them. In refuting an objection, justifying a rule, or defining its range, one may eliminate a doubt, reduce a disagreement, or avoid a dispute that has actually presented itself, and this procedure

*Report presented at the Entretiens de l'Aquila (Italie), of the Institut International de Philosophie, September 15-19, 1964, on *Le Fondement des droits de l'Homme,* Actes (Florence: La Nouva Italia, 1966), pp. 10-17. Translated by George Leibacher from its publication in *Droit, Morale et Philosophie* (Paris: Librairie Générale de Droit et de Jurisprudence, 1976), pp. 67-73.

may furnish a *sufficient* basis for a given situation. But it is always possible that a dispute, temporarily avoided, may emerge later for some new reasons. A sufficient grounding at a given moment may not have the characteristics of an absolute grounding that can permanently forestall disputes concerning this matter. One can understand that the ambition to avoid all disputes forever has moved most philosophers to seek an incontestable, absolute grounding for their assertions.[1] Opposed to the philosophic dogmatism that claims to furnish such an absolute grounding, knowable through some form of evidence, is the philosophical skepticism that denies such a possibility and takes exception to such evidence. But both approaches overlook a "sufficient" grounding, one that eliminates a current doubt or dispute but does not guarantee, once and for all, the elimination of all uncertainties and all future controversies. The history of thought, in all its domains, teaches us the importance of groundings that are not absolute but might appear sufficient to certain minds, in certain ages, in certain disciplines, and manifest the personal aspect of our knowledge and culture, historically and methodologically situated. The search for groundings that are sufficient but relative to a spirit, a society, or a particular discipline becomes philosophically essential for all those who, while refusing to consider self-evidence an absolute criterion, nevertheless cannot be satisfied with a negative and sterile skepticism.

In classical philosophies, which I have elsewhere called first philosophies,[2] the criterion of self-evidence in an ontology or epistemology, whether it concerns intuitions of the reason or of the senses, must permit the distinction between necessary first realities and principles—which require no grounding on anything else—and the realities, truths, norms and values, that must find their grounding in those first realities and principles. That which exists in itself and is conceived through itself provides a foundation for that which exists in something else and is conceived through something else. Thus, in some cases, the modes will find their grounding in substance, contingent beings in Necessary Being, derived truths in evident principles, norms and values in an incontestable reality.

Corresponding to the classic conception of proof,[3] where all that is doubtful must be demonstrated and that which is self-evident has no need of proof, the classic idea of grounding is that of an obvious and absolute foundation. Now, in the empiricist conception of knowledge, only sensation furnishes us this indubitable foundation. Thus, norms and values, which are not given by sensation, would have to be capable of being grounded upon some empirical reality. But as one cannot deduce the "ought" from the "is," norms and values deprived of a valid grounding would be nothing more than the expression of subjective emotions or of commands drawing their weight from the source that imposes and sanctions them.

In a theocratic view of society, when a command is considered to emanate from a perfect source, the norm that it poses cannot be challenged. If the command emanates from the general will, constituted on the basis of a social contract, the norm it establishes is considered obligatory by virtue of the principle *pacta sunt servanda*. The clearly expressed will of the sovereign gives these norms an unquestionable foundation. One sees how, in transferring to the general will the functions previously filled by the divine will (*vox populi vox Dei*), the juridical positivism has thereby succeeded in grounding all positive juridical rules on the legislative power of the state and on the sanction that guarantees obedience to the law. Refusing all other grounding of the law, juridical positivism has denied the existence of any law that is not the expression of the will of the sovereign.

But this conception of juridical positivism collapses before the abuses of Hitlerism, like any scientific theory irreconcilable with the facts. The universal reaction to the Nazi crimes forced the Allied chiefs of state to institute the Nuremberg trials and to interpret the adage *nullum crimen sine lege* in a nonpositivistic sense because the law violated in the case did not derive from a system of positive law but from the conscience of all civilized men. The conviction that it was impossible to leave these horrible crimes unpunished, although they fell outside a system of positive law, has prevailed over the positivistic conception of the grounding of the law.

The renaissance of natural law theories in contemporary legal philosophy is certainly in great part the consequence of the failure of positivism. But, to counter this failure, is it absolutely necessary to fall back on ideological constructions that seemed definitely destroyed by the positivistic critique? More and more, jurists from all corners of the world have recourse to *general principles of law*, which one might liken to the ancient *jus gentium* and which would find their real and sufficient grounding in the consensus of civilized humanity. The fact that these principles are recognized, explicitly or implicitly, by the courts of various countries, even if they have not been proclaimed obligatory by the legislative power, proves the inadequacy of the Kelsenian construction, one which makes the validity of all rules of law depend upon their integration in a hierarchical and dynamic system whose elements would all draw their validity from a presupposed supreme standard. This juridical formalism, whatever its advantages and seductions for a theoretician of systematic mind, does not take into account the aberrant element constituted by the general principles of law. But the lack of a legislative grounding, does not oblige one to seek a foundation for these principles in a permanent natural law which no subsequent reaction of conscience can modify or clarify. Just as the natural sciences have stopped granting their theories and principles the status of final truths sheltered from all refutation by experience, we, too, despite love of system, do not have to shelter our norms and values from challenges our consciences may present. To say that the conscience must limit itself to the domain of morality, without its revolt having any consequences in the juridical domain, is sacrificing more than is necessary to the love of order and a methodologically satisfying construction. That grants to an ideology, whatever its motives and reasons, an untouchable and imperfectible character. It grants to institutions designed to protect the individual and promote the common good an infallible character, one that no contradiction not conforming to the modalities foreseen by these institutions could change. This ideological absolutism, to which the search for an absolute and unchangeable grounding must lead even if this grounding is positivisitic, seems unacceptable to me. But that does not mean that all search for a nonabsolute foundation lacks sense and significance.

Whenever controversies arise about the existence or significance of certain rights, it is normal to link them to an ideological grounding, that is to say, to ontological, anthropological, or axiological principles that, once admitted, would furnish sufficient reasons in favor of a right or of a limitation or hierarchization of rights. Indeed, a conception of the real or of a vision of man does implicitly contain evaluations, hierarchizations, or structuralizations from which an axiology and a link to moral and juridical norms can be made. In structuring the real, based on an ontology, one places a higher value on certain aspects. Quite naturally, one will admit the primacy of essence over accident, of the act over the possible, or of the spiritual over the material. In conceiving the individual in relation to society, or in making the social reality depend on individual wills, in giving preference to that which is unique or reputable, one at least implicitly puts value on *(valoriser)* one or another aspect of the real in his ontology or anthropology. It is this overall and hierarchizing view of the real which distinguishes the ontological from the purely scientific, purely methodological point of view. In preferring an epistemology that favors scientific methods under all circumstances and neglects all others, positivism under its various manifestations arrives at an ontology that retains only those aspects of the real that the methods of the positive sciences permit it to recognize. Thus its case confirms, paradoxically, that there exists no ontology devoid of all value judgments, at least implicit ones.

It follows that the attempt to ground norms in an ontology does not consist of a deduction of an "ought" from an "is," of a *sollen* from a *sein*, but of the structuralization of these norms based on a vision of the real inseparable from a stress, therefore a valuing *(valorisation)* either of certain "beings" or of certain aspects of "being."

When it is a question of norms, the search for a grounding is too often inspired by a mathematical model, as if one could demonstrate them, like the theorems of a system of geometry, starting from axioms both evident and unambiguous. But, in reality, the search for a foundation in the moral and juridical domain is of an entirely different nature.

In the interesting volume published by UNESCO on the occasion of the Universal Declaration of the Rights of Man,[4] several authors state that if agreement upon a list of the rights of man, between representatives of different and even opposed ideologies, has been possible, it is because their sense, their significance, and their hierarchization have not been spelled out.[5] Regarding the rights of man, we find ourselves confronted with the same situation as that indicated in a previous discussion concerning the ultimate principles of morality.[6]

Indeed, it is easy to obtain agreement on general principles, such as "It is immoral to inflict pain unnecessarily"; "We must act in such a way that the maxim of our will can at the same time become a universal law"; or "that is moral which has the greatest utility for the greatest number." As long as these principles remain sufficiently vague, nobody wants to challenge them. But the arguments start as soon as general rules are applied to specific cases. I wrote concerning this:

In fact, the different principles of morality are not challenged by men who belong to different cultural environments but are interpreted in diverse fashions, these attempts at interpretation never being definitive. In matters of morality, the argument differs completely from formal demonstration because it is a constant relating of particular experiences with concepts which are partially undetermined and in constant interaction. . . . Moral philosophy is not worked out by means of axioms and deductions but thanks to a continual development of rules which can guide us in action.[7]

From this perspective, the search for an absolute grounding must give way to a dialectic in which the principles one works out in order to systematize and hierarchize the rights of man, such as one conceives them, are constantly confronted with the moral experience, the reactions of our conscience. The solution of the problems created by this confrontation will be neither obvious nor arbitrary. It will develop through taking a theoretical position resulting from a personal decision, a position that one presents nevertheless as valid for all reasonable minds. This decision, not conforming simply to the evidence, and not presenting itself as infallible, does not risk furnishing a grounding for an enlightened despotism that escapes all checks and critiques. On the contrary, the contingent and obviously perfectible solutions presented by the philosophers can claim to be reasonable only to the extent that they are submitted for the approval of the universal audience, constituted by the totality of mankind who are normal and competent to judge.[8] Indeed the *reasonable* does not refer to a reason defined as reflection or illumination of a divine reason, unchangeable and perfect, but to a purely human situation, with agreement presumed from all those whom one considers competent to discuss the questions under consideration. This presumption permits the working out of a rule or norm, but one which does not escape from a check by the facts. The *norm*, the *normative*, is intimately associated with *normal*, with that which "is." But one sees immediately that recourse to the members of the universal audience, in order to actualize the idea of the reasonable, cannot fail to refer us to an anthropology, a theory of man, just as the *duty of the dialogue,* the fundamental norm in the thought of Guido Calogero,[9] gives rise immediately to the question: "With reference to whom do we have this obligation to dialogue?" If one tries to respond to such questions, and to all that they imply, one will arrive, by a certain point of view, at justifying certain rights of man.

Let us now take the idea of the reasonable, which I believe conditions the ancient ideal of philosophy.[10] Taken as a criterion of conduct and practical norms, the reasonable is, by that very fact, grounded *(valorisé)*. But the reasonable works itself out due to the participation of all human beings capable of integration in the universal audience and necessitates the confrontation of their ideas, the knowledge of their actual reactions. The fruitful development of a philosophy of the reasonable requires an appreciation *(valorisation)* of the men who prepare it, the recognition of all the rights of these men that would permit them to contribute effectively to the progress of thought.

The recourse to the reasonable, as a grounding for the rights of man, that defines and hierarchizes these rights in terms of their contribution to the progress of a concrete rationality, furnishes an illustration of my general thesis. Because it shows that only those who grant some value to the progress of theoretical thought and especially to philosophy, who conceive this progress in the form of historical elaboration of ever more reasonable conceptions, could link to it a theory of the rights of man arising out of a dialectic of the reasonable. But one sees that the grounding thus worked out would be neither an absolute grounding nor the only grounding conceivable, and that the rights that it would permit us to justify would not be defined in a fashion devoid of all ambiguity and indetermination. This example shows in what sense the undertaking is possible and demonstrates that the theory of the rights of man thus grounded would not be the expression of an irrational arbitrariness.

NOTES

1. *See* my article "jugements de valeur, justification et argumentation," in *Justice et Raison* (Bruxelles: Presses Universitaires de Bruxelles, 1963), pp. 236-38.

2. *See* "Philosophies premieres et philosophie régressive," in Ch. Perelman, *Rhetorique et Philosophie* (Paris: Presses Universitaires de France, 1952), pp. 85-109; "Evidence et Preuve," in *Justice et Raison,* pp. 140-54 (trans. as *The Idea of Justice and the Problem of Argument* [London: Routledge and Kegan Paul, 1963]).

3. *See* Pascal, "De l'esprit de géométrie et de l'art de persuader," in *L'oeuvre de Pascal* (Paris: Éditions de la Pléiade, 1941), pp. 380-81.

4. *Autour de la Nouvelle Déclaration des Droits de l'Homme,* texts collected by UNESCO (Paris: Sagittaire, 1949).

5. Ibid., J. Maritain, "Introduction"; R.McKeon, "Fondements philosophiques et conditions matérielles des droits de l'homme"; Don Salvador de Madariaga, "Droits de l'Homme ou relations humaines?"; "Conclusions de l'enquête menée par l'UNESCO sur les fondements théoriques des Droits de l'Homme," pp. 210-14.

6. Ch. Perelman, "Scepticisme moral et philosophie morale," in *Morale et Enseignement*, no. 44 (Bruxelles, 1962), pp. 22-26. Reproduced in *Droit, Morale et Philosophie*, pp. 83-86.

7. Ibid., pp. 25-26; *Droit, Morale et Philosophie*, pp. 85-86.

8. For the idea of universal audience, *see* Ch. Perelman and L. Olbrechts-Tyteca, *Traité de l'argumentation* (Paris: Presses Universitaires de France, 1958), 6-9. English trans., as *The New Rhetoric* (South Bend, Ind.: Notre Dame University Press, 1969).

9. *See* G. Calogero, *Logo e Dialogo* (Milano, 1950); *Filosofia del dialogo* (Milano, 1962).

10. *See* "L'idéal de rationalité et la règle de justice," *Bulletin de la Société française de Philosophie*, no. 1 (1961). Also in *Le champ* de l'argumentation, pp. 287-336.

ABRAHAM KAPLAN —— 2

Human Relations and Human Rights in Judaism*

*Professor Abraham Kaplan addresses the concept of human
rights—how it is defined and conferred—as fundamental to the moral
philosophy of Judaism. He concludes that the link between human
rights and Judaism is virtually self-evident in the traditional literature.
To demonstrate how human rights are particularized in the numerous
aspects of Jewish life and society, he outlines the complex and universal features of modern Judaism, focusing on the various denominational approaches to poverty, freedom, equality, and moral responsibility.*

It is not easy to generalize about Judaism. There is no orthodox doctrine to
serve as a point of reference. Orthodoxy is a matter of *halachah*—ritualistic
and moral observance—while doctrine belongs to *Haggadah*, along with
myth, legend, and other embellishments of practice. Moreover, questions
about Judaism may concern, in addition to the religion of the Jews, their
culture, ethnic identity, or political and social behavior. In all these respects
there is, besides, considerable variation among historical periods, movements, and individual thinkers.

Scattered quotations could be selected in support of quite divergent accounts. When two Jews argue, the folk saying runs, there are four views: the
one each holds, and the one each ascribes to the other; perhaps we should
say six views, for each dialectician by himself is likely to be of two minds.
The reader is warned.

Comparative studies of doctrine run the risk of arriving at invidious comparisons if a clear distinction is not maintained between institutions and the
philosophies that institutions embody, invoke, or suggest to interpreters.
Partisanship usually compares *our* theory with *their* practice, a maneuver
that takes advantage of the gap everywhere between high aspiration (or
pretension) and significantly lower achievement. The rejoinder, of course,

*Based on the Mark Chamberlain Lecture delivered at Lewis and Clark University, January
13, 1978.

compares our *practice* with their *theory*. I deal here only with doctrine, not with institutions.

In relation to human rights, patterns of action cannot be spoken of as Judaic in a strict sense since biblical times. Distinctively Jewish practice in the modern period is that characteristic either of the east European *stetl*, of Western urban and suburban life, or of the Israeli compound of Middle East tradition, the German Enlightenment, Anglo-Saxon law, and early Russian socialism. Jewish theory and practice have also been shaped by many non-Jewish influences; "distinctive" does not imply either self-contained or unique.

The actual patterns prevailing in a given group may be called its *moral code*. The moral code is to be distinguished from the *moral doctrine*, which practice aspires to or pretends to. The code calls for sociological and historical investigation; doctrine may be elicited from philosophical, religious, and political writings, and other such texts. I am concerned here with doctrine, not with code. I also omit any detailed consideration of questions of *ethical theory* (what in modern parlance is sometimes called "metaethics"). Theory comprises the explication and validation of doctrine. I consider only briefly how, in Jewish thought, human rights are conferred, what makes them a matter of right; I am concerned chiefly with what the rights are and how they are conceived to be particularized in social settings.

Human rights are worth only as much as it is worth to be human. The worth of the *individual* human being is another matter; individualism is not logically presupposed by every doctrine of human rights, for the rights might be defined to have their primary locus in some collective entity. A contemporary movement claiming to aim at the "legitimate rights" of a people is notorious for its denial of human rights to individuals, even within the movement. But rights must have *some* locus, whether individual or collective, and that locus must have some worth, or else the rights assigned to it will be devoid of significance. Judaism has much to say in recognition of the worth of man.

The first exponent of a systematic Jewish religious philosophy, Saadya Gaon (882-942), identifies man as "the final object of creation."[1] "The whole work of creation was for the sake of man," he writes (6,3), calling man "the axle of the world and its foundation." The cosmos is no more than the setting for a drama in which man is the central character, and God the Author, Producer, and Director. The events of nature and history are the unfolding of a divine plan; the world is subject to the governance of Providence. To take away from any man what is rightfully his is to act in defiance of the will of God with regard to what He Himself considers of primary importance.

Human rights are, in this sense, natural. Though their *source* transcends nature, they are embodied *in* nature and nature's laws, by way of the special place in nature assigned to man. The theory of natural rights, whatever its roots, is quite congenial to Judaic doctrine, though Judaism did not explicitly formulate any such theory. The Jewish teaching is that the rights of man belong to the way of the world as God meant it to be; to deny these rights is to depart from God's way.

Human rights belong to man, not only because of his place in nature, but by virtue of his own nature. He was created in the image of God, and thus embodies, in his own fashion and within his own limits, ultimate and supreme worth. The proposition that man was created in the divine image (Gen. 1:27) was selected by ben Azzai, one of the sages of the early Talmudic period, as the most important single verse in scripture.[2] The good life for man is that which accords with the divine element in his makeup.

That man should live by what is best in him is a view going back to Plato and Aristotle and forward into a continuing Judaic tradition. This view is retained, at least in part, in Spinoza's doctrine that virtue is nothing but action according to the law of our own nature. Martin Buber restates the position in the traditional religious idioms: "When God created man, He set the mark of His image upon man's brow, and embedded it in man's nature, and however faint God's mark may become, it can never be entirely wiped out.... God's real commandment to man is to realize this image."[3]

In what respect man is like his Maker is not univocally specified by the locution of an "image." Often it is man's reason which is regarded as the gist of his commonality with God. More to the present point is Saadya's view (2,3) that the verse in question is to be explained "in the sense of God bestowing dignity and honor upon man."[4] This is an echo of Psalm (8:5), "You have made him but a little lower than the angels, and have crowned him with glory and honor." Some centures later the Kabbalist rabbi Judah Loew of Prague (1525-1609) argued that because of the divine image, man is superior even to the angels. Whatever man's exact standing, he shares divine attributes and is deserving of high regard. Wherever man goes forth, he is preceded by a company of angels calling out, "Make way! Make way for the image of God!"

The consequences for human rights are immediate and direct. Because man embodies the divine image, there is a certain equivalence between man and God. "Wherever you come across a footprint of man, God stands before you," says a traditional aphorism. Man is to be treated, therefore, with something of the love and respect, not to say awe, which would be evoked by God Himself.

The implications have been made explicit with regard to the ethics of violence. "He who strikes his fellow," the Talmud warns, "strikes, as it were, the *Shechinah* [the Divine Presence]." Commentators have noted that on the two tablets of the Law one side begins with "I am the Lord your God" and the other side with "You shall not commit murder"—which implies, they explain, that murder is a crime directly against God.

The commandment prohibits murder, not, as often loosely rendered, killing. Judaism is not pacifistic. Apart from the violence recorded in the biblical narrative of the attainment of national identity, wars of national liberation have been important in Judaism from the time of the Maccabees and Bar Kochba to our own day.

However, in postbiblical practice the commandment has been strictly construed regarding capital punishment. During the last period of ancient Jewish authority, capital punishment was so hedged round with restrictions and qualifications that a single death sentence was enough to earn for the judicial body which issued it the designation "the bloody Sanhedrin." In the thirty years' existence of the modern state of Israel there has been only one execution, that of Adolf Eichmann.

Judaism begins with an affirmation of the sanctity of life. This is the significance of the *akedah*, the "sacrifice" of Isaac, in which dedication to a way of life replaces sacrificial death, especially of children. (In pre-Judaic times infanticide was associated with a valley in Jerusalem called "Gehennom," a name which later came to be used, understandably enough, for Hell.) The Talmud explains that "man was created singly [from Adam] to teach that he who destroys one soul is considered as if he had destroyed a world, and he who saves one soul as if he had saved a world" (Sanhedrin 37). Much the same formulation appears in other traditional texts: "One human being is worth as much as the whole creation."[5]

The measureless worth of every single life—a worth derived from its creation *by* God and in the image of God—later became a favorite theme of homiletics. We are careful not to swallow an ant, said the Hassidic Reb Baruch (the grandson of the eighteenth-century founder of Hassidism, the Baal Shem Tov), but we are not so careful about swallowing up a human being. Another Hassidic master, Israel of Rhyzn, observed that we treasure the creations of artists, but not the creations of the Creator Himself.

The worth of man derives from his divine origin and nature. It follows that his worth is intrinsic; man is not to be valued for what we can do with him or make of him. The Judaic kingdom of God anticipates Kant's kingdom of ends, in which man is never treated only as a means. This is the core of Buber's conception of "Thou": I am not to use the other or even merely to orient myself in relation to the other, but to realize him and thereby actualize myself.

Being treated as a means *only* is what is in question. There is more in man than the divine image. The earthly man, as it were, may properly be used—if he is used properly. He may even serve as a hired "hand." The gospel teaching that the laborer is worthy of his hire presupposes the Judaic regard for work.

Not even religious ends justify making of man only a means. The Sabbath was made for man, not man for the Sabbath, says the Talmud (Mechilta 80).

Yet man does serve religious ends; in Judaic perspectives, religion *is* service. The Hebrew word *avodah* means both work and worship (like the English word "service," for that matter). In the Kabbalah of Isaac Luria (1534-1572), whatever man does here below brings about corresponding changes in the world above. God needs man to put an end to His own exile: the Redeemer is to be redeemed.

That the cosmic destiny depends on man became a central doctrine of Hassidism, in the teaching of Yaakov Yosef of Polonye, for example. Mendel of Kotzk asks, "Why was man created? To perfect his soul? No. It was to lift up the heavens!"[6] But if the divine in man is a means, it serves as such only for divinity. For other human beings, man's precious essence must be prized as an end in itself, setting limits to our use of man in his earthly nature, and determining the nature of that use.

Man is both end and means to other men. Between Buber's "Thou" and "It" is the workaday "you." If I do not exploit the other, misuse him, the alternative is not necessarily to treasure him. Though I am to love my neighbor as myself, I do not live all wrapped up in myself either. Jewish realism has long recognized that even as much love for the other as is self-directed may be more than can be expected. Do not despair if you do not love your neighbor; it is something if you can live in peace with him.

But the peace is to be *with* him; morality is not sufficiently served by *leaving* him in peace. If I have noxious neighbors I am glad when they leave me alone; but there is something still to be desired if I have been left *alone.* That is inhuman treatment, cold and impersonal. The Judaic ideal was expressed in the Yiddish-speaking subculture as being a *mensch*—literally, a person, a human being—with the connotation in such contexts of being not just human but humane, having compassion, sympathy, and consideration for the other.

The condemnation of our society as dehumanizing has this content, that we treat one another as things, as means only, and at best leave one another alone. A conspicuous exception is the surge of fellow-feeling in the face of disaster, present or impending. If we are human to one another only in the face of disaster, we are headed for disaster. In traditional Jewish symbolism, that is what happened to the Cities of the Plain: characteristically, Abraham was unwilling, even when God's will was made known to him, to abandon the cities to their fate.

Individualism is not logically presupposed by a concern for human rights. Judaism is in fact individualistic, so far as concerns the morality of action. The term "tribalism" is often used nowadays as a pejorative substitute for nationalism or patriotism, as "clannishness" is used pejoratively for solidarity and group loyalty. In a nonpejorative sense "tribalism" may be taken to designate the assignment of moral responsibility (and accompanying praise or blame) to *each* member of a group for the actions of *any* member. One of many ironies of Jewish history is that though Jews are recurrently accused of "tribalism," it is anti-Semitism, like all ethnic prejudice, which is tribalistic, holding every Jew accountable for what is imputed to any Jew.

The Jews repudiated tribalism as early as the age of the prophets. Both Ezekiel (18:1-4) and Jeremiah (31:29-30) insist on personal rather than familial moral responsibility, rejecting the teaching of an earlier time that when the fathers have eaten sour grapes the children's teeth are set on edge. Each man will be brought to account only for his own sins; only the sinner himself is subject to judgment. Isaiah, in Buber's explication, similarly emphasizes personal responsibility as alone being capable of infusing morality into institutional life. "When Isaiah speaks of justice," Buber says, "he is not thinking of institutions, but of you and me, because without you and me, the most glorious institution becomes a lie."[7]

Buber carries moral individualism to the point of making the action of individuals the touchstone of morality. What is wrong for the individual, he declares, cannot be right for the group. This principle may be sound if the action under consideration is being undertaken in the *name* of the group. The right of the individual to act in that name may be morally questionable, as in the case of terrorists acting to liberate a society from "capitalist exploitation" or "imperialist domination," when the society they presume to speak for may share neither their end nor the means they employ to attain it.

But action *by* a group—that is, by individuals duly authorized to act for the group—may be morally right even though it would be wrong for the action to be performed by an individual acting for himself. It is wrong for one individual to extort money from another, but a state may rightfully collect taxes; it is wrong for one individual to resort to force to compel another to his will, but a state may rightfully exercise police power or wage war.

In Judaism there has long been a tension between politico-religious nationalism and moral individualism. The fate of each Jew has been seen, from biblical antiquity to the present, as bound up with the fate of Israel as a people. Yet it is only the individual who can be righteous or a sinner. The Sadducees took the position that God is concerned only with the whole people, in accord with a doctrine widespread in the Hellenistic world, that the gods occupy themselves only with the affairs of nations, or with very special personages such as kings. It is the position of the Pharisees, however, which prevailed in Judaism, and subsequently also in Christianity: God cares for the individual soul, and each soul is of measureless worth in His eyes.

The moral dilemma persists. It has become acute in our time because so much morally significant action in our day is collective—performed by transpersonal entities such as states, corporations, and political groups. The moral dilemma is that the individual cannot control group action, yet it is only individuals who can be held morally responsible. *I* cannot make peace or war, establish or destroy a social order or an economic system. Yet I cannot for that reason claim exemption from moral responsibility for such actions, or no one will be morally accountable for them. The dropout is impaled on one horn of the dilemma and the militant activist on the other; one takes no action at all, the other takes matters into his own hands.

Judaism copes with the dilemma by assuming individual responsibility for *affecting* group decisions, so far as it is in the individual's power to do so. Hillel, the most quoted of the *tannaim* (early Talmudic sages), enjoins, "In a place where there are no men, strive to be a man!"[8] This is usually interpreted to mean that if moral leadership is lacking in the community *you* must take the initiative. The predicament is especially painful when it is the leadership itself which is morally corrupt. It is not easy to be a man—that is, to live up to one's moral responsibilities—even under the best of circumstances. It is almost impossible in a state of subjection to powers beyond one's control, the condition of all Jews through a large part of their history, and of some Jews (like those of the Soviet Union) even today.

Individualism as a social doctrine, as distinct from moral individualism, is on the whole foreign to Judaic perspectives, in spite of the stereotype of the Jewish entrepreneur. Such an individualism conceives of the ends of social action as definable by reference to no more than the welfare of individuals rather than to a common good as well. It conceives of the means of social action as even more individualistic, in a competitive rather than a cooperative framework. Yet collectivist means pursued for collective ends are uncongenial to Judaism. Buber's position is at bottom the traditional one: "Individualism understands only part of man," he says, whereas "collectivism understands man only as a part; neither advances to the wholeness of man."[9]

That the individual needs his fellow man is scriptural wisdom: "Two are better than one . . . . For if they fall, one will lift up his fellow; but woe to him who is alone when he falls, and has not another to help him up. Again, if two lie together, then they have warmth; but how can one be warm alone? If a man prevail against one alone, two shall withstand him; and a threefold cord is not quickly broken" (Eccles. 4:9-12). The Midrash uses the homely phrasing that no barber cuts his own hair (*Midrash Rabbah* on Lev. 14:9).

The medieval Jewish philosopher Shlomo ibn Gavirol (1020-c.1060) (proven in the nineteenth century to be identical with the presumedly Arab philosopher Avicebron) is equally concrete: a man alone is the left hand without the right. Spinoza carries on a long tradition with his remark that to man there is nothing more useful than other men. The strength of socialist institutions in Israel, whatever the politics of a particular government, reflects the influence on the new state not just of Russian intellectuals, but of Russian Jewish intellectuals.

For Judaic practice, the *kehilla* (the congregation or community) takes priority over the individual. Prayers are to be recited communally if at all possible; individual, personal prayers are the exception, and usually only second best. The Talmud rules that a religious practice does not have binding force if it is such that the majority of the community cannot observe it (Horayot 3b, Avodah Zarah 36a). Society is not merely a setting for individual action; it provides the norms for action.

Society does more: it gives substance to individuality. Hillel asks, "If I am for myself only, what am I?" This is not the conventional exhortation to altruism. It points, rather, to the role of identification—involvement, emotional investment—in making up the self. Giving of oneself is the process by which the self comes to be; through the Thou one becomes an I, as Buber has it.

The inverse of the process, introjection or taking the other into oneself, provides the self with content. Moses Cordovero, a sixteenth-century philosopher of the Lurian circle, anticipated modern social psychology with his view that in every man there is something of his fellows. Buber formulates the doctrine in the dictum that all real life is meeting. For man, he says, the primal reality is the *zwissenmenschliche*—what takes place between man and man.

The conception is that elaborated in some detail by G. H. Mead, who speaks of the genesis of the self in the capacity to take the role of the "generalized other." In Jewish society, tightly knit since the tribal period, the other is not generalized without bounds but has a Jewish cast. Similarly, identity is well defined for other social groups with distinctive character. To the question "Who are you?" the reply traditional among Jews is "A Jew!" The group identity is more significant than the individuality. One of the Hassidic masters is even known simply as The Jew ("Yehudi"); he is the subject of a fictionalized biography by Buber, *For the Sake of Heaven.*

The Jewish social identity is made the premise for important conclusions about individual morality. I *must* care for the other because in fact he is not altogether other. The voice of my brother's blood cries out to me from the ground because that blood is my own. "Do not stand idly by the blood of your fellows," the Torah enjoins (Lev. 19:16). Moses did not stand by idly when he saw an Egyptian smiting a Hebrew, "one of his brothers" (Exod. 2:11).

That we are all members of one body may be metaphorical; that we are members of one mind, one soul is a literal truth. *Kol Yisrael chaverim*—all Jews are comrades—is the folk expression of group loyalty and solidarity; underlying it is a psychological reality. Each becomes the person he is because the people is what it is. All for one and one for all is more than a romantic declaration of comradeship; it is the acknowledgment of a personal destiny.

To be a member of a community is one thing; to have a sense of community is another. The community is intrinsic to the identity, but it is no small matter for anyone to come to know who he is. Pirke Avot (a section of the Mishnah known as the Ethics of the Fathers) enjoins us to keep in mind where we have come from and where we are going. The injunction may be given a naturalistic interpretation as well as an eschatological one. To know oneself is to be aware how much of the other we have taken into ourselves and how much of ourselves is a giving to the other. If we do not know the other, we cannot know ourselves.

We do not know either self or other save as we appreciate who and what they are; fact and value are bound up together, suffuse one another, just as self and other do. This is the sense of community: that I and they are one, and that it is good that this is so. To produce and sustain such a sense of community is the fundamental aim of the Torah, the Law, according to Philo Judaeus of Alexandria (c. 25 B.C.E. to 40 C.E.): "What our most holy prophet through all his regulations especially desires to create is unanimity, neighborliness, fellowship, shared feeling. . . . [10]

Community implies the extension throughout the group of the caring of one individual for another. In Buber's locution, "Only men who are capable of truly saying Thou to one another can truly say We with one another."[11] The use of the first person plural may serve instead to gloss over the absence or breakdown of community. A politician who repeatedly calls on his "fellow Americans" may be campaigning for policies to which fellowship is irrelevant or even antithetical. The question whether there is such a thing as a "Jewish vote" points to the deeper question whether there is in truth a Jewish community. The prophet does not speak to the people of Israel; his task is to *make* it a people.

Buber contrasts "community" with "collectivity," which, he says, is "not a binding together but a bundling together." The Judaic emphasis on the need for one another may point to a necessary condition for community; it is not a sufficient condition. One person can make use of another and build a relationship by allowing the other to make use of him in turn. The dehumanization in one direction is not cancelled by its repetition in the reverse direction; it is only exacerbated. A barbed definition of the difference between capitalism and socialism runs: "Capitalism is the exploitation of man by man; in socialism, it's just the other way around." Community is not a matter of *reciprocity*—letting you do to me what I do to you—but of *mutuality*: doing together what we cannot de separately, or would not want to do separately if we could.

In Judaism, caring for the other is not a matter merely of addressing ourselves to our own needs unless we acknowledge that disinterested caring is itself a need. The pragmatic defense of human rights, though valid and persuasive, misses altogether the psychological roots of Jewish involvement in the civil rights movements. Jewish attitudes toward educational opportunity, for instance, have much more to do with the Judaic regard for learning than with concern for enlarging the work force available for a complex technology.

Other verses than the one affirming the creation of man in the divine image have been selected as the most basic in Scripture. Rabbi Akiba (50-135

C.E.), one of the founders of Talmudic hermeneutics, selected the verse "Thou shalt love thy neighbor as thyself" (Lev. 19:18). Writing a generation earlier, Philo Judaeus notes that though "Thou shalt love the Lord thy God with all thine heart" is also an explicit injunction (Deut. 6:5), "He who loves God but does not show love toward his own kind has but the half of virtue."[12] It is, indeed, the lesser half, dependent on the other. "He in whom the spirit of his fellow men does not take delight," Pirke Avot preaches, "in him the spirit of God does not take delight" (3:12). The charm for loving God, Hassidism ceaselessly taught, is to love man.

To love another is to care for *his* needs, not our own. What is more, it is to care for his needs as *he* experiences them, not what *we* judge he needs. Too often, Mendel of Kotzk warns, we occupy ourselves first with our own material needs before the spiritual welfare of the other, rather than the other way around. Yet there is a moral dilemma to be faced here. The greatest need of the other may be to learn to recognize his needs and declare them. The deepest bondage is that which no longer knows the meaning and worth of freedom.

The point remains that in Judaic teaching love presupposes respect. The controlling, manipulative, over protective mother is no more Jewish than, say, Italian, Japanese, or Mexican; in any case, the underlying perspective is not Judaic, whatever its social psychology. There is a crucial difference between being "helpful" and actually helping someone. A recent article elaborating this distinction bears the memorable title, "Chicken Soup Can Be Poison." The client-centered therapy of Carl Rogers formulates in a clinical context a theme expressed in many dicta of the Hassidic masters, like Simcha Bunam. We may place the ladder and hold it firm, but the other must climb it himself. When one wearing a blindfold comes before us, another parable runs, we are not to lead him but to remove his blindfold; then he will see for himself how to go. I can do something *for* another, that is, on his behalf; I cannot do it in his stead.

Awareness of my own needs can heighten my perception of the needs of the other; what I suffer when my needs are frustrated can make me more sensitive to his misery. When Hillel was asked the essence of the Law—what can be taught "while standing on one leg"—he replied with the Silver Rule: "What would be harmful to you, do not do unto others" (Shabbat 31a).

The criterion is whether the act is harmful; the question is not one of subjective likes or dislikes. The revolutionist's handbook appended to Shaw's *Man and Superman* repudiates the rule on the grounds that people have different tastes. Taste is not always at issue—the undeniably bitter pill may be undeniably medicinal; and where the choice *is* only a matter of taste, whether something is *to* one's taste, either your own or another's, is an objective question.

Love and respect for the other imply not that I do something in his place but, as Hillel urges, that I put myself in his place before judging him (Avot

2:5). The sense of community confers the capacity to do just that. This is why Hillel also enjoins, "Do not separate yourself from the community" (Avot 4:7). To go my own way regardless of the other is not only to leave him to his damnation but also to condemn myself to an uncaring, insensitive existence.

Before the rebellious Korah and his company were destroyed, Moses and Aaron and the congregation of the righteous were commanded to withdraw from them (Num. 16:20-21). There was more moral grandeur, and what subsequent history showed to be a more characteristically Jewish response, in the plea of Moses for a sinning people, "If You will forgive their sin . . .; if not, blot my name out of Your book" (Exod. 32:32). Literalists construe this as a reference to the Book of Life—that is, as an offer to die in their stead; the spirit of the verse is Moses' readiness to stand with his people even in confrontation with his God.

Moral autonomy is not being negated, as though I must go along with others even when their way offends my moral sense. What is being negated is the pursuit of a purely personal salvation; redemption is not to be defined for the individual without regard to the community. Noah was a righteous man "in his generation" (Gen. 6:9); at another time he might have been judged differently. Told of the coming Flood, he carried out the directions to save himself and his family without a word of protest on behalf of others, in striking contrast to Abraham on being informed of the imminent destruction of the Cities of the Plain.

This same concern for the other is expressed in the hospitality for which Abraham was noted, sitting at the door of his tent so as not to miss any traveler. Noah was a "just" man, one of the very few explicitly so described in Scripture, but it was with Abraham that God established His covenant. In the cold, said Mendel of Kotzk, there are those who wrap themselves in furs while others light a fire that can be seen from afar and that sheds its warmth all around; Judaism disparages the saint in a fur coat.

The crisis of indifference in our time has often been noted. That people nowadays simply do not want to get involved is not new. What is new is that the conditions of modern life make it plain that we are involved whether we want to be or not. I am my brother's keeper even though I feel strongly that no one keeps *me*. Judaism is at one with other religions in affirming a moral responsibility for the welfare of others. Judaism attaches religious significance to the discharge of the moral responsibility. Deeds of personal kindness were held by Yochanan ben Zakkai, who might be regarded as the founder of rabbinic Judaism, to be well able to take the place of the Temple ritual. Job based his claim for justice on a moral life in which he did more than respond to the needs which were brought to his attention: "The cause even of him I knew not I searched out" (29:16).

A *minority ethics* has been characteristic of the Jews throughout most of their history, in which they lived as a minority or with painful memories of what it means to be a minority. Jews have been responsive to the oppression of any people, having been so much oppressed themselves. Pursuit of the ideals of equality, justice, and freedom has been a matter of simple self-interest. In the two millennia between ancient Israel and the new state, the Jew has been a marginal man, not necessarily with regard to his economic role, but in the sense of living always on the periphery of the larger community. At home anywhere, he was everywhere a stranger.

With the price paid in social standing he bought a priceless basis of moral aspiration. "Love the stranger, for you were strangers in the land of Egypt" (Deut. 10:19). In Buber's Judaism, it is the Jewish vocation to testify to the unredeemedness of the world. The Jew "feels this lack of redemption against his own skin, he tastes it on his tongue, the burden of the unredeemed world lies on him."[13] For the term "Jew" to be anything more than a label of identification is for him to remember that he was once a slave and to await the Messiah with whose coming all men will be free.

The Jew should remember that *he* was once a slave. The Passover Haggadah, the text for the celebration of the Exodus, enjoins that each participant in the ceremony is to experience himself, not merely his remote ancestors, as redeemed from bondage. It is a matter of strength of identifications. Only on this basis can there be a recognition of the correspondingly personal responsibility for pursuit of a social ideal. The Messiah will come only when we are ready for him; each must make *himself* ready. The time is always out of joint, and each Jew knows that he was born to set it right.

The Talmud specifies the obligation in concrete terms. When someone is to be rescued—for instance, from robbers, drowning, or wild beasts—one cannot perform the rescue himself, but nevertheless has the obligation to organize a rescue and at his own cost (Sanhedrin 73a).

The God of Israel characteristically identifies Himself to His people not as the Creator of the Universe but as "the Lord your God Who brought you forth out of the land of Egypt." Since each Jew was himself brought forth, God has an intensely personal significance for each. Each man, says the Talmud (Sanhedrin 37), should have the sense that the entire world was created for his sake.

If God is so concerned with me, it cannot be wrong for me to be concerned about myself—provided, of course, that I know who and what I am. There is no departure from Judaism in Spinoza's dictum (in his *Ethics*, Part IV, Props. 20, 24) that "the first and only foundation of virtue, or the rule of right living, is seeking one's own true interest."

Judaic ethics does not counterpose egoism and altruism (both so-called). By way of identifications and introjections the other enters into the very being of the self. There is nothing morally questionable in caring for self; on the contrary. One is not to clothe others while going about naked (Baba

Bathra 60b). Hillel's question, "If I am for myself only, what am I?" is preceded by the equally pointed, "If I am not for myself, who will be?" Judaism enjoins fulfilling the self, not losing it—even in mystic communion.

The injunction to love thy neighbor as thyself is hardly being followed by one who hates his neighbor with the excuse that he hates himself as well. The most that one can give to another, perhaps all that he can truly give, is himself; if the self has been impoverished, there is that much less to be given. There is no love, Buber has said, without being and remaining oneself.

What is called "self-sacrifice" is often not a genuine giving, but a manipulation of the other by inducing a sense of guilt, or a self-punitive device to alleviate a sense of guilt. Jewish condemnation of reverse discrimination accepted in a spirit of "we deserve it!" is a case in point. Affirmative action— for instance, special programs to raise the qualifications of victims of discrimination—is morally justified; indeed, it is a moral obligation. Lowering standards in certain cases to meet the lower qualifications, on the other hand, is morally wrong, for it creates new victims. It is extraordinary how much rhetoric has been devoted by political passion to obscuring the simple truth that two wrongs do not make a right. It is no service to the black to make him the supposed beneficiary of a reverse racism, "until a balance has been reached."

The anti-Semitic image of the cringing, fawning Jew, whatever the sociological roots of the stereotype, is quite foreign to Judaism, from biblical times to modern Israel. Far more typical is Mordecai's refusal to bow to any man (Esther 3:2), and Job's determination not to resort to "hypocrisy" (more accurately, groveling flattery) to appease an angry God (Job 13:16). According to Saadya Gaon (3,2) "reason lays down that the wise man should not permit himself to be vilified and treated with contempt." If a man bows too low too often, the Baal Shem Tov (1700-1760) warned, he forgets how to raise his head to Heaven.

The confession of one's sins on Yom Kippur has a number of noteworthy features bearing on the Judaic attitude toward the self. The faults and shortcomings are formulated in the plural—"we" have done such and such, not just "I"—so that no one need be shamed before his fellows. They are listed in an alphabetical acrostic, because it is so easy to forget what we would rather not remember. The alphabetical order serves another purpose: though our failings run from A to Z, when we have finished the alphabet there is an end to them, and a basis is left for self-respect. Without that, there is nothing.

Morality is not adequately served by the vague principle of caring for "others"; a great deal hinges on how many others. To love thy neighbor is one thing in a rural society where neighbors are few and far; it is quite another in urban life, as in American cities, where there are, on the average, some tens of thousands living within one mile of one another. Even if the difference between rural and urban communities were obliterated and populations were uniformly dispersed, there are today thirty-five countries in which each inhabitant would have within a mile more than one thousand neighbors. What can it mean to care for such a mass in human, which is to say, personal, terms?

Moral issues hinge not merely on how *many* others we care for, but *which* others. Questions arise not only with regard to the range of our identifications but also their composition; with whom do we identify, and identify most closely? That charity begins at home is an ancient doctrine. Blood is thicker than water: in every society kinship entails special rights and obligations. To care for one's own first or to care more, if it be a moral failing at all, is at any rate a universal one. In this respect Jews have often been denied what is permitted and even applauded in other peoples. In the Soviet Union today a Russian who cares first and most for Russians is a "patriot"; a Lithuanian or Ukrainian identifying with *his* people is a "nationalist"; a Jew wanting to migrate to Israel is a "Zionist imperialist."

Whatever case can be made for a universalist morality must come to terms with the moral demands of more restricted identifications. Discrimination in the strict sense of the term—to respond differently to different stimuli or in different circumstances—not only cannot be condemned out of hand but might even be acknowledged to be the aim of all learning. The question is always whether the difference in stimulus or context is relevant.

It sometimes *is* relevant, as morality itself insists. Philo Judaeus argues on behalf of moral universalism, "He who is fast bound in the love of his wife or under the stress of nature makes his children his first care, ceases to be the same to others and unconsciously has become a different man, and has passed from freedom into slavery."[14] It is not a base jealousy, however, which forbids a man to treat other women quite like his wife and other children quite like his own; if he did, marriage and the family would cease to have meaning. If you are equally a friend to all, I beg leave to doubt whether you are a friend of mine.

Just as there is a tension in Judaism between nationalism and individualism, there is also a tension between the particularism focused on Jews, and a moral universalism concerned with all the nations. The new king of Egypt who knew not Joseph feared that the Hebrews might join his enemies (Exod. 1: 8-10); Haman charged the Jews with not keeping the king's laws because their laws were diverse (Esther 3:8). Since biblical times, Jewish loyalty to others has been challenged because of their loyalty to their own.

Yet a universalist perspective is also intrinsic to Judaism. "It astonishes me," Philo writes, "to see that some people venture to accuse of inhumanity the nation which has shown so profound a sense of fellowship and goodwill to all men everywhere, by using its prayers and festivals as a means of supplication for the whole human race, in the name of all men."[15]

Not only are many Judaic observances performed on behalf of all men; the morality Judaism enjoins is presented as a norm for all men. Nowhere in the Torah or the Talmud is there any reference to a "good Jew" but always only to a "good man." God's law is for a "man" to live by, not just a "Jew" (Lev. 18:5); there is no particularist limitation in the moral ideal formulated, say, in Psalm 15, in Isa. 33:14-16, or in Mic. 6:8.

What God requires is proclaimed to all who can hear the voice of prophecy. True, Amos declares (5:4) "Thus says God *to the house of Israel*, seek Me and live," but in Isaiah we have (56:1-7), "Thus says God, Keep My judgment and do justice. . . . The sons of the stranger that join themselves to God I shall bring to my holy mountain. . . . My house shall be called a house of prayer *for all people.*" Mordecai is introduced with the words, "There was a certain Jew . . ." (Esther 2:5), but Job simply by "There was a man. . . ." (Job 1:1).

The Judaic teaching is on behalf of all and applies to all; the tradition is that it is also taught to all. The Torah, says the Talmud (Shabbat 88b), was revealed in the desert rather than in the land of Israel so that it would be accessible to all; no man's land is every man's. The voice at Sinai spoke in every language, as at the feast of Ahasuerus every prince was served with the wine of his own province and the vintage of his own year of birth. The Midrash (on Num. 1:54a) adds that every line of Torah can be interpreted in seventy different ways (one for each nation of the world).

In spite of the fact that Hebrew is known as the "holy tongue," from the standpoint of *halachah* prayers may be said in any language (Shabbat 12b)—all languages are alike to God's understanding. (A concession to particularism, provided by the Haggadah, is that the angels, however, understand only Hebrew!) Truth is not limited to any one mode of expression. "What is lofty," Maimonides declared, "can be said in any language; what is lowly should be said in none."[16] The same assessment is made by Spinoza: "Books which teach and speak of whatever is highest and best are equally sacred, whatever be the tongue in which they are written, or the nation to which they belong."[17] The position is especially significant in view of the centrality of language in group identities, to this day.

From as soon after the biblical period as Philo Judaeus, Jewish philosophy has been universalistic; Judah Halevi (1085-1141) stands out as an exception. Philo held that there was a law prior to and independent of the Mosaic law proclaimed to the people of Israel. The patriarchs, especially Abraham, lived by this prior law. The name "Israel" he construed, with what I take to be dubious philology, as meaning "one who sees God" (it is more commonly rendered as "Prince" of the Lord—Gen. 32:28). On his reading, the people of Israel includes all who attain to the vision of the divine. All scriptures are sacred, embodying prophetic inspiration. The training of the soul for the vision is open to all, not only to Jews.

Maimonides comes to much the same conclusion, without Philo's meta-physical premises. "Accept the truth from whomever speaks it."[18] It is crucial, of course, what test of truth is invoked. The genetic fallacy narrated in the gospel, "Can there any good thing come out of Nazareth?" is as far as could be from Maimonides's temper of mind. "Whether one should believe a prophet or not depends on the nature of his doctrines," he wrote, "not on his race."[19]

In our age of nuclear weapons and global pollution, there is widespread emphasis on *pragmatic universalism.* We live in one world; we are all in the same boat. Differences are feared as being divisive and therefore mortally dangerous at a time when each holds in his hands the fate of all. There is a strong strain of pragmatic realism in Jewish thought also, especially in the Talmud. Jerusalem was destroyed, as were the Cities of the Plain and the generation of the Flood, because of "gratuitous" hatred—that is, hatred of one another rather than of sin. Such hatred is as vicious as the three cardinal sins of incest, murder, and idolatry (Yoma 8-11). If particularist identities are fed by hatred and in turn nourish it, they may yet destroy us.

More characteristic of Jewish thought than pragmatic universalism is *prophetic universalism:* not just that we risk the same fate, but that we are of one flesh, formed by and infused with the same divine Spirit. The brother-hood of man derives from the common fatherhood of God. Pharisaic Judaism preserved the universalist perspective. For the Sadducees, with the elitism to be expected of their aristocratic bent, the God of Israel was the God of Israel only, and concerned himself only with the Jews. Some distinction between a national god and a universal deity can be recognized in both biblical and postbiblical times. *Yahweh* is often taken to designate the national God and *Elohim* the universal God—as in Ecclesiastes and the Wisdom literature in general.

Since God is the Father of all, the concept of the family of man takes on moral significance. The very first question raised in the Talmud concerns the time when morning prayers may be recited—at any time after midnight, with the earliest flush of dawn, after the sun has wholly risen, or when? Among the answers presented is that we can recite the prayers when there is enough light for a man to recognize his brother. No doubt this can be taken literally, as a purely ritualistic specification, but the ethical reading is inviting.

The Talmud (Megilla 9, Sanhedrin 39) records an unequivocal expression of prophetic universalism. When the Hebrews of the Exodus succeeded in reaching dry land while the pursuing Egyptians sank into the sea, Moses and the children of Israel sang unto the Lord. The angels, says the Talmud, joined in the song, whereupon God rebuked them, "My creatures are drowning, and you dare to sing!" At the very moment of triumph, the end to centuries of slavery, the first breath of a free people celebrating an unimagined victory over those seeking to destroy them—at that very moment comes the affirmation that even their mortal enemies are children of the same God, Who cares for *them* as He does for all His creatures.

There is a third universalism, *rational universalism:* common to all men is a faculty of reason, with its associated principles, a commonality that overshadows the superficial differences between one man or group of men and another. Rational universalism also has an important part to play in Judaism, although it is not as distinctive as the prophetic doctrine. An old-line stereotype contrasts Greek intellectualism with Hebrew moralism. Bertrand Russell remarks somewhere that Jeremiah and Thales were roughly contemporary; had they met, he suggests, the philosopher might have declared, "All is water," to which the prophet would have rejoined only, "Woe, alas!" In fact, a Greek chorus might well have provided the lamentation, while a Hebrew sage might have speculated on the reality underlying the spectacle of the visible universe.

In particular, the *chachamim* of the period of the Wisdom literature—well within the Hellenistic age—elaborated a moral teaching based on principles common to all men. The Book of Proverbs, for instance, makes no mention whatever of Israel, its history, or its mission; the word "man" (*adam*), however, occurs thirty-three times. "Wisdom," "understanding," and "knowledge" (the intellectualist triad important in *kabbalah* and *Hassidism*, whose Hebrew names—*chochma, bina,* and *da'at*—provide the acronym for the *chabad* movement) appear, together with their cognates, more than sixty times each in a book of fewer than a thousand verses.

For Maimonides it is virtually axiomatic that reason belongs to the essence of man; rationality is not, as popular religion often supposes, a consequence of the Fall of man. The intellectualism of the Wisdom literature is carried on by Hillel and Akiba, who are well aware that study will lead to action, whereas action does not necessarily bring one to study.

The rationalism of rabbinic Judaism, to the point of hair-splitting and logomachy, is notorious. It is acknowledged in the Talmud itself: "Three kinds of creatures quarrel: dogs, fighting cocks, and sorcerers. Some say also harlots; and some add, Babylonian scholars"—a remark which appears in the Babylonian Talmud (Pesachim 113). In the Talmud is also to be found the noteworthy statement that "one who has a scientific mind and refuses to apply himself is condemned for indifference to the wonders of God" (Shabbat 75).

Even the Hassidic movement, for all its pietism, did not lose sight of the intellectual virtues and their moral significance. "I would rather be with the wise in Hell than with the fools in Heaven," said Naftali of Ropshitz, adding, "but in Heaven there are no fools!"

Rational universalism merges with prophetic universalism in the view that reason as such is not only common to all men but is the commonality between man and God. "It is because of the divine intellect conjoined with man that it is said of him that he is in the image of God," Maimonides explains at the very beginning of his *Guide for the Perplexed* (1, 1). He was, of course, much influenced by Aristotle, but the same doctrine is to be found also in the neo-Platonist Philo: "It is in respect of the mind, the sovereign element of the soul, that the word 'image' is used."[20] On still another metaphysical basis, Spinoza sees the human mind as "part of the infinite intellect of God" (*Ethics* 2, 11).

There is no essential difference among men, with regard to either their spiritual or their intellectual endowment. They are therefore capable of grasping and adhering to the same moral law. Judaism accordingly imposes the obligation to extend equal treatment to Jew and non-Jew: "The stranger who lives with you shall be to you as one born among you" (Lev. 19:34); "One law and one ordinance shall be for you and for the stranger who is with him" (Deut. 1:16); "The strangers who live among you . . . shall be to you as native-born among the children of Israel" (Ezek. 47:22).

To be sure, universalist injunctions like these do not altogether negate Judaic particularism, which assigns to the Jews a special place among the peoples. Judaism, like only one or two other well-known religions (for instance, Shinto), is intrinsically bound up with a particular people, its land, and history. The doctrine that purports to separate Zionism from Judaism is an absurd political concoction. Anti-Semitism also falsifies Judaism in the reverse direction, construing its particularism in a way that not only leaves no place for the universalist element but also distorts the particularism itself.

I refer, of course, to the identification of the Jews as the "chosen people." The label occurs much more often and with much more emphasis in anti-Semitic propaganda than in Judaic liturgy or philosophy. Even Judah Halevi, among the most particularist of Jewish philosophers, does not use the word "chosen" in connection with scriptural passages referring to God's choice (for instance, Exod. 19:5). He speaks, rather, of man's choice, and specifically, Israel's acceptance of the Torah, with all its burdens. (The myth is that the Law was successively offered to and refused by all other peoples.) More apt than the "chosen" people would be the "choosing" people; better still might be the word "choosy." The Jews volunteered for special duty in the armies of the Lord.

The difference between Jew and non-Jew is not in moral standing but in religious obligation. This is a matter of doctrine, it must be repeated, not of personal feeling or social practice, which—among Jews as among every other ethnic group—makes invidious distinctions between "us" and "them." To be a Jew is declared to be a great privilege, carrying with it commensurately great responsibilities. The Hebrew term for a virtuous action or good deed, *mitzvah*, means literally a commandment; Judaism is a religion of duties. From most of them, all but the purely ethical ones, non-Jews are exempt. The Hassidic rabbi Levi Yitzchak of Berditchev, known as the Compassionate, prays, "Dear God, if Your time has not yet come to redeem the Jews, at least redeem the gentiles!"

The universal obligations are those formulated in the last six of the Ten Commandments, which are sometimes said to make up the "Code of Noah," since he was a righteous man before the time of the Covenant. All who live by the moral code attain to spiritual fulfillment. The position is explicit in a variety of materials from the Talmudic period: "The pious of all nations have a portion in the World to Come."[21] "Whether a person be a Jew or non-Jew, according to the deed which he performs, the Holy Spirit rests on him."[22] The same position is taken by Judah Halevi, and, as is to be expected, by Maimonides.[23]

The range of Jewish identification is underlined in the attitude toward converts. Judaism is conspicuously lacking in evangelism. Far from doing everything possible to propagate the faith, Judaism discourages proselytes; indeed, the restrictiveness of the criteria for acceptable conversions is a matter of considerable debate in Israel today. Judaism looks with the prophet to the day when God will be one and His name one; it will be the day of the coming of the Messiah. That day is not hastened by what we do to others but only by what we make of ourselves.

Reluctance to accept the proselyte is not a reflection on his eligibility but only on the effectiveness of the process of conversion. The Talmud (Hagiga 3) points out that Judaism was founded by a convert, Abraham, who, after all, was not born a Jew. The Book of Ruth traces the ancestry of King David back to a convert; Akiba is another notable descendant of non-Jewish ancestors. Judah Halevi is once more outside the mainstream of Judaism, both before and after his time, in conceiving of the Jewish people as comprising only born Jews. His own major work, however, the Khuzari, nevertheless takes its title from an eighth-century group of converts to Judaism.

Once the conversion has been made, Judaism does not countenance any discriminations between the born Jew and the convert. The Talmud explicitly prohibits any reproach of the convert for the deeds of his fathers (Baba Metzia 4:10). The position taken in practice follows the doctrine stated, for instance, by Philo: "All who spurn idle fables and embrace truth in its purity, whether they have been such from the first or through conversion . . . have reached the higher state, obtain His approval . . . , giving equal rank to all incomers with all the privileges which He gives to the native-born."[24]

Jews identify most closely with other Jews and next with men of goodwill everywhere—that is, those who, whatever their identification, share the Judaic morality and other basic values. (In Israel today, "the righteous among the nations" is an official designation, by which the state honors non-Jews who were instrumental, at considerable personal risk, in saving Jewish lives during the Holocaust.) Only then does Jewish identification reach out to the whole family of man. In practice, much the same three levels of identification apply to every ethnic or religious identity. In theory, Judaism is more egalitarian than many other doctrines.

Equality is a direct implication of prophetic universalism. "If I despised the cause of my servant when he contended with me, what shall I do when God rises up?" Job asks (31:13-15). "Did not He who made me also make my servant? Did not one God fashion us both?" The Book of Proverbs (22:2) draws the same inference: "The rich and the poor meet together, God is the maker of them all." The point is also expressed in Hannah's prayer (1 Sam.2:7). In the same vein the Talmud (Sanhedrin 37) explains that all men were created from Adam, rather than each man singly, so that no one could boast of ancestry superior to another's.

Equality is of special importance in Hassidic teaching, in part because of the social setting of its origin. Eastern European Jewry in the eighteenth century exhibited marked differences in standing in the community—not only as between rich and poor, but also between scholar and peasant (the *talmud chacham* and the *am ha'aretz*) and the rigidly pious and those less strict in their observance because of ignorance or poverty. To the masses, Hassidism brought the message that Judaism acknowledges no elites.

If one appears in the marketplace and thrusts men aside with the words, "Make way for the Messiah!" he is only a false prophet, for the Messiah thrusts no one aside. The Hassidic style of dance, in a circle, was explained by the Baal Shem Tov to have this significance: in the circle, there is no beginning or end; all the dancers are equal links; wherever there is a separation, the circle is broken. Left unexpressed here is the core of the teaching, that the dance can begin whenever men put their arms around one another.

Discrimination based on birth—central to all forms of racism—is wholly absent in Judaism, except in a narrowly religious context. This is the perpetuation of the priestly castes, Kohanim and Levites, by descent in the male line. They do not in fact constitute the rabbinate, have only a very few special functions to perform during the liturgy, and are subject to some special restrictions as to marriage and divorce, participation in funerals, and the like. Beyond that, descent is of no significance in Judaism. Traditionally, a Jew is identified by his given name and the father's given name (in some circumstances, the mother's), but ancestry does not determine in any degree *what* he is.

Birth is also significant in another religious context—that relating to mixed marriages and conversions. Children of a Jewish mother (whether she herself was born Jewish or converted to Judaism) are born Jews; if the father only is Jewish, they are not Jews unless converted to Judaism. This practice might be traceable to primitive matriarchy; the rationale given in Judaic sources is that there can be no doubt of maternal parenthood.

Even in religious contexts the significance of birth is extremely limited. Maimonides was asked by a convert whether converts may recite any of the many prayers addressed to "Our God and the God of our fathers." His reply was that the "fathers" in question are not those in a merely biological sense but in a spiritual sense; in embracing Judaism the convert acquires a whole new spiritual ancestry, "If others taunt you," he adds, "with their descent from Abraham, Isaac and Jacob, you may rejoin that you are descended from God Himself" (Responsa 42).

Another type of inequality, to which increasing attention is being given, is also foreign to Judaism—discriminatory treatment of the aged. The Wisdom literature makes a characteristically pragmatic argument against such treatment: "Do not dishonor the old; we shall all be numbered among them" (ben Sirach 8:6). In Job (12:12) the old are seen as especially qualified by experience to give counsel in the conduct of life: "Wisdom is with the aged, and understanding in length of days."

More fundamental to the status of the aged in Judaism is the importance Judaism attaches to history and tradition, of which the old are an embodiment, symbol, and link. A custom in the *Bar Mitzvah* (confirmation) ceremony is for the rabbi to put the Torah scroll into the hands of the grandfather, who hands it to the father, and he in turn to the boy being initiated—a reenactment of the transmission of the Law, in accord with the injunction (Deut. 6:7) to teach one's children. Even when the old can no longer take part in the transmission, they are to be honored for the sake of the past. "Respect [even] an old man who has lost his learning," says the Talmud (Berachot 8b). ". . . The fragments of the Tablets broken by Moses were kept in the Ark alongside the new."

That Zionism is racism is among the most cynical of the political lies of our time. The discrimination that does deserve attention is that against women.

Here it is especially important to keep in mind the distinction between institutions and doctrines—sexism practiced by Jews as contrasted with whatever discriminatory treatment of women is countenanced in Judaism. For two thousand years Jewish institutions have been those of the encompassing society, especially, till modern times, in the Middle East and North Africa, regions hardly noted for recognizing the equality of the sexes. Politics has so corrupted genuine movements for equality and liberation that a UN-sponsored international conference on women's rights in Mexico City a year or two ago found occasion to pass a resolution condemning Israel, although women enjoy incomparably more rights there than in the countries confronting her. For instance, of the nine states in the world still denying women the right to vote, seven are members of the Arab League.

The characters of scripture include a number of women of unquestioned stature: Eve, Sarah, Miriam, Deborah, Hannah, Esther, and others. Equality, however, is not only a matter of how much can be attained by outstanding individuals. What discrimination most ineluctably denies is the right to be average. Israel is one of the few countries in the world that has had a woman ruler (in contrast to the far more common ceremonial head of state). But women rulers have been known throughout history, in societies where women remained severely discriminated against.

To turn to Judaism rather than to history and sociology, it is often commented that the count of one's blessings in the Judaic morning prayers includes one expressing gratitude for not having been created a woman. Another blessing with the same point is for not having been created a gentile. In both cases, the tacit reference is to the privilege of discharging the religious obligations that fall only on the Jewish male. Even if there were no imputation of inferiority in women's being exempt from certain duties, it is undeniable that a discrimination is being made on a basis which might be judged to be irrelevant. (Even circumcision is in some cultures practiced on women.)

Women do share in religious exercises—for instance, prayer. Inequalities are perpetuated by a separation (*mechitza*), women being restricted usually to a balcony in orthodox synagogues; they must remain on one side of a fence in the area before the Western Wall. Separate facilities are acknowledged to be ipso facto unequal; the inequality is rationalized by the distraction from spiritual concerns that, it is argued, the mixing of the sexes would bring about.

The argument restates a theme running through the Wisdom literature, that women—often "strange" women, but sometimes without qualification—are a snare and temptation which the wise man resists. The character depicted is widely known in the world's mythology: the Greek sirens and Circe; the Hebrew Lillith and the medieval succubi; the Teutonic Lorelei; in modern America the "vamp" (for "vampire"). In the comic strip, "Peanuts," it is Lucy who is depicted as truly destructive, not the Red Baron.

The circle of Isaac Luria introduced the custom, widely observed to this day, of reciting at the festive Sabbath meal—often as a chant or in melodic song—the last chapter of the Book of Proverbs, an encomium on the "woman of valor." She is praised as one who "stretches out her hands to the poor"; "strength and honor are her clothing"; "she opens her mouth with wisdom, and on her tongue is the law of kindness." There is a certain charm, to be sure, in a weekly ceremonial declaration that "her children rise up and call her blessed, and her husband also, [with the words] 'Many daughters have done virtuously, but you excel them all.'"

Yet it is the head of the household who sings *her* praises; *his* virtues presumably go without saying. What is worse, what she is praised for, if taken literally (which is admittedly questionable), reaffirms sexist roles: "she works willingly with her hands"; "she lays her hand on the spindle and takes hold of the distaff"; "she looks well to the ways of her household and does not eat the bread of idleness." It is her husband who is "known in the gates, when he sitteth among the elders of the land" (Prov. 31:23).

Ecclesiastes (7:28) sums up the ancient assessment of woman's frailties, if not downright sinfulness: "One man among a thousand have I found, but a woman among all those I have not found." To this, Robert Gordis has commented that men are being claimed to be not more than one tenth of one percent better. Judaism today exhibits in its several denominations significant variations in the treatment of women. Conservative Judaism has abandoned separations and is extending to women more and more participation in religious observances (for instance, a *Bat Mitzvah*, confirmation for girls). In Reform Judaism, women are occasionally ordained as rabbis.

The equality implied by prophetic universalism is both generalized and made concrete in the Judaic ideal of social justice. The tacit principle is to give to each according to his need. Social justice means particular concern for the welfare of the deprived, those whom either social practice or personal circumstances make especially needy. Job (29:12-15) describes what has been an operative ideal in Jewish society from the time of the prophets to the present: "I delivered the poor who cried, the orphans who had none to help them. The blessing of him who was about to die came upon me; I made the widow's heart sing for joy. . . . I was eyes to the blind and feet to the lame."

Whatever oppositions between priest and prophet there may have been in Judaism as in other religions, social justice remained a basic component of rabbinic Judaism. Such an important contributor to rabbinism as Akiba, for instance, pressed the interests of artisans and laborers, even to the point of opposition to the prerogatives of the priesthood; raised the status of women; championed the rights of aliens; and fostered peace as a religious as well as a political goal. When the Karaites, some centuries later, rejected the prescriptions of rabbinic Judaism, they nevertheless retained the traditional Jewish passion for social justice.

A keen sense of injustice underlies the arraignment of society to be found in Isaiah, Jeremiah, Micah, and other prophets. That there are inequalities is bad enough; that we refuse to recognize them, to acknowledge responsibility for them, and to take action to remove them—that is the grave moral failing. Worst of all, social resources are expended not to promote justice but to perpetuate injustice. "I saw the tears of the oppressed and they had no comforter," says Koheleth (Eccles. 4:1); "and on the side of their oppressors there was power."

The moral obligations engendered here are both negative and positive. We must diligently avoid committing injustice and be diligent also in alleviating the distress of the victims of injustice. "Seek justice," says Isaiah (1:17), "and relieve the oppressed." Do not be among those who exploit the weak and helpless, but more is required of you than a merely negative virtue.

The Wisdom literature is especially aware of the economic dimension of social injustice. "When a rich man does wrong he adds a threat," ben Sirach observes (13,3); "When a poor man suffers a wrong, he must beg pardon." A few verses later (13,19) ben Sirach asks, "What peace can there be between a rich man and a poor one? Wild asses are the prey of lions in the wilderness, just as the poor are pastures for the rich."

The notion that poverty is a particularly spiritual state, that it may even be a blessing, is a rationalization which is by and large foreign to Judaism. Sholem Aleichem's Tevye is quite within the tradition with his complaint that although poverty is no shame, it is no great honor either. The Book of Proverbs (10:15) recognizes that "a rich man's wealth is his fortress; what destroys the poor is their poverty." This assessment is fully substantiated by such observations as are embodied, for instance, in the statistics of the greater proportion of convictions and the greater severity of the sentences imposed upon poor defendants than upon rich ones, even in democratic America.

The difference in the economic functions of employer and employee does not justify significant differences in the standard of living. "You shall not eat white bread while your servant eats dark," says the Talmud (Kadushin 22); "you shall not sleep on cushions while your servant sleeps on straw." That a livelihood must be provided to those who are unable to provide for themselves is enjoined in the Torah: "If your brother has become poor and his hand fails, you shall uphold him, even if he be a stranger" (Lev. 25:35). The concluding phrase is noteworthy—there are no exceptions to the right to a decent livelihood.

Associated with this right, as with any other, is a correlative duty: in this instance, to engage in productive work. "Six days shall you labor" is as much of a commandment as it is to rest on the seventh day (Exod. 20:9). The obligation may fall on others, however, to provide the opportunity to work. Compensation for the unemployed has a moral sanction; morality is even better served, the Talmud emphasizes, by providing employment (Baba Kama 112a). Maimonides distinguishes various grades of charity; the highest of them is to make it possible for the recipient to provide for himself, by giving him work.

The English word "charity" connotes benevolence and goodwill, qualities which, to be sure, are contained in the Judaic conception, though they do not define it. For Judaism charity is not something to be bestowed if and when we feel charitable. Giving is a duty; the recipient is taking possession of what is his by right. The Hebrew word for charity is *tsedakah*, from the same root as the words for righteousness and for justice.

The underlying idea has been made familiar in modern times in the theory of taxation. Taxes have long been recognized to be just when they are a payment for benefits received and are not based merely on the ability to pay. What we have come to see is that the ability to pay is in itself an indisputable mark of a benefit having been received. Jewish philanthrophy is celebrated, and with good reason; Jews have always recognized the obligations of affluence.

To sustain this sense of obligation, one of the Hassidic masters, Moshe Leib of Sasov, even counseled that one must act as if there were no God in the world: You yourself must provide for the needy—you cannot leave them to Heaven. Moreover, you must do it now. Says the Book of Proverbs (3:27-28), "Do not withhold good from him to whom it is due [sic] when it is in your power to bestow it. Do not say to your neighbor, 'Go, and come again, and tomorrow I will give' when you have it by you."

The moral obligation in Judaism is realistically limited: one is not to distribute in charity more than one-fifth of what he has. To impoverish yourself altogether means not only that you can no longer help others but even worse, that you yourself become a burden to others.

That the ideal of social justice defines obligations does not imply that action on behalf of the ideal is necessarily detached and impersonal. On the contrary; it is hard to recognize our obligations toward others unless we feel something of the miseries we are obliged to alleviate. "Let them eat cake!" can be spoken only by someone who has never lacked bread. S. Ansky's drama of Hassidic life, *The Dybbuk*, presents an anecdote also told of Levi Yitzchak of Berditchev. A newly rich man of very limited philanthropies was taken by the rabbi first to the window, then to a mirror, and asked in each case, "What do you see?" "Behold!" said the rabbi; "the window is glass and the mirror is glass; when a little silver is added, we see only ourselves!"

Far from conceiving of charity as enjoined by a sense of duty antithetical to personal feeling, Judaism introduces a category of acts of loving kindness *(gemilut chasadim)*, which it extols above impersonal, often institutionalized, philanthropies. Such acts are carried out not only by what a man has but by what he is in himself; they do not humiliate their beneficiaries or put them under any reciprocal obligation; they can be bestowed upon all alike, rich or poor. "One who performs both *tsedakah* and *gemilut chasadim*," says the Talmud (Sukkah 49), "is as if he filled the whole world with kindness."

What is known as "Christian charity" is so-called in a Christian society; it is not grounded in (nor need it be taken to imply) a virtue contrasting with Judaism in either doctrine or practice. Such contrasts have, indeed, been claimed. A widespread stereotype characterizes the Old Testament as promulgating a religion of law, while the New Testamant proclaims a religion of love. The contrast is as groundless as such stereotypes usually are.

That the God of Israel is a God of love is both scriptural and rabbinic. For the Jews, mercy is as much a divine attribute as is justice—indeed, the more significant attribute, so far as personal religion is concerned. That God is merciful, compassionate, gracious, and slow to anger is a doctrine explicitly formulated in the Torah (for instance, Deut. 4:31), by the prophets (for instance, Neh. 9:17), and in the Hagiographa (for instance, Psalms 136:15).

The Talmud (Berachot 7a) writes that God Himself also prays; His prayer is, "May My mercy prevail over My justice, that I may deal with My children in kindness!" It is not to be doubted that *His* prayers are always answered.

That love covers all sins is an *Old* Testament verse (Prov. 10:12). Innate depravity and eternal damnation are both wholly foreign to Judaic thought. Even popular myth, as distinct from doctrine, is in Judaism strikingly benign: punishment in hell does not last longer than twelve months (Shabbat 33a)! If there is a contrast to be drawn, it is between the humane charitableness of both Judaism and Christianity on the one hand, and on the other hand such inhumanities as those of the Church Father Tertullian, who declared that one of the joys of the righteous will be watching the torments of the wicked, or of the Grand Inquisitor Torquemada, who consigned many victims to the flames in the name of a God of love.

The characteristic Christian doctrine "Love thine enemies" is rooted in Judaic teaching, antedating even the social idealism of the prophets. "If you meet your enemy's ox or his ass going astray, you shall bring it back to him" (Exod. 23:4-5). The passage continues, "If you see the ass of one who hates you lying under its burden, you shall not leave him with it, you shall help him to lift it up." The Book of Proverbs (25:21) is just as explicit: "If your enemy be hungry give him bread to eat and if he be thirsty give him water to drink."

Another stereotype which anti-Zionist propaganda has recently brought to attention is the interpretation of "an eye for an eye" as excusing and even enjoining revenge. The Old Testament verse (Lev. 19:18), which ends with "Thou shalt love thy neighbor as thyself," begins "Thou shalt not avenge, nor bear any grudge...." That vengeance is the Lord's appears in the Book of Deuteronomy (32:35) as well as in Psalms (94:1), and elsewhere in the Old Testament. What the propagandist acknowledges to be acts of self-defense or deterrence in the case of other countries, he calls retaliation in the case of Israel.

In its historical setting, the doctrine of an "eye for an eye" in fact marked a considerable advance for human rights. First, it restricted punishment to something commensurate with the gravity of the offense rather than, as in many countries to this very day, inflicting capital punishment for a whole host of offenses. Second, it made punishment depend solely on the nature of the offense, rather than considering who is the offender, as is characteristic of aristocracies and of present-day feudal societies. In this respect, its point is very like that embodied in the formula "The king can do no wrong," which means, not that the king is above the law, but the very opposite. There is no equality without social justice, and there can be no justice at all without equality before the law.

In democracies, human rights are denied by prejudice and discrimination; in dictatorships the denial is a matter of official government policy. Judaism has taken a very constructive position with respect to the social issues, but rather a less constructive position with regard to the political issues.

Prejudice involves, first, an element of tribalism—responding to a person not as an individual but as a member of a certain group. Second, the group is likely to be characterized by stereotypes rather than in terms of real attributes and their actual statistical distribution. Third, and most important, the attributes are irrelevant to the purposes actually operative in the context, save, tautologically, those served by the prejudicial attitudes themselves. Favorable attributions may therefore be as prejudicial as unfavorable ones; prejudice is very often ambivalent.

Prejudice within the Jewish community has no doctrinal content. Differences between Ashkenazi and Sephardic Jewry in Israel are considerable. They are a matter chiefly of social and economic status, together with the associated cultural advantages and deprivations. The significantly larger families and significantly less schooling of Jews from North Africa and the Middle East, as compared with those from Europe and America, create and maintain a gap that is recognized as a serious social problem today. But there is no doctrinal opposition anywhere to overcoming the gap; there is prejudice, but no bigotry.

For that matter, within the Ashkenazi community itself, in America as well as in Israel, status differences are recognizable, although neither as sharp nor as oppressive as those dividing Ashkenazim from Sephardim. At the top of the hierarchy are Spanish-Portuguese Jews (Sephardim in a narrow sense), who sometimes constitute exclusive elites in relation to other Jews. Next come Jews from Germany, and perhaps other Western European countries; Lithuanian and Russian Jews follow, then Poles, and possibly Hungarians and Romanians. At the bottom of the Ashkenazi scale are Jews from Galicia and Soviet Georgia. Familiar ethnic prejudices about all these groups are expressed in folk humor, beneath which may be a strand of real hostility or contempt. These prejudices invite sociological and psychological examination rather than ideological.

Doctrinally, there have been four major divisions within Jewry since biblical times. That between Sadducees and Pharisees was resolved by the end of the Talmudic period, Rabbinic Judaism being largely shaped by the Pharisees—in rather different ways than is implied by the prejudicial usage of the name in Christian sources. The Karaite schism, the second doctrinal division, was overcome largely by the influence of Saadya Gaon and Maimonides.

The rise of Hassidism in the eighteenth century, the third division, occasioned bitter prejudices that has subsided only in our day. Opponents of Hassidism went so far as to denounce Hassidic leaders to the Czarist authorities as being engaged in subversive activities, and one or two jail sentences were imposed. The acknowledged spiritual leader of Ashkenazi Jewry in Europe in the eighteenth century, the Gaon of Wilna, even pronounced excommunication on the whole Hassidic sect, thereby prohibiting, among other things, intermarriage with them—an injunction of very limited and short-term effect. In the last century or two the impact of Hassidism has been felt not only by Orthodox Jewry, but also by Reform Jewry, whose predecessors in the Enlightenment had contemptuously attacked the Hassidim as superstitious and obscurantist.

The fourth division is that among Orthodox, Conservative, and Reform Jewry. Although denominational differences are sometimes dogmatically adhered to, they are not associated today with significant prejudices in the sense specified earlier. An Orthodox Jew may refuse to eat at the home of the non-Orthodox because the latter modify or reject Judaic dietary laws, but one's own scrupulous observance does not imply prejudice against those lacking in such piety. Reform Jews may continue to regard certain rituals as more superstitious than spiritual, but without prejudice against those who continue to practice them. Strong adherence to one's own convictions does not in itself entail prejudice against all who do not share the convictions.We may still respond to others as individuals, recognize their real attributes, and acknowledge contexts to which the differences in convictions are irrelevant.

Attitudes of Jews toward non-Jews raise further questions. Many features of Judaism developed, as Maimonides and later scholars documented, out of a determination to sharpen and fix the differences between Judaism and the heathen practices of the time. Dissociated from the context of origin, differentiations may be prejudicial in effect, when the former relevance is lost sight of or no longer applies. Wine touched by a non-Jew, for instance, may not be used for sacramental purposes. This has nothing whatever in common with the racism which is embodied, say, in separate drinking fountains; it was meant to ensure that the sacramental wine be wholly distinct, beyond any shadow of doubt, from wine poured as a libation to idols.

Nevertheless, there is a circle of prejudice that may arise out of such contexts. Discrimination, on whatever basis, tends to produce or strengthen prejudices; these, in turn, lead to further or more rigid discriminations. Jews have sometimes been no more than tolerant of the non-Jewish world— which, it cannot be too often repeated, has usually been something less than tolerant of them.

At best, tolerance is a dubious alternative to prejudice; at worst, it even reinforces prejudice. Tolerance implies a fault or shortcoming that is being condoned, like the engineer's acceptable margin of error, or the biologist's concept of how much of a noxious substance an organism can ingest without undue ill effects. Tolerating the other also implies a measure of indifference to *him,* not merely to his faults; we do not pay much attention one way or another to what we merely tolerate. This in turn implies a *guilt by dissociation:* there must be something wrong with those with whom we are unwilling to associate.

Separate facilities are unequal *because* they are separate. One of the most basic human rights is the right to be a member of the community. Relentless hostility to the state of Israel, for instance, repeatedly expresses itself in the attempt to dissociate her from the community of nations by restricting or denying her participation in international activities of whatever kind—cultural and athletic as well as political and economic.

Discrimination is prejudice in action; thought and feeling are expressed in deeds. The circle of prejudice is the reciprocal influence on one another of prejudicial attitudes and discriminatory practices. There is also a *circle of discrimination:* discriminatory practices may produce in their victims certain traits that are then invoked as justifying the discrimination in the first place. Blacks are denied educational opportunity or given only very inferior schooling, patterns which are then defended by reference to the markedly poorer black performance on educational tests and measures. Jews may be socially isolated (the ghetto was originally the Jewish quarter, after all), then condemned for their "clannishness." In thirty years Israel was subjected to four wars by the countries encircling her, attacks which were repeatedly claimed to be justified by Israel's "militarism."

A common response to prejudice and discrimination, a response found among Jews as well as among other victims, is *chauvinism*, in the sense of the conviction that I and mine have no faults or shortcomings. The chauvinist victim sees himself as not only not worse than those who discriminate against him, but indeed as better than all of them.

Chauvinism shares with prejudice the *fallacy of linearity:* the notion that if two people differ in any respect, one of them must be better than the other in that respect. The assumption is that there is always a comparison to be made; every distinction is invidious. In effect, this is a denial of the right to be different, a precious and even vital right for Jews from the beginning. The Seer of Lublin, questioned why Hassidim worshiped differently from others, rejoined, "What kind of God can be served in only one way!" When the premise of linearity is rejected, there is no basis for the conclusion that one must hate others in order to be himself, or to hate oneself in order to relate to others as a decent human being.

Closely associated with the fallacy of linearity is the *fallacy of uniqueness*, the notion that nothing good can be multiple—be found in more than one place, for instance. Based on this premise, if I have something good you don't have it, and if you do, I don't; or else, it is not really good after all. Just as the belief in linearity generates chauvinism, the belief in uniqueness generates what might be called *ego-imperialism:* claiming for oneself all desirable attributes or achievements. The chauvinist formula is, "If it's mine, it's got to be good!" The ego-imperialist claim is the converse: "If it's good, it's got to be mine!" Centuries of persecution or at best the status of a tolerated minority have given chauvinism and ego-imperialism a recognized place in the

Jewish psyche, but hardly a more significant place than they have recurrently occupied in the ideologies and policies of powerful nations.

Discrimination may produce another effect, more marked on those who practice discrimination than on its victims. The self comes to be defined by the discrimination, which provides a negative identity. In the McCarthy era, many citizens knew themselves to be Americans only by their preoccupation with "un-American" activities, as there have been whites whose self-respect rested on little more than a continued emphasis on their not being black, and for that matter, some blacks for whom self-respect seems to demand unremitting differentiation from "whitey." Just so, there are Jews whose Jewishness amounts only to the awareness sustained by prejudice and discrimination that they are not non-Jews. The emptiness of negative identity was memorably declared by Mendel of Kotzk: "If I am I only because you are you, and you are you only because I am I, then I am not I and you are not you."[25]

A widespread contemporary response to discrimination follows a simple logic. Since differences among people are devisive, if we remove the differences there will no longer be any basis for divisions. If the practices of the Jews were not different from those of the rest of the kingdom, Haman would have nothing to say (Esther 3:8). The argument is pointless if applied to the victims of discrimination based on age, sex, birthplace, or skin color.

Even where changes *can* be made—there are, after all, blacks who pass and converted Jews—the outcome is not to protect the self from discrimination but to exchange one self for another. To Judaism, apostasy is especially abhorrent, as combining disloyalty and idolatry with a cowardly and confused self-seeking. Martyrs to the faith are correspondingly honored; memorials to them, in both prayers and monuments, are widespread and frequent occasions for renewed affirmations of faith.

The very existence of the Jews as a tiny minority in a world, often hostile to their identity, is a continuous repudiation of the ideal of a homogenized society. Ecumenism has no place in Judaic doctrine if it means not only respect for and cooperation among differing faiths, but also movement toward obliterating the differences. There is no religious essence to be abstracted as the basis of a living faith which would at one stroke dissipate prejudice as between Jew and gentile. The essence of soup is only water.

On the political side, Judaism since biblical times has taken an activist role in the struggle for social justice and equality. The last chapter of the Book of Proverbs (31:8-9) enjoins the king himself to plead the cause of the poor and needy and to speak out for those who cannot speak for themselves. The contemporary crisis of indifference is anticipated (24:12) with the warning that if you say, "I did not know" or "It is none of my business," He who weighs men's hearts will take note of it and render to every man according to his deeds. Protest movements can find a powerful justification in the Talmud

(Shabbat 54b): "The man whose protest would be of any weight and who does not make a protest when any wrong is about to be committed, is himself held accountable for the wrong."

Yet Judaic doctrine, especially as articulated in the Wisdom literature, is by and large conservative. "My son, fear God and the king," Proverbs enjoins (24:21), "and do not become involved with those who seek change." The most that can be hoped for is the amelioration of misery; there are no radical solutions to social problems. Those who are accustomed to do evil will not suddenly be reformed, the prophet tells us (Jer. 13:23); the Ethiopian cannot change his skin nor the leopard his spots. Social utopias have no more basis than the myth of "the good old days." Koheleth counsels (Eccles. 5:8), "If you see the oppression of the poor and the violent perverting of justice and righteousness in the state, do not marvel at the matter...." "Do not say, 'How was it that the former days were better than these?' It is not out of which that you inquire" (7:10).

Although the prudent man fears the king, the virtuous man knows that no one, not even royalty, stands above the law. Prophets like Nathan and Elijah did not hesitate to condemn the king's crimes even to his face. It may be easier to make the king something of a philosopher than to persuade the philosopher to become king. That is one of the functions of Scripture: "When the king sits on the throne he shall write for himself in a book a copy of this Law ...and it shall be with him and he shall read in it all the days of his life, that ...his heart may not be lifted up above his brothers, and that he may not turn aside from the commandment, either to the right hand or to the left ..." (Deut. 17:18-20).

What the prophet proclaims is the existence of objective moral norms, the sage applies to the concrete affairs of social existence. The priest also is occupied with the same normative system, extended beyond relations among men to the relation between man and God. Even here, social needs remain basic. That ritual has a social function was the teaching of Shimon ben Yochai in early Talmudic times (Baba Metzia 115a), later elaborated in detail by Maimonides.

In a theocracy the distinctions between the moral law, statutory law, and religious ritual are of no importance. Throughout most Jewish history, it is the moral law that remains central, an emphasis that has come to be known as "the prophetic tradition." In Israel today religion is a matter of legal enactment with regard to such matters as the Sabbath, *kashrut* (dietary taboos), and personal status (marriage and divorce).

The Judaic position in law and morality also underlies democratic political theory, which moralizes politics in contrast to the totalitarian political philosophies, which politicize morality. That you cannot legislate morality is as untrue for democracy as it is for Judaism—legislation conforms to moral norms or it has no justification. Conversely, the core of morality cannot be left to pious exhortation, but must be translated into law, as societies have recognized with laws against murder, theft, adultery, and perjury, prohibited in four of the Ten Commandments.

There is an objective moral law that provides the norms for a just social order, but men break the moral law in society just as in individual affairs. "Nature," says Philo (where most Jewish thinkers other than Spinoza would say "God"), "has borne all men to be free; but the wrongful and covetous acts of some who pursued that source of evil, inequality [sic], have imposed their yoke and invested the stronger with power over the weaker."[26] Koheleth states the point in a more general form: "God made man upright, but they have sought out many inventions" (Eccles. 7:29).

In short, the basis of human rights and their content rest, for Judaism, on the divine order of things. Because man, like the rest of nature, has also been created by God, this order has its counterpart in man's makeup, in his conscience and reason. Laws governing relations between man and man, if they accord with the divine law, stand to reason and satisfy our native sense of justice. "Reason," says Saadya Gaon,[27] "prescribes that human beings should be forbidden to trespass upon one another's rights by any sort of aggression"—any sort, even that which claims to be justified by its noble goals. Commentators have explained that the Law proclaims "Justice, justice shall you follow!" (Deut. 16:20), repeating the word "justice" to convey that we must pursue justice in the means we employ as well as in the ends to which we aspire.

God is the Author of human rights, and of man's capacity to discern and defend them. In this discernment, we come to know the divine. We know God by exercising justice and righteousness, says the Mishnah (Avot 1), echoing such prophets as Jeremiah (22:16). When this knowledge is the guide to action, we are in the service of the divine. The sage joins the prophet in insisting that to do justice is more acceptable to God than to perform the sacrifices (Prov. 21:3). Above all, economic needs must be acknowledged and fulfilled. When a poor man stands at the door, says the Talmud, God stands at his right hand. If the poor are invited to share our own food, the dining table takes the place of the altar (Berachot 55a).

Human rights, like other moral ideals, make apparent the emptiness and even hypocrisy of what is often only a lip service. Action has a fundamental role in Jewish doctrine, to the point, indeed, that Judaism must be defined by characteristic actions rather than by a set of beliefs. It is a faith, not a creed, a faith which can find expression only in commitment to appropriate action. "Both the palm tree and the cedar stand tall," said the Baal Shem Tov, "but only the palm bears fruit—be like the palm!" Theories and symbols also have their contribution to make. "Between the mind and the heart," said another Hassidic master, Simchah Bunam, "the distance is as great as that between heaven and earth." Then he added, "Yet the earth is nourished by rain from heaven."

NOTES

1. Alexander Altmann, ed., *Saadya Gaon: Book of Doctrines and Beliefs* in *Three Jewish Philosophers* (New York: Meridian Books, 1960), Ch. 7, Sec. 1.

2. Jerusalem Talmud, Nedarim 69:4.

3. "The Two Foci of the Jewish Soul," *The Writings of Martin Buber*, ed. Will Herberg (New York: Meridian Books, 1956), pp. 268-9.

4. Altmann, ed., *Saadya Gaon: Book of Doctrines and Beliefs*, Ch. 2, Sec. 3.

5. Midrash Tehillim 55:19.

6. Martin Buber, *Tales of the Hasidim: The Later Masters* (New York: Schocken Books, 1948), p. 276.

7. Martin Buber, "Plato and Isaiah," in *The Writings of Martin Buber*, pp.236-7.

8. *The Fathers According to Rabbi Nathan*, trans. Judah Goldin (New Haven: Yale University Press, 1955), p. 233.

9. Martin Buber, *Between Man and Man* (Boston: Beacon Press, 1955), p.200.

10. Hans Lewy, ed., *Philo: Selections* in *Three Jewish Philosophers* (New York: Meridian Books, 1960), p. 102.

11. Buber, *Between Man and Man*, p. 176.

12. Louis I. Newman, ed., *The Hasidic Anthology* (New York: Block Publishing Co., 1944), p. 451.

13. Buber, "Israel and the World," in *The Writings of Martin Buber*, p. 37.

14. Lewy, ed., *Philo: Selections* in *Three Jewish Philosophers*, p. 51.

15. *See, Philo: Selections*, p. 102.

16. Isadore Twersky, ed., *A Maimonides Reader* (New York: Behrman House, 1972), p. 392.

17. Tractatus Theologico-Politicus 10.

18. Maimonides, *Commentary on the Mishnah*, introduction.

19. Maimonides, *Iggeret Teman* 10.

20. Lewy, ed., *Philo: Selections*, p. 54.

21. Tosefta Sanhedrin 13:2; See also the fourth-century *Mishnah* of Rabbi Elieer.

22. Midrash Tanna Eliyahu.

23. Maimonides, *Mishnah Torah, Hilchot Tshuvah* 3:5, 5:3, 5:6.

24. Lewy, ed., *Philo: Selections*, p. 62.

25. Buber, *Tales of the Hasidim*, p.283.

26. Philo, *On the Contemplative Life*, pp. 3,22-37.

27. Altmann, ed., *Saadya Gaon: Book of Doctrines and Beliefs*, Ch. 3, Sec. 2, p. 96.

R. J. HENLE, S.J. —— 3

A Catholic View
of Human Rights:
A Thomistic Reflection

In his approach to human rights, Professor R. J. Henle examines the meanings of human nature, morality, and justice expressed in the writings of Saint Thomas Aquinas. He uses the Aquinian interpretation of these ideas as a basis for a Catholic point of view, to portray the theoretically inseparable relation between human rights and the inviolate value of each human being.

When Yahweh revealed Himself to the Hebrew people and thus entered human history, He stood apart from all the multitudinous gods of the Middle East not only as the one true God, the Creator of Heaven and Earth, but also as the God of righteousness and justice.[1] Although these biblical terms— "righteousness" and "justice"—do not exactly match modern usage it is clear that justice included what we now call human rights.[2] This is illustrated by the repeated emphasis on the protection of the widow, the orphan, the "alien in your midst," and the poor.

The terrible condemnations of injustice in the Psalms and the Prophets, the absolute demand for justice—which transcended sacrifices and prayers— have echoed through the Christian tradition, in the fathers, theologians, pastors, preachers, and in the encyclicals of the modern popes.

The 1971 Synod of Bishops declared:

In the Old Testament God reveals himself to us as the liberator of the oppressed and the defender of the poor, demanding from man faith in him and justice towards man's neighbour. It is only in the observance of the duties of justice that God is truly recognized as the liberator of the oppressed.[3]

Since the great encyclicals of Leo XIII, the Catholic church has continued to issue official statements on human rights.[4] The most authoritative current Catholic statements are those contained in the Vatican II document

Gaudium et Spes[5] and in the document "Justice in the World" issued by the 1971 Synod of Bishops.[6] Important also are the two historic encyclicals of John XXIII, *Mater et Magister* and *Pacem in Terris* as well as the *Progressio Populorum* of Paul VI. The American Catholic hierarchy, since the inception of the labor movement (which was defended by Cardinal Gibbons), has repeatedly emphasized "social" justice. An important annual event has been the Bishop's Labor Day Statement.

These magistral documents and the activism that they have inspired are in full accord with the traditional Catholic teaching on charity (in the theological sense) and justice.

The Catholic ethical and moral tradition is a development of the classical philosophy of Greece and Rome, of the Hebrew scriptures and commentaries, and of the Christian gospel.

The tradition has not been and is not a simple syncretism, nor has it been a rigid repetition of established rules. It is a living tradition, making critical and reflective use of the cultural and religious traditions from which it comes. It absorbs new knowledge and insights and profits from new experiences. It has its phases, retrogression, and renewals, yet it has always been based on substantially the same fundamental view of man and vision of human goodness.

Man is made in the image and likeness of God (Gen. 1:26). Christian metaphysics finds a reflection of God in all created things—the heavens show forth His glory—but in man there is a sharing—formal though analogous—in the highest attributes of God. Man is intelligent and capable of self-giving love and in virtue of these capabilities he is called a "person." He is self-aware, self-directing, and ordered to values and goals that transcend the material universe and relate him to the absolute reality that is God. He is the peak and pinnacle of our created universe; all things are ordered to him and through him give glory to God. He is not only at the highest level of the created universe, he is the meaning of the universe, its finalizing goal, its supreme ontological value.

As Kant said, man is an end in himself; he cannot be made a pure means. No man can be totally subordinated to any other man or group of men, nor to his family, his tribe, or his nation. Total subordination to another's purposes is exemplified in absolute slavery,[7] in which a man is reduced to a pure means equivalent to a mule or a tractor.

The value and finality of man is thus intrinsic to his nature and can be philosophically recognized independently of revelation or theology, as it was, at least to a large extent, by Plato, Aristotle, and the Stoics.[8]

For the same reason, the rights of man are "unalienable" because they are based on human nature. They are not dependent on law, ecclesiastical or civil, or on any covenant or basic document. The Bill of Rights of the United States Constitution gives legal protection but does not create human rights. Human rights are prior to society and the state, although positive refinements and additions can be made by human law (that is, there are some rights that are simply "legal").

For most Catholic thinkers a complete doctrine of human rights cannot be drawn from the teaching of the scriptures or deduced from the law of charity. Philosophical reflection is necessary to develop a full theory of ethical living, or moral standards, and of moral decision. In the greatest of all Catholic moral treatises, the *Pars Secunda* of the *Summa Theologiae*, St. Thomas Aquinas carefully maps the details of man's moral life with philosophical acuteness. But there is an enormous difference from, for example, the Aristotelian analysis; all morality is brought under the imperium and the motivation of divine charity. At the head of the treatise stands his magistral treatment of the love of God. The moral life is seen as a development of the love of God. This changes the attitude of the Christian toward men especially in matters of justice. The love of the neighbor is seen as an intrinsic consequence of man's love for God and as a formal correlate to God's love for man. The enormous energy of divine love drives the Catholic, especially the Catholic activist, to the fulfillment of justice. The rights of man are not only brought under the protection of divine righteousness—as so often in the Old Testament—but become the very test of the love of God.

Now that I have given some general Catholic background, I propose to set the doctrine of "rights" in a special perspective by studying the relationship between the current thinking about rights and the Thomistic view of justice.

What do we mean by a "right"? We talk about a right to something or a right to do something. I have a right to a piece of property. My ownership of this piece of property does not refer to any ontological characteristic of the property itself. If the right is viewed only in connection with the thing claimed, it makes no sense. This can be brought out by asking what my right to a piece of property would mean if all other people on earth were annihilated and I alone remained. The property would not have changed; I would have changed; but to talk of my right to anything would have become meaningless. Clearly human rights must be put into the background of human relationships.

In fact, the language of rights is legal language. The concept of a right is a legal concept and, indeed, a legal fiction. Law is not a purely theoretical discipline; it is a practical system for dealing with the public aspects of human relations. Since these aspects are by nature multiple and complex and are refined and added to by positive custom and positive law, some system of classification is necessary. By identifying and distinguishing various aspects and crystalizing them in distinct concepts—concepts of rights—the law found a way to deal with the fluidity of human relations and the infinite variations of singular cases.

The concept of a right is a constructural concept and functions in law somewhat as the ‚athematical constructs of physics do in natural science. In both cases human versatility has developed a mode of thinking that gives control of and a second-level understanding of first-level reality. These constructural concepts are not simple transcriptions of reality, but they have a definite and justifying foundation in fact.[9]

When we establish a right as a relationship to a thing or an action, we tend to absolutize it. Property rights have tended to be crystallized and formalized to such a degree that, when we try to replace them within the perspective of equity, we must construct other legalistically conceived restraints and limitations. As in all constructural models, reality becomes foreshortened and distorted, and various dialectical impasses are reached. When the use of property is maintained at the ontological level of reciprocal human relations, the flexibility of equity is there from the beginning and does not have to be added as a legalistic afterthought.

What then is the foundation for the conceptualized rights? They are derived from insights into the moral interrelationship between men, taken as individuals or as groups. This means that these concepts are expressions of justice.

In the Thomistic view the vrtue that governed the relations between men under a moral perspective is the virtue of justice. Temperance and fortitude are primary virtues of the individual: prudence also is individual in the sense that it enables a man to judge more easily and more correctly in moral matters.

But justice orders all man's relationships to other men insofar as these relations are brought under a moral perspective. One isolated man, solitary and alone, could not practice justice, but as soon as one other man appears, the basic paradigm of justice appears.

The basic paradigm is that of *one man* to *one man,* a relationship of equality, the original and most universal principle of equity that lies behind all moral and legal determinations. This relationship, however, is not numerical or quantitative, it is not *one* to *one,* but individual *man* to *man.* Equity is qualitative because it is based upon the intrinsic value or ontological goodness of human nature and its transcendent finality. This value and finality is realized fully in each human being, in the sense that there are no degrees in human nature. One is either a human being or he is not.

Of course, this does not mean that the human potential intrinsic to man's finality is always fully developed; on the contrary, at least in this life, it never is.

Justice is defined as the right relationship between men with reference to things and actions. This immediately subordinates the things that concern justice to the reciprocal relation between men. The right to a piece of property is, first, a relationship between men with reference to the use of the property.

At each terminal of this relationship is a human being (or human beings). Therefore, through all the variations of the justice relationship, the individual value of each person must be maintained inviolate. Any relationship that reduces a man to the status of a pure means for another man or group of men—as in slavery, in an unjust labor contract, in the terrorist taking of hostages, or in the obtaining of sexual "services" through force, fear, or purchase—is an unjust relationship. The real evil of prostitution is not that it violates chastity (as it does) but that it uses a human being simply as an instrument of pleasure.

The justice relationship assumes a variety of forms depending on the complexity of human situations, on the accidental variations among individuals, and on the determination of positive law and custom. But if the primal paradigm of the justice relationship is kept in mind, the value of each individual will always be taken into account and the essential reciprocity and proportionality of the relationship will be maintained. The conceptualization of rights tends to make it possible to think of rights as terminating in things (as in a piece of property) or actions (as in freedom of speech), without a clear reference to other men. This entails a tendency to absolutize rights (as we have done to a large extent with property rights) and to make them functions of each individual rather than of a reciprocal relation between individuals.

My right to a piece of property is my right to use it with some degree of exclusion of others from this use. As soon as it is so considered, the possible range of property rights becomes obvious. There can be the sort of temporary exclusive use assigned annually to women in some tribes on the basis of mouths to feed.

The reciprocity also reveals limits imposed by the equal value of others. Thus, if the use becomes such that, in a given circumstance, the basic finality of other persons is interfered with, value reciprocity demands a new mode of usage.

The basic variations of the justice relationship have generally been identified as that between individuals, that between an individual and the community of which he is a member, and that between a community and its members. In these variations, the importance of the philosophical view being proposed here becomes evident. When an individual stands in relationship to his community, the numerical superiority of the latter does not overwhelm the intrinsic value of the individual. Of course, in many ways individuals within communities have roles of service and sacrifice to play, but they cannot be reduced to a pure means for the benefit of the rest of the community. Thus, in Thomistic philosophy, the "common good" is the finality of society that cannot be defined as the "greatest happiness of the greatest number" or as the "interest of the majority" (as in democratic practice it so often is). The common good must be in the interest of each person; when it is not, even one person can justly stand over against an entire community. The level of intrinsic value in a group is no higher than the level of intrinsic value in a single human being.

My purpose is not to object to the well-established conceptualization of "rights" current in our day. Rather, I am proposing that for understanding and clarification it is philosophically necessary to recognize the constructural character of the concept of rights and to explore the more basic foundation in reality, namely the objective *justum*—the right relationship between men with reference to goods and actions. This requires a recognition of the intrinsic inviolable nature of man, in its substance and in its finality; it establishes human relationships on a reciprocity between men that grows out of that value. It grounds all human relations in qualitative equality and restores the delicate variations in the reciprocal relations that tend to be crystalized into limited categories of rights. An illustration is the fact that in both civil and canon law there is a recognition that established definitions and procedures do not always achieve justice in individual cases, and that, therefore, the more universal principle of "equity" may be appealed to against precedent and law. This "equity" is precisely the general qualitative reciprocal paradigm of human relations.

Thus, the Thomistic analysis of justice brings us back to the fundamental view of man described above as underlying the Catholic tradition. In that tradition and in view of St. Thomas, the living out of justice becomes a living out of the love of God.

NOTES

1. John R. Donahue, S.J., "Biblical Perspectives on Justice," in *The Faith That Does Justice*, ed. John C. Haughey (New York: Paulist Press, 1977), pp. 68-78; also in *God's Call to Public Responsibility*, ed; George W. Forell and William H. Lazareth, (Philadelphia: Fortress Press, 1978), pp. 20-35; Philip Land, S.J., *An Overview*, Pontifical Commission: Justice and Peace (Vatican City, 1972); Juan Alfaro, S.J., *Theology of Justice in the World*, Pontifical Commission: Justice and Peace (Vatican City, 1973).

2. Some have thought that there is no recognition of "natural law" in the scriptures. It seems to me that the presentation of the themes of God's righteousness and man's justice clearly implies that the standard is objective, that God is demanding the observance of the objective right and not merely positive regulations like the ceremonial rules of the Mosaic code.

3. Alfaro, *Justice in the World*, p. 13.

4. The teaching of human rights and practical related actions, of course, did not begin with Leo XIII. For example, Gregory the Great (590-604) protested the persecution of the Jews and their forced conversion; Pius II in 1462 condemned the Portuguese slave trade; in 1537 Paul III condemned the enslavement of South American Indians, whether Christian or pagan.

5. *The Documents of Vatican II*, ed. Walter M. Abbot, S.J., (New York: Herder and Herder, 1966), pp. 199-237.

6. A comprehensive listing of such documents may be found in *The Gospel of Peace and Justice*, presented by Joseph Gremillion, Maryknoll, N.Y., 1976, based upon the 1971 Synod of Bishops.

7. As described, for example, in Cato the Elder, *De Re Rustica*, trans. Ernest Brehaut (New York: Columbia University Press, 1933).

8. The Protestant tradition has tended to reject the use of philosophy and to base Christian ethics exclusively on the Bible. Catholic thinkers have usually incorporated a complex philosophical structure into both ethics and moral theology. Today, there are new directions in both traditions. *See* James M. Gustafson, *Protestant and Roman Catholic Ethics* (Chicago: University of Chicago Press, 1978), especially pp. 1-29; Donahue, "Biblical Perspectives", p. 68.

9. They are what the Scholastics call *"entia rationis cum fundamento in re"* (beings of reason with a foundation in reality).

SEYYED HOSSEIN NASR —— 4

The Concept and Reality of Freedom in Islam and Islamic Civilization

Professor Seyyed H. Nasr approaches the concept of human rights from a religious perspective of Islam. He concludes that the foundation of human rights is essentially theological and is rooted in the obligations owed by human beings to God.

The discussion of the concept of freedom in the modern West is so deeply affected by the Renaissance and post-Renaissance concept of man as being in revolt against heaven and master of the earth that it is difficult to envisage the meaning of freedom in the context of a traditional civilization such as that of Islam. It is necessary, therefore, to resuscitate the concept of man as understood in Islam in order to be able to discuss the meaning of freedom in the Islamic context. It is meaningless to try to study the notion of freedom in Islam from the point of view of the meaning that has been attached to this term in the West since the rise of humanism.

It might be said that most of the discussion in the West concerning freedom involves in one way or another the freedom to do or to act, whereas in the context of traditional man the most important form of freedom is the freedom to be, to experience pure existence itself. This is the most profound form of freedom, but it is forgotten today because modern man, who is so fond of collecting experiences, has ceased to remember the meaning of the experience of pure existence, which is a reflection of Being Itself and is at once beauty, consciousness, and bliss. Therefore the freedom that makes this experience possible is inexpressably precious.

Humans are, according to the Islamic perspective, created in the "image of God" and are also God's vicegerents (*khalīfah*) on earth. But they are both by virtue of their servitude to God, which makes it possible for them to receive from heaven and to administer on earth. By virtue of their centrality in the cosmic scheme, proven in reverse, if proof is necessary for the skeptic, by the nearly complete destruction they have brought upon the environment, they participate in the Divine freedom, and by virtue of being early creatures they are beset by all the limitations that a lower degree of existence implies. God is both pure freedom and pure necessity. Man as the theophany of the Divine names and qualities, or as the "image of God," participates in both this freedom and this necessity. Personal freedom lies, in fact, in surrendering to the Divine Will and in purifying oneself to an ever greater degree inwardly so as to become liberated from all external conditions, including those of the carnal soul (*nafs*), which press upon and limit one's freedom.

Pure freedom belongs to God alone; therefore the more we *are*, the more we are free. And this intensity in the mode of existence cannot come, save through submission and conformity to the Will of God, who alone *is* in the absolute sense. There is no freedom possible through flight from and rebellion against the Principle, which is the ontological source of human existence and which determines ourselves from on high. To rebel against our own ontological Principle in the name of freedom is to become enslaved to an ever greater degree in the world of multiplicity and limitation. It is to forfeit the illimitable expanses of the world of the spirit for the indefinitely extended labyrinth of the psychophysical world where the only freedom is to pursue an ever more accelerated life of action devoid of meaning and end.

Infinity resides in the center of our being, a center that is hidden from the vast majority of those who live on the periphery of the wheel of existence. Yet, only at the center are we free in an absolute and infinite manner. Otherwise each of us is limited in both our powers and rights vis-à-vis God, nature, and other human beings. To seek infinity in the finite is the most dangerous of illusions, a chimera that cannot but result in the destruction of the finite itself. "Infinite freedom" exists only in the proximity of the infinite. At all lower levels of existence, freedom is conditioned by the limitations of cosmic existence itself and is meaningful only with respect to the limitations and obligations that the very structure of reality imposes upon us.

The principles outlined briefly thus far form the background of all Islamic thought on freedom, but the degree to which they are explicitly formulated depends upon the perspective within Islamic civilization in question. The Islamic intellectual world is a hierarchical one in which the same truths are reflected in different forms on various levels and modes of understanding, ranging from the exoteric law to pure esotericism. Here it is sufficient to discuss the concept of freedom as understood by the jurisprudents (*fuqahā'*), theologians (*mutakallimūn*), philosophers, and Sufis to grasp its basic meaning within the Islamic worldview.

The jurisprudents are concerned with the codification of Islamic law (*Sharīᶜah*), and their discussion of freedom is naturally from a juridical point of view rather than a metaphysical one. Nevertheless, the metaphysical background is present in their juridical discussions, for they are dealing with the same *homo islamicus* to whom the whole of the Islamic revelation is addressed. The jurisprudents envisage human freedom as a result of personal surrender to the Divine Will rather than as an innate personal right. For them, since we are created by God and have no power to create anything by ourselves (in the sense of creation *ex nihilo*), we are ontologically dependent on God and therefore can only receive what is given to us by the source of our own being.

Human rights are, according to the *Sharīʿah*, a consequence of human obligations and not their antecedent. We possess certain obligations toward God, nature, and other humans, all of which are delineated by the *Sharīʿah*. As a result of fulfilling these obligations, we gain certain rights and freedoms that are again outlined by the Divine Law. Those who do not fulfill these obligations have no legitimate rights, and any claims of freedom that they make upon the environment or society is illegitimate and a usurpation of what does not belong to them, in the same way that those persons who refuse to recognize their theromorphic nature and act accordingly are only "accidentally" human and are usurping the human state which by definition implies centrality and Divine vicegerency. Islam holds this conception not only for its own followers but also for the followers of all other religions who, therefore, as religious minorities are given rights under their own religious codes.

The technical discussion of freedom (*hurriyyah* in Arabic and *āzādigī* in Persian), as far as jurisprudence is concerned, usually involves the question of slavery, the means whereby slaves are freed, the duties free men have toward them, and so on. But in a more general sense, not necessarily bound to the technical term *hurriyyah* itself, jurisprudence defines human freedom in the context of a Divine Law that concerns not only our own relation to God but also our relation to nature, to other men, and even to ourselves, since we are not free to do anything we wish with our own lives which we have not created. For example, suicide is considered a great sin because it is the usurpation of the right of God. Man is not free to take his life because he did not bring it into being in the first place. In this question, Islam stands at the very antipode of the agnostic existentialism that envisages complete freedom for human existence without considering the source, and also the end, of this existence. The *Sharīʿah* also imposes limitations upon human freedom, but in return bestows a sacred character upon human life that in turn makes possible a greater inner freedom. Ultimately, the limitations imposed by the *Sharīʿah* are in the direction of removing from human life certain negative possibilities and freedoms to do evil and of establishing the maximum amount of equilibrium in the human collectivity, which then serves as outward basis for the inner life leading to freedom in its most universal sense.

As far as the theologians are concerned, the most famous school among them, namely, the *Ashʿarite*, negates human freedom (*ikhtiyār*) completely in favor of a determinism *(jabr)* that is all-embracing. Other theological schools, such as the *Mu^ctazilite* and most of the *Shi^cite*, do believe in human freedom and reject the total determinism of the *Ash^carites*. Altogether the debate concerning free will and determinism is a central one to *Kalām*, and nearly every theologian has participated in it. The debates are in many ways the reverse of what is seen today among philosophers; some seek to safeguard the free will of the individual in one form or another of materialistic determinism whether it be biological, behavioral, or something else, and others try to defend these forms of determinism. Among Muslim theologians there has been, of course, no question of an outward "material" factor determining human freedom. The problem is the relationship of human will to the Divine Will and the extent to which the latter determines the former.

Muslim theology, especially in its prevalent *Ash^carite* form, tends toward a totalitarian voluntarism not usually seen in Christian theology, but there are many other views among Muslims. It is also important to remember that despite all the debates among theologians, men did and do continue to live with a consciousness of their free will and hence responsibility before God. As the remarkable dynamism of Islamic history proves, the Muslims are not at all the fatalists they are made out to be in Western sources. But their reliance upon the Divine Will and awareness of the operation of that Will shown in their incessant use of the term *inshā'Allāh* (if God wills) in daily discourse is more noticeable than in most other cultures. The debates of the theologians reflect this general religious concern for submission to the Divine Will and conformity to Its injunctions, although the shortcomings of all rational theologies in overcoming certain dichotomies and polarizations, which the theological debate of the subject created, pushed certain hardened positions to extremes and went so far as to deny human freedom against both the immediate experience of man and religious injunctions concerning man being held responsible before God for their actions.

The philosophers in general reacted severely against the theologians on this question and asserted fully the reality of human freedom. The early Muslim Peripatetics such as al-Fārābī, Abu 'l-Hansan al-^cAmirī, Ibn Sīna (Avicenna), as well as the Andalusian philosophers such as Ibn Bājjah (Avempace) and Ibn Rushd (Averroes), were greatly interested in political philosophy and well acquainted with Plato and Aristotle and even with some of the Stoics. On the question of freedom, however, they regarded the problem from the point of view of the Islamicized political philosophy of al-Fārābī rather than in purely Greek terms. For all of them the *Sharī^cah* (which al-Fārābī equated with the Pythagorean-Platonic *nomos*) was a reality in the Islamic community *(ummah)*, and the legitimacy of political rule was derived from the source of revelation, in terms of either *Sunni* or *Shi^cite* interpretations. They supported the reality of human freedom, but in the context of the nomocratic society of Islam and not from the point of view of a secularist humanism. Later Islamic philosophers such as Mullā Sadrā reverted mostly to a more theological and religious debate about free will and determinism and shied away from the discussions on political philosophy of the kind seen in an al-Fārābī or Averroes. But they, too, were adamant in asserting the reality of human freedom and also the necessity to conform to the Divine Will that rules over both the cosmos and human society and that alone can prevent men from becoming imprisoned in the narrow confines of their own passions.

Finally, something must be said about the Sufis who more than any other group in Islam have spoken about freedom. The verses of such Sufi poets as Rūmī and Ḥāfiẓ are replete with the word *āzādigī* and similar terms denoting freedom. In one of his most famous verses Ḥāfiẓ says:

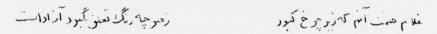

I am the slave of the spiritual will of him who under the azure wheel

Is free *[āzād]* from whatever possesses the color of dependence.

The goal of Sufism is union with the One Who is both Absolute and Infinite, Who alone is beyond all limitation. The Sufis therefore consider freedom *ḥurriyyah* or *āzādigī*, as being almost synonymous with the goal of Sufism itself. However, for them freedom does not mean individualism, for their whole aim is to integrate the individual into the universal. Rather, for them freedom means to gain inner detachment through the help of the revealed forms, whether they be cultic or artistic, forms which are outwardly limited but open inwardly toward the infinite. Sufis therefore have always been the most rigorous in the observation of forms, of regard for the *Sharīʿah* and its meticulous practice, yet they have "broken" these forms from within and attained complete freedom. They have, moreover, done so not in spite of the revealed forms but because of them. No one can transcend what one does not possess. The Sufis transcended forms not by rebelling individualistically against them but by penetrating into their inner dimension that, because of the sacred character of these forms, opens unto the Infinite. Sufis also practiced detachment and were often indifferent toward worldly authority. But there were also those among them who were outwardly rich or who even wielded political power. In both cases there existed inner detachment and spiritual poverty (*faqr*) that alone make inner freedom possible, for men lose their freedom to the extent that they become enslaved not only by external factors but also by their needs, whether these be artificial or real. Freedom in Sufism means ultimately deliverance (*najāt*) from all bondage and an experience of the world of the Spirit, where alone freedom in its real sense is to be found.

As far as the realization of freedom in Islamic civilization is concerned, it too must be studied on several levels, especially those of action and thought as well as the actual possibility of attaining inner freedom and deliverance. On the level of external action, the immediate question that arises is that of political freedom vis-à-vis forms of government that, from the Ummayyad period onward, did not have a completely religious character and were supported by nearly unlimited military power. Much has been written about "Oriental despotism" and the lack of freedom of men in the face of the state. But it must be remembered that for ages the Divine Law remained as a protective code whose bounds even the most ruthless ruler could not transgress. There remained within Islamic society a continuous tension between the political authority of the caliph, sultan, or *amīr* and the religious scholars (*ᶜulamā'*) who played a major role in protecting the *Sharīᶜah* and, therefore, those freedoms of the individual guaranteed by the *Sharīᶜah*.

Also it is important to mention that the *ᶜulamā'* do not play the same role in Islam as the clergy do in Christianity, because the priestly function in Islam is divided among the male members of the whole community. There is no sacerdotal hierarchy in Islam, and there is an element of "sacred democracy" in this tradition that enters directly into daily religious life and has much to do with the guarantee of a great deal of freedom in the life of individuals and the community. The role of the *Sharīᶜah* and its institutions as protection of the community against arbitrary military and political oppression needs to be emphasized, especially since most modern studies on the subject only view the external political institutions and not the personal relationships, family structure, individual rights, among others that are all embraced within the comprehensive fold of the *Sharīᶜah*.

The lack of an organized religious structure is combined in Islam with the lack of a strictly defined credo in the Christian sense and therefore a much less rigorously defined notion of what is doctrinally acceptable. In Islam, orthodoxy is defined by the testimonial of Islam or *Shahādah, Lā ilāha illa'Llāh* (There is no divinity but the Divine), which is the most universal formulation possible of Divine Unity and not a closely defined theological formulation. There has also been no institution in Islam to define the meaning of the *Shahādah* and its legitimate interpretations. Of course, there *is* orthodoxy in Islam without which, in fact, no truth and no tradition is possible. But this orthodoxy has not been defined in any limited sense nor has there been a particular religious authority to decide who is orthodox and who is not. Those in Islamic history who were persecuted or even put to death for their words or writings, such as Ibn Hanbal the jurist, al-Hallāj the Sufi, or Suhrawardī the Sufi and philosopher, were all involved in political situations with religious implication—the problem of al-Hallāj being, however, of a special nature. But even cases of persecution such as those cited are few in comparison with what is found elsewhere. By and large the Islamic tradition has provided a vast umbrella under which views as different as those of a Rhazes and an Ibn ʿArabī have been expressed and taught. If there has been a tension, it has usually been between the exoteric and the esoteric dimensions of the tradition, but this is a tension that is of a creative nature and lies within the structure of the Islamic tradition itself.

The most crucial test for the actual realization of means to attain freedom in Islam has been the degree to which it has been able to keep alive within its bosom ways of spiritual realization and inner freedom. And in this matter of central concern as far as man's entelechy is concerned, Islam has been eminently successful. Over the ages and despite all the obstacles that the gradual darkening of man's outward nature has placed before authentic spiritual paths, Islam has been able to preserve intact to this very day ways of attaining freedom in its absolute and unconditional sense, that is, in the sense of complete detachment from everything except God, which is in fact exactly how Sufis have defined freedom or *hurriyyah*. Its spiritual techniques and methods, contained mostly within Sufism, are doors opening inward to the only freedom that is real and abiding but imperceptible to the outward eye. Any discussion of the concept and reality of freedom in Islam must take into account, besides outward manifestations of freedom on the plane of action, the inner freedom that is related to the experience of being itself and transforms us in such a way that outward forms of freedom gain a completely different meaning for us. In modern terms, we may have gained many freedoms, but we have also lost the most fundamental freedom to be ourselves, not the coagulated cloud of the ego with which we usually identify ourselves, but the immortal self that resides in the proximity of the Self and enjoys immortality and freedom because of its very nature.

REFERENCES

Lings, M., *What is Sufism?* (London: Allen and Unwin, 1975).

Northbourne, W.E.C.J., *Looking Back on Progress* (London: Perennial Books, 1970).

Nasr, S.H., *Islam and the Plight of Modern Man* (London: Longmans Green, 1976).

Rosenthal, F., *The Muslim Concept of Freedom Prior to the Nineteenth Century* (Leiden: Brill, 1960).

Shuon, F., *Logic and Transcendence*, trans. P. Townsend (New York: Harper & Row, 1975).

ISHWAR C. SHARMA ——— 5

Human Rights and Comprehensive Humanism

Professor Ishwar Sharma presents his paper from a crosscultural and metaphysical perspective: as an Eastern philosopher in the Hindu tradition reflecting on the concept of human rights and on its treatment in Western philosophy. He believes that a sound philosophical basis for human rights would necessarily emerge from a comprehensive humanism stressing the freedom of the self.

The problem of human rights has gained prominence among philosophers recently. It appears that philosophical interest in this area is partly an intellectual reaction of the contemporary thinkers to the human misery caused by the two world wars. The use of an atomic bomb has brought home to man the truth that, in case human rights are transgressed wantonly in the future and in case a nuclear war were to break out, neither the victor nor the victim can survive. Before man commits atomic suicide even inadvertently, it is the duty of philosophers who represent Socrates as a gadfly, to point out that human rights are invariably linked with human obligations and are indispensable to human dignity. Most philosophers are in the habit of raising questions, creating antinomies, and ending up with skepticism and doubt. Any suggestion to solve controversies would be unwelcome to them since they believe such an attempt might thwart pure philosophy, which in their opinion is nothing but an insatiable intellectual curiosity. This chapter does not support such a view. Socrates, as depicted by Plato, cannot be dubbed either a skeptic or a dogmatist. It appears that the contemporary empiricists, in spite of their dogmatic adherence to an ethical relativism born of skepticism, would not begrudge affinity with Socrates. This chapter does not make any claim to an absolute or indisputable answer to the philosophically disputable question of human rights. Instead it gives a perspective emphasizing the aspect of man that seems to be at the core of his nature. The recognition of this core may not only provide a basis for human rights, but also may encourage intelligent study that results in the highest philosophical activity.

This presentation, therefore, would avoid both absolutism and skepticism. The problem of right is intimately connected with and dependent on the performance of duty, moral obligation, or virtue. Socrates' life and his heroic death demonstrate that a true philosopher is not one who has a mere intellectual concern with virtue as a concept, but one who applies it in his practical life. In the application of virtue, which is "true knowledge," a philosopher gains the highest freedom, the freedom of self that is the core of human personality, and by doing so he protects human rights. Unrefuted until today are the arguments offered by Socrates in the *Crito*, in defense of a categorical adherence to democratically constituted laws of the state that an individual has voluntarily chosen and the rights he has enjoyed all his life. Socrates refused to avoid a death sentence and to live longer and benefit the people of his time with his wisdom, thus demonstrating that respect for democratic law alone can preserve human rights. Even at the cost of exaggeration, it may be said that humanity is indebted to Socrates for the preservation of democracy and the championship of human rights. He did not fail to adhere to his duty as the price for the protection of freedom for posterity.

Whenever and wherever human rights have been crushed, revolution and violence have invariably ensued. In spite of the revolution and wars enacted in the name of social, religious, political, and economic freedom, man is not yet free. Rousseau was disturbed at this pitiable plight when he remarked, "Man is born free, and is everywhere in chains. One thinks himself master of others, and still remains a greater slave than they. How did this come about? I do not know. What can make it legitimate? That question I think I can answer."[1]

While answering this question Rousseau arrives at the conclusion that the freedom of man can be restored when he is governed by the law legislated by himself. He favors a republican type of government and justifiably rejects aristocracy and monarchy. He also categorically denies the use of force to create "right." His theory of social contract is a form of humanism that advocates self-limitation and self-government. His definition of law to be obeyed by man in order to enjoy the right of freedom, indicates that freedom consists in self-restraint and not in an unlicensed exercise of will. In his words: "Laws are, strictly speaking, the conditions of civil association. The people being subject to the laws, ought to be their author: the conditions of society ought to be regulated by those who unite to give it form."[2] Rousseau did not advocate revolution and the use of force to change a government that enforced legislation contrary to the general will and common good.

Revolutionary interpretations of the social contract theory have been advocated since Rousseau's time. However, the use of force in claiming rights for Rousseau was self-contradictory. It cannot be universalized. Yet the history of the American, French, and Russian revolutions has shown that civilized people do resort to "might" for securing right.

Almost all wars in the past and in our own time have been fought with the pretension of securing rights and liberties. Medieval Europe was a scene of brutal wars, massacres, and crusades, presumably to secure religious rights. Today we can say with some justification that the medieval wars were unjust and irrational because Christians killed Christians in the name of the Prince of Peace and because the parties belonging to one religion were not wise enough to rise above denominational differences.

In the twentieth century two world wars have been fought to preserve equality, liberty, justice, and peace. Both the Allies and the Axis powers during the World War II, categorically declared that they were fighting for human rights. It must be confessed that in spite of all the scientific progress and unprecedented intellectual advancement, twentieth-century man has not yet risen above the use of brute force as long as there is war, as long as there is oppression and violent exploitation of one group by the other anywhere in the world. Perhaps in fifty years posterity may blame us, the proud product of an era of science, spaceships, and nuclear revolution, because we kill one another in the name of political affiliations.

Is man a religious animal? The religious wars have answered the question in the negative. Had man's essential characteristic been profession of a religion, had his basic right been religious in nature, he would not have committed homicide in the name of God.

Is man a political animal? The answer again is no! The history of the past three hundred years, which have been devoted to man's political emancipation and to the procurement of "equality," "liberty," and "fraternity," is again our witness. If man had been merely a political or social animal, or if his only demands had been for the freedom to govern himself, the abolition of monarchies would have brought nations of the world closer and solved all human problems. The political aspect of man, like the religious aspect, renders only a partial definition of his nature. Hence, the procurement of religious and political freedom will not suffice to resolve conflicts and bring peace to mankind.

The Marxist approach to the problem is based on another narrow definition of man, namely, the economic definition. Marx, like Rousseau, claimed that he wanted to free man from the chains of slavery. But his diagnosis was different. For him the sole cause of this slavery was economic inequality. In his words:

The general conclusion at which I arrived and which, once reached, continued to serve as the leading thread in my studies may be briefly summed up as follows: "In the social production which men carry on they enter into definite relations that are indispensable and independent of their will; these relations of production correspond to a definite stage of development of their material powers of production. The sum total of these relations of production constitutes the economic structure of society—the real foundation, on which rise legal and political superstructures and to which correspond definite forms of social consciousness. The mode of production in material life determines the general character of the social, political, and spiritual processes of life. It is not the consciousness of men that determines their existence, but, on the contrary, their social existence determines their consciousness. At a certain stage of their development the material forces of production in society come into conflict with the existing relations or production, or—what is but a legal expression for the same thing—with the property relations within which they had been at work before. From forms of development of the forces of production these relations turn into their fetters."[3]

Even though Marxism has been adopted as a philosophy of the Communist countries, historical happenings in our own time have amply proved that this extreme political ideology is not an absolute truth. Communism is not a monolith today. The procurement of economic rights alone cannot lead to peace and harmony, because man is not merely an economic animal.

The philosophic problem may be outlined briefly as follows: What is the sanction of the source of human rights? If the source is universal in character, it would not represent a lopsided aspect of human nature and we would be nearer the truth. There could be greater agreement between the contending views and greater possibility of the controversy being resolved. As long as there is controversy, as long as human rights are supposed to have been based on flimsy grounds, neither philosophy, theology, economics, nor political theories can be of any help.

The intention of this chapter is not to deny the religious, the political, and the economic aspects of human nature, but to evaluate their relative importance. What is being stated here is that these aspects are not comprehensive in their own right. The theological basis of right is external and authoritarian. It cannot be denied that the development of modern democracy has been influenced to some extent by the Judaeo-Christian concept of the equality of men. The article on democracy in the *Encyclopaedia Britannica* states the following:

Closely allied to the idea of liberty in democratic theory is the idea of equality. The early Christian idea, inherited from the Jewish tradition and enunciated by Jesus and elaborated by St. Paul, was that all men are equal before God, being descended from the same first parents, who were created by God, and being redeemed by the death of Christ, and hence are all brothers and can boast no inherent distinction one over the other because of race, fortune or other accidental inequalities . . . .

As the Judaeo-Christian doctrine gradually took possession, equality became a fundamental tenet in theory, and the much-quoted dictum of Pope Gregory the Great (590-604), that "all men are by nature equal," was maintained as the universal teaching for many centuries.[4]

There are two important implications of the statements quoted above. First, the basis for equality and hence for liberty, according to this view, lies outside human nature. Hence, it cannot be acknowledged as inherent in man. Second, this basis, besides being anthropologically supernatural with reference to the concept of God, excludes an overwhelming non-Judeo-Christian majority of people all over the world. Any sanction of human rights that is outside human nature is bound to be relative, limited, and hence discriminative. The rights of equality and liberty as advocated in the modern concept of democracy, on the contrary, were the outcome of opposition to the doctrine of the "divine rights of kings" sanctioned by medieval theology. It has therefore to be admitted that,

The extension of this right [of equality] to all men . . . without regard to status, economic position, religious belief, or race is essentially a modern idea, and with a few exceptions the application of the idea in the contemporary democracies dates back only to the last quarter of the nineteenth century.[5]

Although not altogether free from theological bias, modern philosophy, determined to shake off "the handmaiden" yoke of religion, has turned toward science, naturalism, and materialism, thereby advocating a secular source of human rights. Even in the American Declaration of Independence, in spite of the recognition of "the laws of Nature and of Nature's God," the secular basis of human rights has been explicitly emphasized:

We hold these truths to be self-evident, that all men are created equal, that they are endowed by their creator with certain unalienable rights, that among these are Life, Liberty and the pursuit of Happiness—that to secure these rights, governments are instituted among Men, deriving their just powers from the consent of the governed. . . .[6]

The inalienable rights of men can be secured by the institution of a government that derives its just powers from human beings and not from any external supernatural source. It is therefore evident that the American concept of liberty is secular and that American humanism is secular in character.

The concept of liberty as a political idea is both theological and secular. Its theological character was influenced by the philosophy of Saint Augustine and Thomas Aquinas who emphasized that it is in the interest of the members of the community to exercise the right of liberty to be ruled. This idea makes the authority of the government a necessary ingredient of freedom. This stemmed from the theocratical concept of liberty that dominated Europe for centuries. The modern concept of liberty is secular and is opposed to the theocratical concept. It recognizes the right of man to be free and his right to be the arbiter of his own political destiny without any external intervention whatsoever. In this sense, liberty is opposed to authority.

American revolutionary thinkers steered a middle course and suggested that liberty is complementary to, and not the antithesis of, authority, as long as authority is legal and as long as it is exercised with the sole purpose of protecting the right of liberty. This approach appears to be more logical because it advocates political and social equality, without denying religious freedom. This appoach is nearer comprehensive humanism than the purely theological and purely secular types of humanism. However, the question arises whether economic equality is necessary for the establishment of political equality. It is here that the philosophy of capitalism comes in conflict with that of communism. Both represent extreme attitudes. If man is considered only a social animal or a political animal or an economic animal, conflicting philosophies of life are bound to emerge.

All three (social, political, and economic) secular concepts of man, respectively, point to the dichotomies between individual and society, ruler and the ruled, those who have and who have not. Secular humanism, in its anxiety to get rid of the anthropomorphism of traditional religion, falls victim to the fallacy of accepting a too narrow definition of man. In its fanaticism to eliminate God and religion, it resorts to the bigotry of rejecting every method of inquiry other than the scientific. The only assumptions, postulates, and discoveries accepted by secular humanism are those of modern science. One example of this type is to be found in Auguste Comte's "Religion of Humanity," which creates a dichotomy between man and nature and ends in what may be called anthropocentrism. Another extreme type of such humanism is Marxism, which declares that "Religion is an opiate" for man. The question arises: Why do such radical ideologies including the "Death of God" radical theology so vehemently oppose a theocratical concept of man? It is likely that a right answer to this question may suggest a reconciliation between secular and religious and between scientific and metaphysical notions of man, God, and nature. This answer could also be the answer to the question: What is the basis of human freedom?

Science and religion have been drifting apart for a long time, and the separation continues to widen day by day. One reason for this opposition on the part of religion appears to be that, in spite of the recognition of God as the Supreme Being who is omnipotent, omniscient, and omnipresent, traditional theology has always overemphasized the concept of God as a transcendental Person and as an external authority who constantly intervenes in human affairs and whose wrath inflicts severe punishment on those who transgress His commandments. Morality, therefore, is imposed from above; it is not an inner growth, but rather a response to external constraint. Nowhere do the Old and New Testaments mention God as a man with physical dimensions. On the contrary, they always designate Him as the "Light, Spirit, Truth, Love, and One Lord, beyond all names." It is strange that the traditional interpretation of theology has externalized God as a Supernatural Person, wrathful Judge, and an Autocrat of a high order. This has resulted in a parochial approach to the concept of liberty, with the suggestion that man has no right to be happy unless he is the member of a church or a temple that has a monopoly or eschatological insurance. According to this view, science, philosophy, and all intellectual pursuits are not only futile but present great obstacles in the progress of man due to his arrogance.

This antirational, anti-intellectual, and antiscientific attitude of traditional religion during an age of scientific discoveries and technological triumph over time and space, and a period of political, social, and cultural advancement the world over has been responsible for outbursts of radical ideologies and antireligious movements. Whereas science has helped man to rise above social, political, geographic, and racial boundaries, religion seems to have created artificial walls between groups. Hence, scientific humanism is preferred to any religious humanism by many philosophers. The "Humanist Manifesto" of 1933, issued by a group of thirty-four persons including the American pragmatist John Dewey, is worth mentioning in this context:

The manifesto stated that humanists hold an "organic view of life," reject the "traditional dualism of mind and body" and believe that "man is a part of nature and that he has emerged as the result of a continuous process." Man with all his faculties is a part of one all-embracing natural order. He is the highest product of the creative forces of the universe with "nothing above or beyond him" but his own aspirations.[7]

Although this manifesto appears to be an article of faith in gross materialism, its implications go beyond such an attitude. It purports to point out that the nature from which man has emerged is not absolutely extraneous to him. If this nature is a "continuous process," and if man "is the highest product of the creative forces of the universe," then whatever is at the root of the universe, that "x," must necessarily be creative and not, in any case, less intelligent and less powerful than its product. It appears that the metaphysics of the Humanistic Manifesto is not basically different from that of any philosophic religion or of any religion that declares its God to be an all-powerful Supreme Being. The only difference is that the "x" from which nature and men emerge is being referred to here, as "nature" and "creative forces," as organic and monistic, because the "traditional dualism of mind and body" has been abandoned. The same "x" is designated as God in religious terminology. If God as the creative force from whom man has emerged as "the highest product" (in scientific terms), or as the "crown of creation" (in religious terms) is the Supreme Source of all that lives, exists, and has its being, then that element in man that manifests a "creative force" in him must be the core of his personality.

"Creative" and not "destructive force" in man is the highest and most expressive of his innermost self. When man's thoughts are creative and positive, when his feelings and emotions are harmonious and permeated with love, and when his volitions and actions are motivated by goodness and benevolence, his personality becomes integrated and his self, from which intelligence, love, and good will emerge, becomes highly manifested. Recognition of this self as the author of ethical, political, and social judgments is the presupposition of what may be called comprehensive humanism.

Comprehensive humanism explains why respect for life is necessary for claiming the right to live, why respect for property is the precondition of the right to possess property, and why respect for the opinion of others is the presupposition of freedom of thought. Comprehensive humanism contends that moral obligations are to be discharged voluntarily by every normal individual, because such behavior, being the flow of the creative force of the human self, leads to the integrated development of personality, ultimately bringing him the highest freedom, the "freedom of mind," referred to by Dewey as "the basic freedom."

Man has the option to use nature and exploit its resources either wantonly and recklessly or on a reciprocal basis without creating an imbalance in nature resulting in environmental pollution. Any imbalance created by man in the natural environment is bound to result in dangerous consequences, as it would be hazardous to all life on our planet. If man adopts a friendly attitude toward nature, he will not have to face the problems of environmental ecology. Man's physical well-being depends on his reciprocal relation with nature.

In like manner, man's mental well-being, his happiness, peace of mind, and enhancement of personality depend on his reciprocal relation with society and state. He may either choose a selfish attitude of disregarding obligations and harping on rights only or a liberal attitude of discharging his duties honestly and thus acquiring human rights as a natural consequence. Comprehensive humanism neither creates a fear complex in man, as the dogmatism and excesses of orthodox religion have done, nor overemphasizes the successes of science as the basis for its claim to absolute truth. Science itself makes no such claims. Philosophers who espouse scientific humanism do overshoot the mark and seem to be overwhelmed by its achievements in the same manner as philosophy was overawed by religion in the Middle Ages.

Where does the locus of human rights, human freedom, and particularly "freedom of mind" lie? Does it lie in the state as "social contract," in an external supernatural authority, such as God, or in a "proletarian dictatorship," the transitional stage to the classless humanism of Marx? Comprehensive humanism would contend that the sole grounding for human rights is that aspect of man that is designated as the self, the pivot of intellectual, emotional, and volitional functions in him. Overemphasis on any one of the three functions of intelligence (reason), feeling (fear or dread), and volition (the leap of faith or will to power), at the cost of man's self, might result in the acceptance of a partisan philosophy. Although intellect is near to objective truth, the self that generates intellectual understanding of truth, aesthetic apprehension of beauty, and ethical adoption of goodness should be the main concern of philosophy in this context.

Science, no doubt, gives us cogent knowledge of a small part of truth. Yet its correctness, based only on intellect, though universal, does not give a comprehensive picture of human nature. In the words of Karl Jaspers:

This correctness, in its universal validity, does not unite us completely as real human beings, but only as intellectual beings. It unites us in the object that is understood, in the particular, but not in the totality. . . . To the intellect all else, in comparison with what is correct counts only as feeling, subjectivity, instinct. In this division apart from the bright world of the intellect there is only the irrational, in which is lumped together, according to the point of view, what is despised or desired.[8]

It is in this sense that scientific humanism, if it were to exist as a philosophy, would be incomplete and lopsided. Similarly, religious humanism, which is opposed to reason and scientific objectivity, would not grant liberty to man qua man.

Comprehensive humanism with its genuine concern in the understanding of the totality of human nature could provide a sound basis for human rights. Even though the 1933 Humanist Manifesto was framed mainly by scientific humanists, it appears to imply a comprehensive humanism. However, the second Humanist Manifesto issued in 1973 by a group of more than a hundred persons, including scientists, philosophers, and theologians, inadvertently appears to have advanced a step further toward comprehensive humanism. In this context it would be proper to conclude this chapter with the remarks of Harold Titus:

While the first Manifesto set forth humanist values in general terms, the second, lengthier, statement is more scientific and affirms the right to birth-control, abortion, divorce, social freedom, euthanasia and privacy. The document also stresses freedom of the individual, participatory democracy, a minimum guaranteed annual income, universal education and worldwide ecological planning. It deplores or opposes war, nationalism, and any dogmatic or authoritarian religion that places revelation, God, and creed above human need and experience. The goal is the "fulfillment of the potential for growth in each human personality"; and the use of reason and intelligence in the building of a "world community in which all sectors of the human family can participate."[9]

The declaration falls short of another step toward comprehensive humanism, because it fails to assert that intellectual dogmatism is to be avoided along with credal tenacity.

NOTES

1. Aubrey Castell, *An Introduction to Philosophy* (New York: Macmillan and Co., 1976), p. 281.

2. Ibid., p. 286.

3. George P. Stein, *The Forum of Philosophy* (New York: McGraw-Hill Book Co., 1973), p. 320.

4. *Encyclopaedia Britannica*, vol. 7 (Chicago: Encyclopaedia Britannica, 1957), p. 184 c.

5. Ibid.

6. Ibid., p. 125 b.

7. Harold Titus and Marilyn Smith, *Living Issues in Philosophy* (New York: D. van Nostrand Co., 1974), p. 416.

8. Ibid.

9. Ibid.

PETER K. Y. WOO —— **6**

A Metaphysical Approach
To Human Rights
from a Chinese
Point of View

*Chinese philosophers commonly acknowledge that the conception of
individual human rights was introduced into early twentieth-century
China from its origins in Western philosophy. Professor Peter K. Y.
Woo contends that the Western idea of human rights has never been
widely accepted in China because it is rooted in metaphysical concepts
that had been foreign to traditional Chinese culture. He shows how an
examination of certain vital ideas provides a basis in Chinese philosophy for an acceptance of human rights.*

SOME BASIC CONCEPTS

The issue of human rights becomes a problem only when it is present in
our awareness as a privation. Hence, for the issue to become a problem within a culture, it presupposes this awareness of privation. Otherwise, one may
say that there is no such problem within the given culture.

The subject of human rights may be considered superficially in its political
and social aspects. It is, however, essentially a philosophical or metaphysical
problem. Only when the issue is studied from this standpoint can one get at
the basic issue and its possible implications.

The general tendency of the Chinese philosophy of life is at variance with
the Western perspective. In philosophical research of the issue of human
rights, it is necessary to have recourse to historical comparisons and analogi-
cal thinking to make clear the difference in positions.

This chapter consists of three sections dealing separately with historical
development, the concept of human rights, and its contemporary significance.

HISTORICAL DEVELOPMENT OF HUMAN RIGHTS

Chinese culture was founded on agriculture. In the earliest records, the ordinary people, as the backbone and working force of the economy, were already regarded as the center of interest and the reason for the political formation.[1] This is to say that the political leaders were to concern themselves with, and aim their activities at, the welfare of the ordinary people. With this in mind, the aim of benefiting the people was regarded as the original purpose of government. To have this aim for government was to negate the legitimacy of the self-seeking of power and advantage for the leaders, if they were to be consistent with the basis for government. This purity of government was well kept in the early years of Chinese communities, and the faithfulness to the purpose of government can be seen from prehistoric times. One example of the freedom of the people is reflected in this lyric, common at the time: "Working as the day breaks, retire as the evening comes. We dig wells in order to drink; we cultivate the land to eat. What can the emperor do to us?"[2] We can also witness the same phenomenon of ungoverning government from Mencius's (372-289 B.C.) view: "The people are the most important element in a nation; the spirits of the land and grain are the next; the sovereign is the lightest."[3]

Early Chinese history showed how a system of selecting rulers for the community evolved in relation to this particular view of the nature of government.[4] The system, known as "selection according to virtue and ability,"[5] led to a morality of "letting the better man rule,"[6] even at the sacrifice of one's own political position.

This state of ideal government, however, did not last. It was followed by a period in which governments were filled with power-oriented leaders. This period was the well-known period of "the warring states" (403-221 B.C.) when there were endless struggles among the leaders for dominance and the people were reduced to war refugees with no protection for either life or property.

Political upheaval usually brings changes in the development of ideas as part of the social transformation. In Greece, the establishment of the Olympic games resulted in the recognition of slavery as a natural state of things. Externally, to maintain slavery, the Greeks were by necessity imperialistic. These new instiututions caused reactionary phenomena in philosophical ideals, represented by the Platonic *Politeia* and the Aristotelian *Ethics*. These philosophies were to teach about, and to oppose, the deplorable state of society by rediscovering the essential nature of man from a cosmological foundation.

Similarly, the historical change of the warring states in China caused a series of new movements leading to political and social ideals known as the "hundred schools." These Chinese philosophers had the same intention of solving social problems through metaphysical ideas. For example, both Confucianism and Taoism are known for their radical investigations from a metaphysical basis into philosophies of life to reclaim a true existence for man. Confucius claimed that the ideal relationship between rational beings is ultimately a compassionate and benevolent one. For the Taoists, the recognition of the ontological connection between the being of Tao and man is the necessary link toward having an authentic existence within the harmony of Tao.[7] Both these philosophies eventually became integrated into the practical aspects of living in Chinese culture, and they helped significantly in shaping the traditional Chinese view of life.

Another factor in the shaping of cultural tendencies in China is the interaction with foreign cultures. In viewing Greek civilization, one can see that, at least for a historical moment, neither the Platonic *Politeia* nor the Aristotelian *Ethics* had arrested the general acceptance of slavery and political imperialism. It remained for the Judeo-Christian influence to dissolve the institution of slavery at a much later time.

In China, the hundred schools also failed to put a stop to the warring states. In addition, these philosophical schools gradually declined into such activities as fortune-telling and alchemy to such a degree that, when Buddhism was imported into China, it became almost immediately the central philosophy.

Foreign cultural influences also became generally accepted. In the West, Genesis, in its biblical sense, had long been considered the major evidence to sustain the dignity and value of man's existence. Yet Buddhism in China ignited the desire in every man for the self-realization to become Buddha, since the nature of that perfect being is considered inherent in every single man. The state of nirvana shared, with the Confucian ideal of the compassionate man, supreme position in the value system of Chinese thought. In fact, as a final goal of life, they became paramount because the two ideals are quite compatible, and both stress a similar state of unity and harmony in which man wants to live with others and the universe.

This universal unity later became the only noticeable motive for the combination of three essential philosophical schools: the Confucian, the Taoist, and the Buddhist. The consequence of this combination is the substantiation of the general view that repudiated any attempt to separate, conceptually and ontologically, the essential being of man from the universe as a whole. It also generated a compassionate feeling in man toward all beings.

In view of the acceptance of universal unity and harmony, the issue of individual rights among men did not take the shape of a problem, nor did any form of struggling for rights become recognized as a legitimate activity. The role of the ideal of unity awoke the compassionate feelings and the desire for cooperation, rather than the consciousness that the individual needs to be protected. This philosophical trend did not encourage the struggling for power or dominance. For example, the theory behind "the ways of the king" is that of invoking the feelings of righteousness in the ruler to benefit the general populace, and not the ways to power or to control.

Since Tung Chung-shu's (179-104 B.C.) effort to reinstate the authority of Confucianism in state politics, by the repudiation of all other philosophical views, the Chinese people have had one political ideal. It was to aspire for the rule of one emperor who would be true to the original purpose of government, to benefit all without active control or domination. All the moral reflections of Confucianism addressed to the rulers were aimed at showing them their duties to the people. There are four main steps for the ruler or, for that matter, for all men to follow as moral beings. One must first cultivate oneself in all virtuous aspects, as the basis for forming a harmonious family. Only after this can one attempt to govern people without enforced dominance. The last step is to influence the world and give it peace and harmony by exercising the virtues of a moral ruler. For the general populace, Confucianism was to inculcate the acceptance of fate or of any living conditions, since all forms of revolt were ruled out in the conceptual scheme of Confucianism.

For the ruler, this philosophy was to instill the desire to assist heaven in realizing the kind of political state in which people might enjoy, and not suffer, their fates.[8]

After the period of neo-Confucianism, the rationalism advocated by the philosophers in the Sung (A.D. 960-1279) and Ming (A.D. 1368-1644) dynasties was a metaphysical intuition of the aforementioned universal unity and harmony. Man is identified in both substance and essential virtues with all other kinds of beings. The philosophers formulated a cosmic principle, "the endless creative creativity" from the I-Ching (Book of Change). I-Ching posited a circular dynamic process of the manifestations of the basic metaphysical substance to explain the being of man as well as the rest of the universe.

Within the formulation of the ideal of harmony and unity, the issue of human rights cannot obtain the status of an independent and genuine problem, because the relations among men are only a step toward a much higher goal of the harmony of all beings. Whatever grievance an individual person may have must be reconsidered in relation to the value of universal unity. Hence, conceptually, not only were the actual experiences of human relations ignored, but the issue of human rights never arose. For example, the ideal of righteousness was not regarded as the central idea to deal with human relations. The harmony and the consequent equality of men were to be arrived at through compassion and the mutual, conscious striving for harmony.

The historical evidence for the general inclination toward the philosophies of harmony can be seen from the fact that the legalistic school, the philosophers who advanced the idea of righteous human relations, had never gained any real influence in the Chinese mentality. Their social positions were always secondary in relation to the schools that upheld universal harmony.

We have seen that the trend of political views, as well as of the philosophies of life, had always been more conducive to the promotion of virtuous sentiments in rulers than to the desire for rebellion to gain rights for the people.[9] Unquestionably, there had been bad rulers who did not recognize that ideal, and there had been wars. But neither the bad rulers nor the wars came to be seen as cases for gaining rights for the oppressed. The wars were rather the aberrant behavior of rulers who fought for their own dominance. Most probably, the people were never quite conscious of having rights as citizens.

But, after foreign invasions and the opium wars of 1840, the Chinese became conscious of the threat to the lives of their community and culture. This awareness was naturally more acute among the educated. They saw that the philosophical ideals were no safeguard against the mechanical weapons of foreign powers. From that historical moment, there emerged the need and the desire for self-protection, and this need triggered a series of social movements for advocating social, political, and military reformation. Among these movements, the most notable was the May 4, 1919 demonstration for political and economic self-determination that set off a new idealism to promote the military efficiency of China with the aid of new technologies. This new idealism removed, in part, the impact of Confucianism and the pacifist attitude. It was a new consciousness that identified itself with the general desire to Westernize, to catch up with the progress of technology through struggle instead of submission. This was virtually the beginning of a consideration of the problem of human rights in China.

The first actual incident produced by this new consciousness was the people's revolution against the ruling Manchurian government led by Dr. Sun Yat-sen (1866-1925). It was a revolution of the Chinese people to free themselves from foreign dominance. In spite of Manchuria's occupation of China for 300 years, and its gradual assimilation into Chinese culture, it was still, strictly speaking, a foreign power. After the success of the people's revolution, a new Western type of government was created, with the concepts of protection for the individual citizens and their property, of establishing legal rights of the people, and of a government elected by the people. These ideas were incorporated in the "Three Principles of the People" by Sun Yat-sen, to safeguard the freedom of the people during a transition to constitutional government. It was also the conceptual bridge between the ideals of universal harmony and the independence and freedom of the individual.

Early twentieth-century China was imbued with an enthusiasm for human rights, ranging from a concern with the nature of the family and its components of individual persons, and the status of women in society, to the balancing of the rights of individuals with the community as a whole. The efforts in dealing with these problems led necessarily to more reforms, most significantly, in education and in the consciousness of what it means to be a person. It has been seen that, before this consciousness, people had unquestioningly accepted government by privileged individuals.[10] With this new consciousness, it became possible for an individual to strive for whatever rights he felt entitled to. The concepts of legality and of a constitution are the natural consequence of this consciousness. Furthermore, the "Three Principles of the People" guarantee such rights as freedom of speech, of religion, of assembly, and of choice of residence.[11]

In 1911, after the overthrow of the Manchurian government, these rights were legalized with the establishment of the republican government in China. The "Three Principles of the People" of Sun Yat-sen were patterned after the old ideal of universal harmony and equality, along with the specifically Western concept of the individual person. In a practical sense, their combination was to balance the power of the central government with that of the individual citizens in such a way that both elements could be preserved without sacrificing one or the other within the existing Chinese culture. Sun Yat-sen also felt that the "Three Principles of the People" could bring a new vitality to the Chinese culture. However, the promotion of these principles had been difficult, for there were periods of disruption by the warlords, by the Japanese invasion, and by the uprising of communism. These incidents had again and again immersed China in wars and unrest. In mainland China today, the issue of human rights is entirely supressed under the totalitarian communist government. On the other hand, the Republic of China, after its retreat into Taiwan, made good progress in that regard.

The following is a recapitulation of the essential historical and cultural facts in the rise of the problem of human rights.

In the very earliest period, there was the idealism for the universal unity that predominated the social and political scene. Man was said to have an ontological connection with the universal substance, and the attempts to actualize the natural state of harmony with all beings were expressed in the formulation of moral codes for both the ruler and the people. Especially for the general population, the acceptance of its state of existence in society was stressed. Thus, the relations among men were a moral rather than a legal problem. But the moral impact lost its strength with the decline of Confucianism and Taoism, later replaced by the influence of religious Buddhism. During the period of rationalism in the Sung and Ming Dynasties, moral philosophies had again assumed a prominent role in the philosophical creation of the ideal society. This endeavor lasted until the political transition to a republican democracy at a much later time. The ideal of harmony had persisted for a long time because there was no clear consciousness of the meaning of a person independent of the family and the society. Although there were many changes in the various groups that held political power, the people maintained the mentality of "accepting" whatever living conditions were thrust upon them.[12]

In the past thirty years, the republican government in Taiwan has energetically cultivated the understanding and general awareness of the rights of a person through the new educational system and the establishment of a democratic constitutional government. Even in mainland China, we can see that the escape of the refugees from behind the Iron Curtain is a positive gesture of the desire for and the awareness of human rights.

CONCEPTUAL DEVELOPMENT OF HUMAN RIGHTS

It may strike one as an amazing fact that there is no individual character in the Chinese language to signify the "person." From the pre-Ching philosophies, the goal of self-realization was not the obtaining of personal advantage but a rational and moral concern for the welfare of other members of a family or a community. Thus, to be a gentleman or a sage who wishes to perfect himself is to pattern himself after the ideal of the compassionate man. This kind of life perspective cannot allow the struggle for personal freedom, at the expense of other people's happiness, to be a genuine goal of morality. In other words, the general view of life, for a Chinese person, is to submerge his ego, to disappear, and to be absorbed into the universal harmony.

The concept of nirvana has also contributed to the overall importance of the idea of a universal harmony. It is quite impossible, in this cultural atmosphere, to develop the idea of a person apart from other beings.

The Chinese philosophical view, however, should not be seen as a despising of the individual person. Instead, the perception of the individual person as a part must be conceived from the general scheme of the whole *(sub specie universismi)*.

The Chinese hold this view because no man lives independently of other people or of his community. The individual existence must be defined as an existence in and with the world.[13] The Chinese philosophical view has never departed from the perspective of this unity. One can thus see that the idea of a "natural man," man without the artificiality of conventions, is already associated with the idea of a moral man, since the Chinese are convinced that man is inherently both rational and moral. The feeling of concern for others has underlain all Chinese philosophies and motivated people to realize themselves by being naturally and morally harmonious with others.

This concern for others also removed the barrier between the empirical and the transcendent worlds, because it was founded on the theory that all beings share the same metaphysical substance. Because of the immanence of the metaphysical substance, the Chinese philosophies do not involve the struggle between the being of man and the being of God, as in Christianity.

The Christian faith takes its philosophical departure from the empirical ego, and God is not immanent therein. The ontological division between God and man is also characterized socially in isolated empirical persons and their strifes and competitions with one another. Later, when social morality was on the wane, the compassionate feeling was sustained by the religion of Buddhism. The purpose of universal harmony requires a moral awareness, and not legal consideration. We can understand the importance of moral concern from its philosophical status in the concept of "righteousness," but this was always regarded merely as a stage of awareness in moving toward the higher concept of "propriety." The latter is stressed much more, since it would lead to harmony, whereas "righteousness" is a concept that usually implies an enforced legal activity. To strive for righteousness for oneself or for others is directly opposed to what is a natural and moral attitude of life, because this activity destroys the presumption of the natural harmony. Compassion and humility are the logical consequences of the ideal of harmony as the appropriate means of dealing with human relations.[14]

In the Western conceptual framework, there is a duality within the nature of man: the physical aspect, which includes all the undesirable appetites, and which is considered to represent the evil in the nature of man; and the spiritual aspect, which has a divine origin and, hence, contains all the good qualities. With this duality comes the division between the mundane world and the transcendent world. The postulating of this dualistic nature of man makes it necessary for an external, supernatural cause such as God to intervene to sustain man's dignity. For example, the social consequence of the belief that God is the cause of all good qualities in men was the removal of the institution of slavery.

The Chinese view of human nature, represented by Confucianism, advocated the idea of "divine duty" or "fate," which is the force immanent in human nature that drives man toward being good. Buddhism also claims that there is goodness in everyone, as in the nature of Buddha. Thus, both of these philosophies are founded on metaphysical presuppositions, and human values are based upon the divine gift of awareness. This kind of divine endowment of value is translated politically in China to mean that the emperors are also a divine gift and that their powers are foreordained for the realization of universal harmony.

The concept of a person obviously cannot be easily derived from the idea of a divine gift. It must come from the frequent association of equal beings. To have this concept, one must, first of all, require a definition of the intension of this term. In China, there are two occasions on which the idea of the individual arises. The first instance occurs in the philosophical reflections that determine that a person is essentially "within the universe." The second occasion for the consideration of a person is in the moral reflections that assert the person to be "existing with others." Neither of these occasions makes it easy to define a person apart from other contingencies. The freedom to do what one likes was, in China, translated into the freedom to do what one does not like to do when a higher goal is to be obtained by a concern with the welfare of others. This difference in defining freedom is also the difference between the Chinese and Western attitudes in the understanding of "rights."

Generally speaking, since the Renaissance, the Western point of departure for the ideal freedom of the person is the ego. This point of departure tends to ignore the extensional meaning and the associations that are connected with the idea of a person. This becomes apparent in considering the way that the problem of suicide is handled. Suicide is outlawed in most of Western civilization. The recourse to the legal system to prevent the taking of a life is an indication that the moral aspects of the concept of a person are not considered. This is because the idea of an isolated person dictates the logic that he should deal with his own life as he pleases. In the Chinese mentality, the reflection that a person exists for others and is dependent on other people makes it morally impossible to deal with one person while disregarding other people's feelings. Because a person exists as a necessary contingent part of the whole, he has a duty and an obligation to continue his existence. In viewing the concept of a person, the totality of a person's life must be seen both from the extension and the intension of that concept. The consideration of these two elements makes it possible for us to define rights as well as obligations, and thereby to prevent a person from drifting into random desires.

The investigation of the concept of a person permits us to trace philosophical ideas from the natural moral person to the religious person. Their interplay formed the core of the Chinese view of life.

In Western culture, the idea of the natural man can be understood from the idea of social Darwinism, which implies that a person is an independent element within the universal competition for survival. The person must engage in the struggle and acquire the "rights" to live. On the level of such a moral person, the emphasis is really on the creation of laws to protect the individual and to create righteousness, rather than to evoke a moral sense for human relations. The general decline of religion in the present day has made it more difficult to hope for compassion as an influence in human relations.

When the Chinese began to adopt the Western concepts of human rights, it was an undeniable indication that the moral and religious sentiments could no longer hold human relations in harmony.[15] The subsequent strife and struggle for individual rights are, strictly speaking, not consistent with the original metaphysical reflections. To allow the free reign of the empirical ego is to fall inevitably into superficial economic and social considerations. The value system must also fall into a state of relativeness, pragmatism, and utilitarianism, as characterized by the mentality of the nineteenth century.

CONTEMPORARY SIGNIFICANCE OF HUMAN RIGHTS

The Chinese people had started their economy and culture with an agricultural background. In the historical progression, they had lived through the Taoistic ideal of natural harmony, the ideal of the compassionate man of Confucianism, and the universal benevolence of Buddhism. They were, for a long time, then, strangers to the concepts of human rights. The contemporary Chinese, however, are very far from the social phenomena of an agricultural environment. In the military encounter with foreign powers, they discovered that they must also join in the general struggle for survival. As a result of the establishment of a republican government, the Chinese also became acquainted with constitutions embodying human rights.

The original Chinese ideas of laws about human relations are derived from the concepts of "oughtness" or duty. There is also the idea of propriety, which is the emotion or behavior appropriate for different types of human relations. So, when it came to the establishment of a republican government, it became apparent that the new constitution must take account of the traditional values. In addition to the laws, there were also considerations of duties and of propriety. The ultimate ideal for the Chinese Republic is naturally the utopia of universal peace and equality under law, as well as the traditional value system of a universal harmony. The republic has also the more immediate function of protection from Communist and other totalitarian political institutions. Dr. Sun Yat-sen's concept of the "Three Principles of the People" was, at first, an adjustment for Chinese society to become industrialized and democratic. Therefore, its composition had, in theory, contained the elements of the traditional ideals of duty, propriety, and compassion, coupled with the universal love of the Christian faith. His reason for this conception was that religious sentiment would supplement the insufficiency of the legal point of view.[16]

Whether it is possible for the Chinese republic to escape a Communist dictatorship, and whether every Chinese will become conscious of the idea of a person and the ideal of democracy, will hinge largely on the correct practice of the "Three Principles of the People." This practice presupposes an understanding of the old cosmological unity and the exercise of the compassion and universal love of the Christian faith. Only in this way can the political view encompass the subtlety of the conceptual unity of the world with the practical recognition of the dignity and values of individuals specified by modern constitutions.

The contemporary significance of human rights relies on balancing the interests of individuals with those of the community as a whole. The balancing must make use of the moral and religious sentiments that were so carelessly discarded by movements such as the May Fourth movement in 1919. The idea of human rights also requires the goal of self-realization for everyone to become a moral person in order that the universal goal of harmony and peace may be reached. The movement toward democracy is not merely a transition economically from agriculture to industrialization. In addition, the influence of the Western world upon Chinese society cannot be regarded solely in terms of technology. Only today have people become aware that the philosophical background, especially that of a moral and religious reflection, is the true foundation from which human rights can be derived.

NOTES

1. The earliest records of the Chinese classics about Fu-shi, Shen-nung, Sui-jen, Yu-tsao, and others regarded as prehistoric saints, involve the welfare of the masses.

2. The freedom lyric, also known as the Tsi-jong lyric found in the classical "Ti-wang shi-tsi," traditionally records that at the time of Emperor Yau there were eighty or ninety old men singing this lyric.

3. "The works of Mencius, Tsin-sin," *The Four Books,* trans. James Legge (Oxford, 1892), pt. 2, p. 483.

4. Shu-ching (Book of History), the lyric of Five Masters.

5. Shu-ching (Book of History), Hung-fan.

6. The principle of "letting the better man rule" is traditionally understood as a prehistoric occurrence, beginning from Emperor Yau's (ca. 2297-2255 B.C.) abdication to Shun (ca. 2255-2205 B.C.), and from Shun's to Yü's (ca. 2205-2198 B.C.).

7. The authentic existence within the harmony of Tao is known as "universism," which comes from the Latin, *versus unum; see* Hermann Koster, "Was ist Eigentlich Universismus?" in *Sinologica, Separatus,* vol. 9, no. 2 (Basel, 1967).

8. Under the influence of religious feeling, people did not calculate their own individual advantages. And it would not occur to people to begin to consider personal rights. The revolutions were considered not as the means to liberate the oppressed but as a way to obtain a better ruler, as dictated by the heavenly duty of the people to assist their rulers. This view was exemplified by all the political revolts in Chinese history, such as the revolution of the Yen dynasty (A.D. 1280-1368), the struggles of the Three Kingdoms (A.D. 220-265), and the overthrow of the Ching dynasty (A.D. 1661-1911).

9. Mencius had centered his philosophy on the concept of "righteousness," which is not similar to "justice" in the West, but an extension of Confucian compassion.

10. In the institution of the empire in China, the subjects could counsel the king on his mistakes. This counseling process was not a way to obtain personal power for the

subject. This can be seen from the fact that some subjects killed themselves in front of the king in order that their advice might be heeded.

11. The Chinese Constitution, Numbers 7-22.

12. Not all political reformations in China were for the purpose of establishing democracy, but were changes to make way for a better ruler.

13. Here we use Martin Heidegger's "In-der-Welt-Sein" and "Mit-Sein" to explain the human relationships of Taoistic philosophy.

14. The Chinese still use the linguistic expression, "humbleness," which has come down from the customs and attitudes in relations among people.

15. The Westernization of China, as centered in the May Fourth movement (1919), not only renounced the Confucian tradition, but also accepted the anti-Christian movement (1922) that had inclined toward an atheistic worldview. *See* Kun-yu Woo, "The Anti-Christian Movement of Chinese Students in 1922," *The South Asia Journal of Theology*, 15, 1 (Singapore, 1973):57-69.

16. *See* the speech of Dr. Sun Yat-sen to the Christians in Peking, September 5, 1911, *Opera Omnia of the National Father*, vol. 8, 2d ed. (Taipei, June 1974), pp. 33-34.

PART 3

The Meaning
of Human Rights

R. S. DOWNIE —— 7

Social Equality

In the tradition of philosophical analysis, Professor R. S. Downie portrays human rights as characteristically different in meaning from "social equality." He addresses the controversy about whether social and economic (as distinct from political and civil) rights should properly be considered as human rights.

The term "human rights" is the more recent label for what in earlier centuries were called "natural rights" or "the rights of man." The tradition of rights in this sense is itself another expression of an even older tradition of "natural law," to the effect that over and above particular systems of positive law there is a higher law to which human beings can appeal and in terms of which they may judge the adequacy of existing systems. Developing out of natural law, the central idea of natural rights is that, underlying the legal and moral rights a person has as a consequence of belonging to a given society at a given time, there are rights that belong to him simply because he is a human being.

Now there have been various lists of these rights, but traditionally they all tended to be confined to what might be called civil or political rights—rights to life (against arbitrary execution), to liberty (against arbitrary arrest), to freedom of movement, to the protection of property against arbitrary expropriation, and so on. The UN Declaration, however, as is well known, included additional types of rights, such as cultural, social, and economic. For example, Article 24 states:

Everyone has the right to rest and leisure, including reasonable limitation of working hours and periodic holidays with pay.

And Article 25(1) states:

Everyone has the right to a standard of living adequate for the health and well-being of himself and his family, including food, clothing, housing and medical care and necessary social services, and the right to security in the event of unemployment, sickness, disability, widowhood, old age or other lack of livelihood in circumstances beyond his control.

There has been considerable philosophical controversy as to whether such nonpolitical rights are properly classified as "human rights." Does their inclusion represent a legitimate expansion of the original natural law tradition, or does it create a breach within it? It would be wrong to regard such a controversy as "purely academic." Thus, some philosophers would argue that illegitimate widening of the tradition could bring the whole issue of human rights into disrepute and that this could have serious practical consequences, whereas others welcome the widening of the tradition, seeing thereby a way of basing the provision of welfare services on the ancient tradition of human rights.[1] I shall attempt to throw some light on this dispute, first by examining the concept of social equality (by which I mean the combination of social and economic rights with the right to equality) and then by using the conclusions of this analysis to suggest an important difference between social equality and the more traditional human rights.

The UN Declaration, like many before it, gave great emphasis to equality: "All human beings are born free and equal in dignity and rights." Article 2 further emphasizes the egalitarian principle:

Everyone is entitled to all the rights and freedoms set forth in this Declaration, without distinction of any kind, such as race, colour, sex, language, religion, political or other opinion, national or social origin, property, birth or other status....

Let us combine the ideas that there are social and economic rights and that these belong to all men equally. For convenience, I shall call this the right to social equality. Is social equality acceptable as a human right, or even as a moral ideal? In considering this question we are hampered by ambiguities in the concepts of equality and rights. Let us look first at the concept of equality.

As an approach to the set of problems I propose to discuss, it is helpful to draw a broad contrast between the ideal of equality of *opportunity*—equality in the starting and running conditions of the race of life—and equality of *satisfaction*—the ideal of proceeding side by side throughout the race to a "tie" at the finish. It is fairly common for moderates to commit themselves to the first of these ideals rather than to the second. But it seems clear that the second ideal is held also at the present time by many politicians who cannot be regarded as extremists.[2] Moreover, the truth may be (although believers in equality of opportunity have not always faced up to it) that the first cannot be secured independent of the second. For if you provide equality of opportunity, given the truth of propositions about the variation in human ability and industry, the tendency will be toward inequality of achievement and reward. The more successful will use their resources to produce *advantages*, opportunities, for their own children or friends without, in effect, destroying to a greater or lesser extent the *value* of the reward of their own success. Indeed, for some people the creation of inequality of opportunity for their relatives or friends is part of their satisfaction. Thus, someone might say, "I've worked hard to provide advantages in life for my children that I never had." Perhaps, we should understand that anyone who is really concerned with equality as an ideal is, in the last resort, concerned to secure not just "equal opportunities" but also "equal satisfactions."

What is the relation between such a concern and the concern for social justice? And what is the moral importance of social justice? Social justice certainly requires us to treat people equally in the sense of giving equal consideration to the claims of all. But this is not to say that each is *entitled* to receive as much satisfaction from life as any of the others: to say that people ought to pay all their bills is not to say that their bills are all for the same amount! No answer can be given to the question whether people are entitled to the means to equal satisfactions without some discussion of the nature of rights.

What we ordinarily call rights may be distinguished as consumer rights (or rights to something for the good—in the last resort the happiness—of the person whose right it is) and *producer* rights (or rights to the conditions for the efficient performance of a job presumed to be worth doing). It would seem that, so far as producer rights are concerned, there is scope for an indefinite amount of justifiable inequality, such as special rations in times of scarcity for special classes of worker. But it is difficult to see any ground for inequality in the case of consumer rights. One person's satisfaction, viewed simply as satisfaction, seems neither less nor more important than that of any other. It may be suggested, therefore, that social equality is a sound *ideal* so far as consumer rights are concerned, although the *practical* approximation to it will be difficult, quite imperfect, and as a *principle*, it will have to be limited by the requirement of unequal producer rights.

It may be further suggested that *only* consumer rights are, strictly speaking, rights at all. The defense of this suggestion is that only consumer rights aim at the good of those who have them. What a worker's extra rations aim at is not the worker's good but increased production and, indirectly, the good of the community as a whole. It is, therefore, plausible to suggest that producer rights are better viewed as trusts. If, then, social justice is concerned with securing for people what they have a right to, it will be concerned only with consumer rights, and the ideals of social justice and social equality will coincide. Viewed in this way, anyone who believes in social justice must likewise believe in social equality. And since all who are concerned with welfare policy are concerned with social justice, it follows that they must also be concerned with social equality, thus trying to bring about equal satisfactions of what I have called consumer rights. However, it does not follow that social equality is the only or, indeed, an entirely sound ideal for the guidance of welfare policy, for the question remains: How important for the creation of welfare policies is social justice? I shall now turn to this question.

Those concerned with welfare tend to rate social justice too highly for several reasons. The first relates to contemporary rhetoric. Such is the emotive force of the term "social justice" that all writers on welfare or social policy must favor it wholeheartedly—just as a theologian must be against sin. The second reason is that policies aimed at providing equal satisfaction of welfare rights are more easily comprehensible and realizable than those concerned with the more nebulous matters I shall mention shortly. For the same reasons, issues of social justice are more politically persuasive than others I shall discuss. I do not propose to enlarge on the first two reasons for the dominant position that social justice occupies in welfare policy because the issues they raise are primarily not philosophic. Rather I shall concentrate on a third reason for the preeminence of social justice in welfare policy—the failure of writers on welfare to note a distinction between two concepts: a person's *good*, and his *goodness*. There is a parallel distinction between the good of a community and its goodness. Let us examine this distinction, first as it applies to the individual.

A person's good consists of his satisfactions or his interests (those things he is interested in obtaining, the objects of his wants or his deeds). Moreover, the terms "good," "interest," "satisfaction," can be analyzed hedonistically. By this I do not mean that a person cannot pursue anything other than his own satisfaction; rather whatever he is pursuing, if he is pursuing it as part of his good, he is logically committed to justifying the pursuit of it in hedonistic terms; and whatever the object of his desire, its justification is self-satisfaction. By contrast, a person's goodness does not refer to his satisfaction, but to the *quality* of his life. A person's life exhibits goodness to the extent that he participates in activities worth pursuing for their own sake; in short, to the extent that he pursues *the good*. Thus, we say "Virtue is good" or "Music is good" or "Knowledge is good" and mean, not that these will bring pleasure (although they may well do so), but rather that they are ends of human endeavor that have an intrinsic dignity; a person's life has goodness to the extent that it is dedicated to the pursuit of these worthwhile ends.

Turning now to the social side of the distinction, we can say that it is a distinction between what we may call welfare (the material provisions for the happiness of the members of a society) and what we may call culture (the development and transmission of art, pure science, and scholarship more generally). The latter is not, of course, concerned exclusively with the interests of those who are often said to make up social elites; rather, it is concerned with the quality of life in all segments of society. For example, it may exhibit itself in state expenditure on the conservation of ancient monuments open to all, on subsidies for the maintenance of property of architectural interest, on the provision of culture classes for adults, on subsidized theaters, on grants for worthwhile television, on the funding of exchange scholarships, and so on. There is some danger, of course, when a state concerns itself with those matters, because those who "pay the piper may also wish to call the tune." But it is a risk that many artists and scholars would be willing to take. The greater danger is that, if social equality were pursued as the only ideal, a society would become a "moralized barbarism"—"moralized" because it would display a concern for others, which is excellent in itself, but a "barbarism" because it would *not* be much concerned with culture.

What is necessary for a morally healthy society, and also one with the energy to develop itself and to flourish, is that its members should recognize that there are two quite different ways in which we may exhibit respect for our fellowmen. There is, on the one hand, respect for their *social rights;* and here we should be thoroughly egalitarian. But so long as we limit ourselves to this aspect of the matter, we are acting as though happiness were the only good. There is, on the other hand, the respect we show to our fellowmen in treating them as cooperators in the service of ideals that are in a sense *impersonal.* In secular language, this involves the achievement of knowledge and moral goodness and the production of what is beautiful, and in religious language, this is service rendered "to the greater glory of God." Service of this sort has nothing to do with rights, justice, equality, or inequality. It is, nevertheless, essential to the culture and the dignity of a society. The conclusion is, therefore, that social equality (social justice) is valid as an ideal, but only as one ideal among others, and that the ideal of culture is quite distinct from it and is in no less essential to the flourishing of a society.

The further, very troublesome, question arises as to whether these ideals may be not only distinct, but also in actual conflict. In other and sharper words, the question can be raised as to whether social *inequality* may not be a condition of his cultural achievement. There is no certain answer to this question. In the past, such achievement has rested on social inequality, indirectly when it was a matter of patronage of the arts and directly in the case of forms of social life dependent on economic privilege that seem to have an intrinsic grace and dignity. These social inequalities are now rightly in the process of being abolished in many present-day societies, but it is an important matter that their function should be taken over by alternatives compatible with a more egalitarian society. For example, as I suggested earlier, they can be taken over by the state, by wealthy industrial concerns, even by trade unions, and so on. However, the point I wish to stress is that a concern for what I have broadly called impersonal cultural values is as important for the flourishing of a society as a concern for the personal satisfaction of the members. I shall return to the problem of the relative weight that should be given to each social ideal.

It might be objected that to have reservations about the acceptability of social equality as an ideal is to have reservations about democracy itself. But to raise this sort of objection is to confuse social equality with political equality. It might be thought that there can be no reservations about the endorsement of political equality as an ideal, however the approach to this idea is to be achieved in a given society. But "political equality" is an ambiguous term. It can mean one or both of two types of equality.

Political equality might men an equal "say" in the determination of political policy, or, an equal "say" in the determination of the arrangements by which political policy should be determined. The second possibility gives the essence of democracy, and it does not entail the first. Indeed, the mark of an enlightened democracy might be that it deliberately erected, on the basis of the second sort of political equality, a structure of government that gave different amounts of political powers to different individuals or sections of the community. Equally, the mark of an enlightened democracy might be that it distributed political powers in terms of equality in the first sense. Decisions as to the best sort of structure for a given society ought to be based on the outcome of discussions of that mixture of practical and moral points that we call political debate. For my purposes the point is that the criteria for political democracy are satisfied by the second definition of political equality. To put the matter another way, there is nothing necessarily undemocratic about having as an organ of government a "second chamber" that is not elected on the basis of universal suffrage. What matters from the point of view of political democracy is that the decision for or against the existence of a second chamber should rest with the people as a whole, and that there should exist some mechanism by which they can alter the structure of this form of government if they so choose.

The relevance of this point to a discussion mainly concerned with social equality is that it should clarify that a democrat is not necessarily committed to the acceptance of social equality as an ideal. If it is possible to be a political democrat and still allow that in some sense political inequalities can be justified, then *a fortiori* one can be a political democrat and still allow that social inequalities in some sense and to some extent can be justified. In other words, the pros and cons of social equality as an ideal must be considered on their merits. Since the whole area of equality is one in which rhetoric and emotional language often cast out clarity of conceptual distinction, it is important to be aware of two dangers: first, the danger of translating opposition to social equality into opposition to democracy itself, and, second, the consequent danger of too cavalier an acceptance of the ideal of social equality in the name of democracy.

Let us return to the original question about the relationship between social and economic rights and traditional human rights. Can social equality be accommodated as a legitimate extension of the tradition of human rights, as enthusiasts for welfare rights may want to argue, or should we regard it as a worthwhile ideal outside the tradition?

An argument to the effect that economic and social rights are not in the same category as human rights has been put forward by Maurice Cranston.[3] Cranston suggests that to be properly a human right, a right must pass three tests: its implementation must be practicable, of paramount importance, and the right must be universal. He then argues that social and economic rights do not pass these tests. Cranston's tests and his application of them to human rights have been much discussed and criticized, and it is doubtful if they can be regarded as convincing in the form he proposed.

I shall therefore look at a more recent argument against including social and economic rights in the list of human rights. This argument, propounded by J. Enoch Powell,[4] is worthy of attention because Powell, a former British Conservative party minister of health, represents the point of view of realistic, hardheaded politicians. Moreover, the disentangling of his argument takes us forward in our discussion of whether social and economic rights are human rights.

The substance of Powell's argument, insofar as it is relevant to our concerns, can be stated as follows: (1) Rights presuppose the existence of society. (2) Rights entail the exercise of compulsion against those other than the right-holders. (3) Compulsion can be either arbitrary or lawful. (4) No compulsion can be lawful unless it can be uniformly applied, and uniform applicability requires unambiguous statement. (5) Article 25(1) of the UN Declaration cannot be so stated. (6) To claim rights to benefits mentioned in Article 25(1) is therefore to endorse arbitrary compulsion. (7) In the case of Article 25(1) the claim is such that the benefits cannot be achieved within a given society; it is therefore a threat to carry out unlimited global compulsion.

There are two main theses in this part of the argument. The first and more radical, expressed in the propositions listed above, is that Article 25(1) morally should not be regarded as declaring any sort of right, because it entails endorsing arbitrary compulsion. All the steps in the argument for this conclusion are dubious, but I shall confine myself to (2) and (5).

It is not true that all rights entail the exercise of compulsion. Legal rights may do so, but moral rights characteristically do not. Someone who claims a moral right would like to see others observe it, or he would like to see it implemented, but that is quite different from regarding it as either practicable or desirable that it should be *enforced.* On the contrary, in declaring a moral right we do not "commend the use of compulsion," but rather we express a judgment that others have an obligation to observe it, and a hope, which is happily often realized, that they will do so.

Turning to (5), I do not think it is true that terms such as "adequate," "well-being," and "medical care" are purely subjective. What is true is that there will be variations in different societies as to what is possible in terms of well-being or medical care. But it seems obvious that where famine is prevalent or certain diseases endemic we have societies which have fallen below adequate standards of well-being and medical care. And in more prosperous societies we can rely on welfare workers of all sorts to provide information on social groups in which standards of living have fallen below what is publicly considered acceptable in that society. There will be variations in assessment, but that is totally different from regarding the whole matter of assessing standards of living and care as purely subjective. There is nothing, therefore, in propositions (1) to (6) that leads us to conclude that Article 25(1) cannot embody acceptable moral rights, which we hope governments will try to implement in their welfare legislation and individuals will try to uphold in their everyday lives.

The second main thesis is that Article 25(1) cannot or should not be regarded as embodying specifically *human* rights, human rights making up that subset of moral rights that all men hold against all men. From a *practical* point of view, it does not matter whether we regard these social and economic rights as human rights or not, for presumably the *moral* purpose of the UN Declaration is to express a judgment that all governments and individuals should work toward the elimination of the large-scale social and economic ills of the world, and we can agree on this whether or not we regard social and economic rights as human rights. From a *philosophical* point of view, however, there is at least one important difference between social and economic rights and the political rights that all agree are human rights: whereas the latter can be fully granted and implemented without prejudice to other moral values of social significance, the same is not true of social and economic rights. The reasons are that the general ethos of a state that concentrates exclusively on material goods is not ideal, and the financing of such concern will starve of resources the equally legitimate concern of cultural standards.

Somehow or other we must strike a balance between the claims of culture and the claims of social justice. There are no rules for doing so, but a minimum principle would be that when what is vaguely referred to as the "standard of living" of a section of the community falls below a certain level, social justice becomes a priority for that section. One way of developing the idea of a minimum principle of social equality might be to distinguish between a person's basic needs and his more complex wants. The fulfillment of his basic needs—to food, shelter, medical care, and so on—can then be regarded as constituting legitimate social rights about which there can be no moral reservations. Indeed, the fulfillment of these minimum social rights can be regarded as a necessary condition for the exercise of any rights whatsoever: there can be no rights to life or liberty without bread to sustain the possessors of these rights.

But problems arise when we begin to extend the range of these social rights. And the problems are acute because a person's pursuit of his own good can come to dominate all aspects of his social life. His consumption increases and his fellow citizens claim their rights to equal consumption. This is the pathology of advanced industrial societies. There is, therefore, a problem as to the relative weight to be given to social equality in this sense, as opposed to other social goods. In this chapter, I have concentrated on the collision between social equality and cultural standards, but social equality as an ideal will collide also with other moral values, such as natural liberty. The problem in each case is the same, however; when we take social equality beyond minimum standards, it not only enters into competition with other goods, but may actually engulf them. This suggests that there is an important difference between social equality and the traditional human rights.

NOTES

1. For example, *see* David Watson, "Welfare Rights and Human Rights," *Journal of Social Policy* 6, pt. 1, (1977).

2. *See,* for example, Anthony Crosland, "Social Democracy in Europe," Fabian Tract 438 (London: Fabian Society, 1975).

3. Maurice Cranston, "Human Rights, Real and Supposed," in *Political Theory and the Rights of Man,* ed. D. D. Raphael (London: Macmillan, 1967).

4. J. Enoch Powell, "Human Rights," *Journal of Medical Ethics* 3, no. 4, (1977): 160-62.

ANDREW LEVINE ——— 8

Human Rights and Freedom

Presupposing a Hobbesian view of freedom, Professor Andrew Levine considers human rights discourse to be inherently inadequate. In his view, claims that invoke human rights have not been well-founded theoretically and hence are essentially arbitrary. However, he does suggest a potential role for a human rights theory in philosophy.

Right is, by origin, a legal concept that, since the seventeenth century, has figured prominently throughout moral discourse. In its original sense, a *right* is a claim advanced by an individual or group, enforceable by law. Some prominent exceptions notwithstanding,[1] the concept has nearly always been understood normatively. To talk of rights is to talk of what the law *ought* to enforce, not of what it does in fact enforce. But, as a normative concept, it seems unduly restrictive to limit talk of rights to particular juridical frameworks. And so, very early on, the concept of right outgrew its strictly legal sense. By *right*, then, is understood any legitimate claim advanced by an individual or group.

In general, rights continue to be claimed within social frameworks. Rights are possessed in relation to others; and rights claims are directed, forensically, to these others. To talk of rights is to presuppose the existence of a community in which rights claims are advanced and in virtue of which rights are "possessed." A *human right*, then, is a claim advanced within the "human community," which is possessed by virtue of being human, and advanced to all other humans. For those who regard the concept of right as unproblematic, the existence of human rights depends upon the cogency of conceiving a human community; and the nature and extent of human rights depends upon the character of that community.[2]

But whatever special problems must be surmounted in developing a theory of human rights, defenders of human rights ultimately must establish the viability of the concept of right in general, in its normative, extralegal sense. Talks of rights today has become so natural, so pervasive, that it is easy to lose sight of this problem. Yet it is far from clear that there can be a nonarbi-

trary, theoretically well-motivated way to assign rights to persons; or even
that it makes sense to talk of persons "possessing" rights. My own view is
that the concept of rights is indeed deeply problematic and that rights ascriptions, in the final analysis, *are* arbitrary. However, I will not attempt a full-
fledged defense of this suggestion here because, I think, ultimately what has
to be assessed in evaluating the concept of rights is the entire conceptual
framework, the system of moral concepts, within which rights in general,
and human rights in particular, play specifiable functions. My aim here is to
focus on these functions by pointing out some conceptual links between the
concept of right and another central moral concept—liberty. I will argue that
talk of rights in general, and *a fortiori* of human rights, at least as we encounter such talk today, presupposes a particular view of liberty; the dominant, liberal view, derived from Hobbes, that to be free is to be *unrestrained*
by others in the pursuit of one's ends.[3] My aim, in other words, is to exhibit
the role of rights, and particularly human rights, within liberalism or, more
generally, within any social philosophy presupposing the Hobbesian view of
freedom.

I will not argue here that liberalism generally, or even its notion of liberty,
is conceptually inadequate or historically particular; although I think such a
case could be made,[4] and what I say here may be colored by this assessment.
Neither should what follows be understood as an argument *against* human
rights. On the contrary, I shall argue *for* human rights, not, to be sure, "under the aspect of eternity," but within the framework of the dominant theory
and practice of politics. As will become evident, the concept of human rights
serves as a *corrective* within a politic that tends to fragment social solidarity
while promoting an individualism that threatens respect for persons. Within
the political tradition we inherit, the possession of human rights is the principal means for maintaining a notion of human dignity. This is why human
rights, unlike other "possessions," cannot normally be traded off, why
human rights are, in the traditional idiom, *inalienable*. To truck and barter
in human rights is to detract from essential humanity, from human dignity;
and to reduce persons to mere things.

Of course, respect for persons, and the radical distinction between persons
and things can and have been theorized differently.[5] But whatever the merits
or defects of alternative accounts, the prevailing political tradition can only
support respect for persons through the ascription of rights. So long as our
practice of politics remains within this tradition, we have only human rights
protecting our dignity as human beings. But this protection is fragile and incapable, apparently, of shoring up: the extent, nature, and even the grounds
for rights ascriptions seem irremediably arbitrary. In day-by-day political
practice, then, we should seek to further and to defend human rights.[6] But
we should never lose sight of their theoretical vulnerability. Ultimately, one
would expect that what the dominant tradition articulates through recourse

to human rights is better conceived, and better defended, otherwise. However, it is idle to speculate on the character of a new theory and practice of politics. It is enough, for now, to probe the fragility of the tradition we inherit.

WHAT ARE HUMAN RIGHTS?

Needless to say, there is scant consensus on what human rights persons "possess." It is, therefore, impossible to list human rights exhaustively or to everyone's satisfaction. However, some generalization, and even classification, is in order. It seems that human rights fall into three relatively distinct categories.

First, there are those human rights associated with traditional liberalism: free speech, the right to worship as one pleases, the right to live as one wishes (so long as no one else is harmed), and so on. Such rights imply a correlative duty on the part of all individuals, and particularly the state, not to interfere with individual behavior.[7] Thus, the power of the state is limited by the rights of its citizens. Liberalism does not, strictly, require the concept of human rights. Indeed, its most important defender, John Stuart Mill, following in the wake of Bentham's scornful rejection of rights as "nonsense on stilts," defends liberty largely without recourse to any notion of rights. However, from time to time, liberals have found the concept useful for articulating their most fundamental and characteristic position on the limits of legitimate societal and state interference with individuals' activities; and today it is most often in this sense that human rights claims are advanced.

Traditionally, such rights have not been ascribed to human beings as such, but only to human beings assumed capable of exercising them responsibly or for some good end. Thus, for Mill, children, idiots, lunatics, and (significantly) colonial peoples—that is, all who have not developed moral and intellectual capacities in the framework of liberal institutions—are excluded from the blessings of liberty advocated for adult Englishmen in possession of their faculties. To the extent that these exclusions are maintained, it is not quite correct to call the traditional liberties human rights, contemporary usage notwithstanding, since there are human beings for whom they are not claimed. However, in what follows I will observe current usage with the implicit understanding that many of the so-called human rights, in this category and in others, are, in their intended scope, somewhat less than human rights in the literal sense.

To the rights of traditional liberalism are sometimes added certain specifically political rights: the right to vote, the right to fair treatment in courts of law, the right to travel or emigrate, among others. Plainly, these rights claims are advanced within specifiable institutional frameworks. It is as a citizen of X, that I claim the right to vote in X, or to fair treatment in its courts, or to a passport. If these rights are construed as human rights, we can suppose that citizenship itself, indeed, citizenship in a political community of a sort that maintains these rights, is being claimed as a human right. Citizenship (of the requisite sort) is not a liberty, a right to be left to do as one pleases, but *a status incumbent with benefits and duties.* Our human rights, falling under this category, would consist of those benefits and duties that are thought proper for all persons, regardless of membership in particular political communities. Presumably, those who would advance human rights claims of this sort, would want to specify these rights minimally, as lowest common denominators of (acceptable) forms of citizenship. Thus, the right to fair treatment in courts of law might count as a human right, whereas the right to "due process" (in the specifically American sense) or the right to avoid self-incrimination would more likely count as rights enjoyed in virtue of membership in a particular political framework. However, in all cases, the implementation and enforcement of such rights is a task, a "correlative obligation," of governments.

Sometimes, especially in recent years, human rights claims of a rather different sort have been advanced. Thus, the Preamble to the United Nations' Universal Declaration of Human Rights (1948) announces that at least some of the rights that document claims should be construed as "a common standard of achievement for all peoples"; and this is sometimes understood to mean that human rights claims articulate basic human needs without specifying correlative obligations on the part of government (or anyone else, including international organizations) to implement these needs.[8] It is in this spirit, it is argued, that the UN Declaration announces human rights to "social security" (Article 22), "to a standard of living adequate for the health and well-being" of all persons, "including food, clothing and housing" (Article 25), and others. It is indisputable that in declaring a human right, say, to clothing adequate for health and well-being, no one is claiming that the government has an obligation to supply clothing to its citizens (except perhaps in cases of extreme indigence or misfortune, where there is no other means for a person to acquire adequate clothing). However, it is less clear that an obligation to ensure the conditions (other things being equal) in which citizens can be adequately clothed is not being ascribed to governments (and perhaps to others as well). Lest this discussion digress needlessly, I will not pursue this question further. What is important is to note how, with the advent of such pronouncements about human rights, the range of the concept is significantly extended—beyond liberties, beyond rights of citizenship—to include at least minimal levels of social welfare. Whether this extension involves a different concept of human rights, or instead a modification of a more familiar concept, is ultimately less important, I think, than what this extension indicates about the role of rights ascriptions.

What claims for noninterference with individuals' activities, for citizenship (and its attendant benefits and duties), and for a minimal level of social goods share is respect for persons, for human dignity. These rights are claimed for persons just in virtue of their being human (exclusions apart), and not in consequence of voluntary agreements or social arrangements of any sort. Our humanity is bound up with the possession of these rights. Thus, it is thought by most liberals (and, of course, by many others as well) that human life cannot be fulfilled, that "powers" (in Hobbes' sense) cannot be developed, if liberty is unduly restricted.[9] So, too, it is thought by many that a fully human life cannot be achieved if citizenship is effectively denied, and if the availability of social goods is so reduced that life itself becomes nothing more than a struggle to survive. It is by articulating these claims forensically, by claiming rights to the conditions for being fully human, that respect for persons is asserted. Within the dominant, liberal tradition, human dignity is asserted in no other way. But this assertion is made in the face of a powerful countertendency, implicit in the dominant tradition's core notion of freedom.

RIGHTS AND FREEDOM

At first glance, it may seem odd even to suggest a conflict between rights and freedom when a principal use of the concept of right within liberal social philosophy is precisely to formulate the view, characteristic of all strains of liberal thought, that to be free is to be unrestrained by others in the pursuit of one's ends. Nonetheless, it must be realized that for a person to claim a right is to claim moral justification for limiting the freedom of those to whom the rights claim is addressed. To have a right is to limit others' freedom de jure, and, so far as rights are enforced by law, to limit their freedom de facto as well. Thus, if I have a right to worship as I please (or not to worship at all), others (in this case, presumably, all others) are morally unfree to interfere with my activities in the matter of worship. Likewise, where there are thought to be rights to some benefits and duties of citizenship, neither the state nor the individuals acting outside the state apparatus can rightfully interfere with the enjoyment of such benefits or the exercise of such duties. And where it is claimed that there are rights to the enjoyment of social goods (at some specifiable level), to the extent that such claims do specify correlative obligations, directly or indirectly, they morally restrict the liberty of persons to act in violation of these obligations.[10]

As is particularly evident when we consider rights to noninterference, what is at issue here is the well-known Hobbesian insight that absolute freedom, the complete absence of restraint, is inconceivable; that a condition for the possibility of any freedom is the subordination of all persons to a common framework for regulating conflict and competition. Thus, paradoxically, the condition for freedom is a diminution of (absolute) freedom; one gives a little to gain a lot. It is not necessary, as Hobbes' own case attests, to use the language of rights to formulate this insight; but in this regard, as in so many other contexts, the concept of right proves especially useful. In any case, the tension between rights and freedom I have in mind is of a different sort.

Freedom, on the view in question, is always a social relation; one is free or unfree with respect to other persons. Thus, in general, freedom may be viewed as the absence of restraints or impediments, contrived by others, in the pursuit of one's ends. Moreover, these ends are always, as it were, extrarational. A person's ends are ultimately reducible to his wants; and wants, in this tradition, are not candidates for moral scrutiny. Thus, reason is purely instrumental. It does not legislate ends, but only the adaptation of means to ends.[11] A person's ends are whatever he takes them to be. This is why one can never be "forced to be free," as Rousseau would have it, by being coerced into pursuing ends not actually willed, but rather "discovered" by others. Contrary to what Rousseau and the idealist tradition generally held, the individual, in the dominant, liberal tradition, is the final arbiter of his ends. Reason, as such, neither prescribes nor proscribes the ends of rational agents.[12]

That the content of persons' ends, ultimately, is incorrigible is not, by itself, sufficient for establishing an *atomic individualist* view of society, according to which the ultimate constituents of social reality (descriptively and normatively), the atoms, are individuals, essentially independent of one another and of society. The ends of atomic individuals are such that others figure only instrumentally in their realization. Where others figure intrinsically, as "ends-in-themselves" (Kant), atomic individualism does not pertain. It is clear, then, that atomic individualism does not follow from the incorrigibility of persons' ends precisely because wherever reason is exclusively instrumental, no constraints whatever are placed on the content of our ends. Rational agents may seek to realize ends that are social or altruistic. They might value association or community, not just as means for realizing other (egoistic) ends, but for their own sake. And thus they might, in consequence, value other persons as "ends-in-themselves," and not purely a means.

But if this view of rational agency does not strictly entail atomic individualism, it certainly inclines toward it. So far as there is no principle for bringing persons' ends together into a common framework, so far as it is natural to regard everything and everyone as means for the satisfaction of antecedently given ends, things and persons tend to be treated the same way—as instrumentalities only. This atomic individualist picture, to repeat, is not entailed by the dominant tradition's conceptions of freedom and rational agency, but only suggested. To remove the suggestion, a functional equivalent must be maintained of Kant's radical distinction between persons and things, where things are means only while persons are also ends-in-themselves. But this distinction evidently cannot be maintained, as in Kant, by appeal to a noninstrumental notion of practical reason.[13]

It is noteworthy that throughout its history, critics of the dominant tradition, from both the Left and the Right, have reproached liberalism for its (atomic) individualism and consequent inability to theorize persons as other then mere instrumentalities. Nowhere is this kind of reproach more appropriate, and more telling, than in reflections on "free markets"; that is, on the institutional arrangement that, as much as any other, embodies the liberal concepts of freedom and rational agency. Market exchanges are, by definition, voluntary or freely chosen; and participants in market transactions, characteristically, seek to do as well for themselves as possible (given the constraint that others, with different and independent ends, also seek to do as well for themselves as they can).

In markets, products of labor exchange as commodities with determinant values measurable against other commodities. In capitalist markets—that is, in the only historically viable form of market arrangements—labor, too, exchanges as a commodity.[14] To the extent that this exchange is subordinated to the requirements of capitalist accumulation, to the extent it is (in Marx's sense) exploitative, any difference in treatment between persons (as workers) and things (as products of labor) is effectively undone. Each becomes neither more nor less than a determinate exchange value, to be used as the accumulation process requires. It is this treatment of workers as means only that motivates well-known attacks on capitalist markets for producing "alienation,"[15] or for fragmenting and commercializing social life, thus reducing the bases for social solidarity and even political legitimacy.[16] Despite very different political motivations, what such charges share is the realization that human dignity is jeopardized in capitalist markets: that the worker, in being treated as a commodity, becomes a thing, while the capitalist, qua "economic man" (subordinate to the "laws" of capitalist rationality), reduces himself to an atomic individual for whom persons are means only.

What is decisive for producing this unhappy result is the additional stipulation, noted above, that economic agents seek always to do as well for themselves as possible, to maximize utility without limit. Characteristically, this stipulation is extrapolated from behavior in markets to behavior generally (or at least to behavior outside the family or among small groups of friends); and it is thus that society comes to be viewed as a collection of atomic individuals. Were we to deny atomic individualism, to suppose, in other words, that rational agents will ends wherein persons (themselves and others) are viewed as "ends-in-themselves" and not merely as means, it could only be for reasons that are, ultimately, psychological; because human nature is thought to be essentially sociable. Historically, however, as we know, the opposite assumption has been made. Hobbes and his successors among economists, but also among nearly all liberals, deny essential sociability. Instead, human beings are thought to be acquisitive by nature, seeking to appropriate both human and natural resources ceaselessly.[17] In this way, a society of rational agents is seen generally as a society of acquisitive, rational egoists for whom others can only be means. Thus, the ground has been prepared by the dominant tradition's concepts of freedom and rational agency, yet atomic individualism established itself, finally, through psychological claims about human nature.

Lacking grounds for ascribing essential sociability, and historically committed to a view of human beings as acquisitive, rational egoists, liberalism, or any social philosophy that shares its notions of freedom and rational agency, needs the concept of (human) rights to save (free, rational) human beings from themselves and thereby to maintain and promote dignity. Without human rights, a free society of "economic men" threatens to become a society of things, of instrumentalities, a collection of atomic individuals for whom everything and everyone are only means.

We have already seen that rights claims provide moral justification for limiting the freedom of others and that without their doing so, or a functional equivalent, freedom could not be exercised at all. A state of nature, of absolute freedom, is untenable; it is a ruthless war of all against all, in which a person's ends generally cannot be realized. We have seen too that the free market is the clearest institutional embodiment of that diminished freedom that supersedes the absolute freedom of the state of nature. The free market retrieves much from the state of nature: it is a nonauthoritative mechanism for allocating benefits and burdens. However, it is not itself a state of nature, but a system of rules, a framework, for regulating conflict and competition. Given the untenability of absolute freedom, this diminished freedom is perhaps the best feasible alternative. But its price, if left unchecked, is a continual assault on human dignity. Accordingly, even within the framework that best salvages what can be saved from the state of nature, rights are, as it were, called upon again to limit the freedom of others. Thus, rights limit markets;[18] more accurately, *inalienable* rights limit markets.[19]

By definition, inalienable rights cannot be bought or sold. Neither are they, in general, subject to other market criteria: they are distributed equally, rather than as incentives, and they are exercised, theoretically at least, without monetary charge. The possession of such rights, accordingly, limits not only the freedom of others but also one's own freedom to *exchange* these rights like other possessions.[20] Were we to deny this restriction and assume that market relations pertain even in the domain of inalienable rights, we should have to conclude that these rights are literally priceless and that there is nothing in principle for which they could be reasonably (advantageously) exchanged. Roughly, such a view would parallel the Kantian thesis that what is essentially human has dignity (*wurde*), whereas all else merely has a price (*preis*). But for rational economic man, this claim is plainly false. It is easy to show that an exchange of many inalienable rights—for example, selling one's vote—would increase the welfare of both buyers and sellers.[21] It must be, therefore, that where inalienable rights are thought to pertain, markets are thought to have no legitimate place. In the end, the tendency to treat persons as things is countervailed, without recourse to psychology—indeed, in terms compatible with the characteristic view that persons are by nature acquisitive and "economic." It is, in short, by stipulating inalienable human rights that liberalism meets the challenge posed to human dignity by human nature (or what it takes human nature to be): a challenge aided and abetted by its concepts of freedom and rational agency.

It has been taken for granted throughout this discussion that liberalism's strategy for saving human dignity is irremediably ad hoc and that there is no theoretically well-motivated way to assign rights to persons. Nonetheless, human rights ascriptions do seem to fulfill their intended function tolerably well. My aim in subjecting these claims to critical scrutiny is not so much to underscore their arbitrariness, but to point out what these (arbitrary) claims reveal about the tradition in which they function. The liberal recourse to human rights is *symptomatic* of a tension between human dignity, on the one hand, and some of the most salient features of the dominant tradition, on the other. Most charitably, human rights function within liberalism as a *corrective*, a concept introduced apart from the core notions of liberal theory with a view to saving liberalism from some of its consequences. But, ultimately, this corrected liberalism is a *contradictory* configuration which simultaneously defends and attacks human dignity, distinguishing and confounding persons and things. Can human rights survive in such a configuration?

BEYOND HUMAN RIGHTS?

Plainly, human rights—in theory and practice—must be made to survive, as long as the dominant tradition in politics continues to hold sway. Liberalism "with a human face" requires human rights.

But liberalism today is vulnerable. It is vulnerable conceptually, of course; but, more important by far, it is vulnerable in its practical implementations. Even in the countries of its origin, it is far from clear that liberalism can adapt to changing social experience and new political exigencies. And the viability of liberalism elsewhere on our planet is even more strikingly doubtful. Needless to say, this situation is very dangerous, particularly in view of recent and contemporary examples of nonliberal forms of politics. But it is also very hopeful. For with the demise of liberalism, or at least the weakening of its hold, the possibility emerges, as a live historical option, to ground what is positive in liberalism on different and more secure foundations, and thus not to lose but rather to supersede what, within liberalism, human rights claims articulate.

It would be idle to speculate what role, if any, human rights might play in such a reconstructed politics. It is worth noting, however, that every major tendency in political philosophy except liberalism, from Plato through Kant and beyond, either excludes the notion of rights (and thus of human rights) altogether, or assigns it a different and far less important role than that discussed here. The reason is plain: these alternative moral philosophies make use of a different notion of freedom. Where individual liberty is not conceived and valued in the way liberalism supposes, moral justifications for restricting the liberty of others takes on diminished importance. And where human dignity is not threatened, as in liberalism, rights are not required as a countertendency.[22]

Human rights save us from our institutions and their *effects* upon ourselves. Were our institutions otherwise, were they of a sort to promote social solidarity and respect for persons rather than atomic individualism and treatment of persons as means only, the need for human rights would diminish accordingly. Doubtless, this is why human rights play no role in political visions such as Rousseau's in *The Social Contract* and elsewhere, where the institutions of society work together to form "the general will," by promoting virtue and citizenship and undoing the individualism that, on Rousseau's account, threatens what is essentially human. For Rousseau, the alternative to human rights is education—education in the broadest sense, by no means limited to the schools, that transforms a collection of atomic individuals into a body politic wherein, so to speak, human dignity is inscribed in each person's will. In this de jure state, human rights drop away for want of sufficient reason, as much as for want of theoretical justification.[23]

However, ours is not Rousseau's de jure state. Within the framework of our institutions, so far from "withering away," the need for human rights is intensified. Doubtless this need will persist as long as political arrangements, unlike those Rousseau envisioned, coordinate independent and (sometimes) conflicting rather than harmonious interests, private rather than general wills. But there is no reason to suppose that this function can be fulfilled only by the concept of human rights; that in the framework of a theory and practice outside the dominant, liberal tradition, what human rights claims articulate might not be theorized differently and more soundly. It must be acknowledged, of course, that the theoretical apparatus for fulfilling this function outside the dominant tradition remains largely undeveloped.[24] But the theoretical vulnerability of human rights claims and of the dominant tradition generally, in both theory and practice, renders the need for such investigation crucial. It is in this sense, and to this end, that the criticism of human rights need not be incompatible with their defense. Ultimately, I think, the best defense of human rights or, rather of what they aim to articulate, is their *reconceptualization* and implementation in the framework of a different politics, with institutions embodying a different tendency, a tendency to promote social solidarity and respect for persons and thus to realize in different ways what, against the tendency of the dominant tradition, human rights claims assert.[25]

NOTES

1. Among the most prominent exceptions are the legal realists, such as Jerome Frank or K. N. Llewellyn, for whom ascriptions of rights are just predictions of what the courts will do. However, even those who construe strictly legal rights in this way understand *moral rights* normatively.

2. *See* Martin Golding, "Towards a Theory of Human Rights," *The Monist* 52, no. 4 (October 1968): 521-49.

3. It should be evident that Hobbes' is not the only extant concept of liberty. Consider, for example, Rousseau's or Kant's view that to be free is to be *autonomous*, that is, subject to a law of one's own legislation. Whatever the underlying affinities in these accounts, there is indisputably also a difference; freedom of autonomy is compatible with restraint by others. Indeed, for Rousseau, such restraint is sometimes in order "to force [persons] to be free" (*The Social Contract*, bk. 1, chap. 7).

4. *See* my "Foundations of Unfreedom," *Ethics* 88, no. 2 (January 1978): 162-72; and *Liberal Democratic Theory* (tentative title, forthcoming).

5. The best-known attempt to do so, roughly contemporaneous with the dominant, liberal tradition, is of course Kant's in part 2 of *The Foundations of the Metaphysics of Morals* (Indiana: Bobbs-Merrill Co., 1975).

6. In the present conjuncture, particularly in the United States, where the concept of human rights has been co-opted with unprecedented gall, as an instrument of a predatory foreign policy, the day-by-day defense of human rights will very often devolve into a struggle to distinguish legitimate human rights claims from their not very subtle, but nonetheless influential, misappropriation. On this problem, see Noam Chomsky and Edward S. Herman, "United States versus Human Rights in the Third World," *Monthly Review* 29, no. 3 (July-August 1977): 22-45.

7. Following Hohfeld, we know that a *liberty* or *privilege* is only one kind of right: that which has as its "jural correlative" a nonright on the part of others (to interfere with individuals' activities). Hohfeld distinguishes three other definitions of the term, each with different "jural correlatives." These other meanings, however important for the analysis of the strictly legal role of the concept of right, seem less important for articulating the objectives of liberal social philosophy. *See* Wesley N. Hohfeld, *Fundamental Legal Conceptions*, 2d ed. (New Haven, Conn.: Yale University Press, 1964).

8. *See* S. I. Benn, "Rights," *The Encyclopedia of Philosophy*, Vol. 7 (New York: Macmillan, 1967), pp. 198-99.

9. For those categories of human beings that are excluded (in varying degrees) from possession of such rights—children, the mentally deficient—it must be concluded that their lives cannot be fulfilled precisely to the extent that they are incapable of forming and implementing individual "life plans." Paternalism in the liberal tradition is an expedient for helping along those on the threshold or the peripheries of full humanity. It is emphatically not a treatment deemed proper for human beings in general.

10. The nature and extent of these restrictions, particularly for this last category of rights, have never, to my knowledge, been investigated adequately. There are two obvious reasons for this state of affairs: first, it is only quite recently that such rights claims have been advanced at all, particularly as human rights; and, second, most persons who do acknowledge such claims are reluctant, as were the framers of the UN Declaration, to suppose that they imply *any* correlative obligations. But even if we grant that there are such rights and that they do specify correlative obligations, it is far from clear what these obligations might be, especially if, as seems likely, we would not want to say that others have a duty to provide the goods in question, so much as a duty to create the conditions for securing such goods.

11. *See* David Gauthier, "Reason and Maximization," *Canadian Journal of Philosophy* 4, no. 3 (March 1975): 411-33; and my "Foundations of Unfreedom," *Ethics* 88, 2.

12. However, there are formal standards for assessing ends; and, to that extent, reason does at least proscribe certain choices. Thus, inconsistent orderings of alternative options in contention are ruled out. The rationale for this prohibition is readily apparent. If a person's orderings of alternatives are inconsistent (intransitive)—if he prefers x to y and y to z, but z to x—then, in a situation where he is confronted with a choice between all three alternatives, he is unable to act in accordance with his ordering. For any choice the person might make, another outcome would always be preferred. Thus, while not providing standards for assessing the content of our ends, reason is not entirely indifferent to the ends we hold. Reason is, in Hume's apt expression, "the slave of the passions." But it must, on occasion, impose requirements on these passions, in order to serve them.

13. *See* note 5. For Kant, by prescribing a system of ends, practical reason gives rise to a "harmony of rational wills"; to a principle according to which persons' ends are not at all disjointed, but rather harmonious. It is in this regard that Kant speaks of rational agents coming together in a kind of internally ordered association, a Republic (*Reich*) of ends. *See The Foundations of the Metaphysics of Morals*, pt. 2.

14. Evidently, this exchange, however voluntary, is not free in quite the sense that an exchange of products of labor between relatively self-sufficient producers is free. The institutional setting in which the exchange of labor power for a wage occurs effectively necessitates that exchange, even without direct coercion.

15. The best known of these critiques is, of course, Marx's in his early writings: *The Economic and Philosophic Manuscripts* (1844), especially the final section of the first manuscript. I have argued elsewhere that, for the early Marx, alienated labor is an "inversion" of the ideal Kantian order in which persons have dignity (*wurde*), while things merely have exchange value (*preis*). *See* my "Alienation as Heteronomy," *Philosophical Forum*, forthcoming.

16. This conservative lament is echoed in Joseph Schumpeter's speculations on the likelihood of capitalism's demise. Schumpeter did not look forward to capitalism's passing, but he considered the prospects of a fully commercial society to be grim indeed. *See Capitalism, Socialism and Democracy* (New York: Harper and Brothers, 1942), pt. 2.

17. The point is not that "rational economic man," as a consumer, always seeks more of all commodities, but that he always seeks more commodities. Thus, where money is a universal medium of exchange, rational economic man will never evidence a negative utility for more money, although, of course, there will be diminishing marginal utility for additional units of money beyond some point. That is, at some point

the "cost" of acquiring more money will outweigh the gain. But if money could be acquired and held without cost, like manna from heaven, rational economic man would always want more.

18. *See* Arthur M. Okun, *Equality and Efficiency: The Big Trade Off* (Washington, D.C.: Brookings Institution, 1975), chap. 1.

19. Many of the rights assigned by courts are indeed alienable and, on some views, are (and should be) assigned on grounds of economic efficiency. For a sustained defense of this view, *see* Richard A. Posner, *Economic Analysis of Law* (Boston: Little, Brown and Co., 1973). However, those who talk of human rights, although they may disagree on their scope and content, agree that such rights are inalienable.

20. It is curious that in practice courts often do allow inalienable rights to be alienated. It is common for the courts to take a dim view of a person's selling his vote (alienating his right to vote), yet there is characteristically considerable tolerance of buying and selling silence (thereby diminishing, if not removing altogether, a person's right to free speech).

21. *See* James Tobin, "On Limiting the Domain of Inequality," *Journal of Law and Economics* 13 (October 1970):9.

22. These remarks should not be understood as a defense of moral relativism and the political experience they articulate. Quite the contrary: my intention is to suggest that the concept of human rights, and the concept of freedom with which it is so intimately associated, are ultimately *inadequate*, bearing the limitations of the political practice that emerged in the course of the seventeenth-century English revolutions and their aftermath.

23. For a fuller treatment of these themes, *see* my *The Politics of Autonomy: A Kantian Reading of Rousseau's Social Contract* (Amherst: University of Massachusetts, 1976).

24. It is noteworthy that the best and most likely alternative to liberalism, theoretically and historically, the political theory of Marx and Lenin, at least in its present state of underdevelopment, adds nothing in this respect to what can be found in *The Social Contract*. However, for Marxists, the state is not, as for Rousseau, the vehicle for harmonizing interests, even if the burden of Marxian political theory is to show that the proletarian state, "the dictatorship of the proletariat," *tends* toward the obliteration of antagonistic interests, toward a classless society, and thus toward a kind of Rousseauean harmony of interests. For Marxists, the state is always an instrument of class *domination*. To the extent that struggles in and over the state promote classlessness, these struggles promote the demise of the state itself. But class domination, as much as the "blind" operation of "free markets," puts human dignity into jeopardy; and it is far from clear that Rousseau-type interventions on the level of "opinion," education in the broad sense, will suffice to guarantee respect for persons. Apparently, it will not do just to *import* the notion of human rights into Marxian political theory from the quite different conceptual framework in which it now, arbitrarily but vitally, functions. However, at present, it is not clear how else Marxian political theory (or practice) might proceed.

25. I am grateful to Marie McGinn, Francis Schrag, and Daniel I. Wikler for the many helpful criticisms they made of an earlier draft of this essay.

EFRAIM SHMUELI —— 9

The Right to Self-Realization and Its Predicaments

When speaking philosophically of human rights we must raise the question about the nature of the human self, that is, what it is and how it should be understood. Throughout the course of Western philosophy, this question has been raised repeatedly, particularly in connection with the moral dimension of human life. In his chapter, Professor Efraim Shmueli presents an analysis of this complex phenomenon and explores the great philosophical traditions related to the concept of self-realization.

This study attempts to clarify the problem of human rights, and particularly the so-called right to self-realization, through a refutation of the claims to "absolute freedom" as *self-creation* and as radical *self-determination*. These concepts are first illustrated by reference to the attempts of Nietzsche and Sartre to elevate the activity of human selfhood to a godlike power and responsibility of self-creation, as well as by reference to the radical version of self-determination expressed by Hegel and Marx.

The idea of the so-called right to self-realization, most fashionable in our days, assumes a variety of meanings. The chapter next examines three different central ideas, or forms of freedom: the "constitutive," the "dominative," and the "regulative," with their three correlated degrees of genuineness in the unfolding of selfhood. Each idea of freedom has its radical and its moderate aspect. The three central concepts of freedom are related to sociopolitical and economic claims of liberalism, anarchism, conservatism, and socialism. Abstract freedom is particularized in concrete liberties or rights. Since the manifestations of freedom are always historically conditioned, no matter how deeply the experience of freedom is rooted in the ultimate interiority of selfhood, the last part of the chapter addresses itself to the recently emerged dangers of losing freedom. It has long been noted that the creative realization of selfhood, in its intimate as well as its public interaction, is threatened by economic, social, and political controlling agencies made most efficient by the achievements of modern science and technology.

The theoretical exploration of the claims of individuals and groups can be easily supported and illustrated by the ongoing struggle for individual and collective rights. The study then warns against the dangers inherent in the rights of self-realization when not properly restrained.[1]

SELF-REALIZATION AS SELF-CREATION

In a certain brand of modern thought, self-realization has become identified with the activity of man as his own creator, that is, as finding the source of his life—its significance, truth, and responsibility—within himself. This idea is notorious for its disregard of moral and religious ties. Self-creation claims primarily freedom from restrictions ("negative" freedom), as well as the right to acts of self-assertion ("positive" freedom). Friedrich Nietzsche is perhaps the most outstanding representative of the idea that man is his own creator and thus has the right to free himself from his past, from his beliefs, even from his companions or disciples, from all obligations, in order to reach out for authentic creativity, that is, to the highest achievement of which human beings are capable. However, simply cutting the bonds in a negative "freedom from" and indulgence in a life of mere impulses or whims is for Nietzsche abhorrent. Man must give laws to himself. But these laws have to be higher and stronger than the traditional obligations. They must be in accord with "that impulse to a sacred selfishness which is the impulse to obey the highest commandment."[2] This new "master morality," no longer being "God's vessel," has to be established without transcendence. Nietzsche's description of the "slaves" and "masters" in his *Genealogy of Morals* is well known. The former live on resentment and, deprived of the proper outlet in action, are forced to find their compensation in "values" full of the spirit of revenge, whereas the latter create an aristocratic morality with its triumphant affirmation of one's self.

As Karl Jaspers makes clear in his book on Nietzsche, a morality that replaces any transcendent "ought" by the "necessity" of the natural development of these two classes of people, falls easily into the trap of naturalism, like many "become what you are!" conceptions of self-realization. The assertion of natural facts of human life and features of human nature easily replace the reality sought by the concept of positive freedom. An ethics of "become what you are!" is easily exposed to all kinds of misunderstanding, particularly to the dangerous opinion that creativity is stifled by following the factual process of psychological interplay of determining desires.

The idea of self-creation absolutizes freedom but is unable to apply valid, universal standards of judgment to its claims. This is clear not only in Nietzsche's idea of a self-creating superman but also in Sartre's account of the relation between consciousness and ego, perhaps the second best-known example of the idea of self-creation in modern philosophy.

Consciousness, according to Sartre, is that reality "that is not what it is, and is what it is not."[3] It does not have an interior life, that is, the power of adhesive existence in itself, but it is rather always passing over objects like a "clear wind," touching them without changing them. Consciousness for Sartre is neither Descartes' *res cogitans* nor Husserl's *transcendental ego*. It is, rather, a prepersonal and nonpositional intentionality that produces the ego. For itself, consciousness is an impersonal spontaneity, an operating intentionality that objectifies itself in acts, roles, and psychic states but is always ahead of its own objectification. It can never be grasped, but it can become an object for itself as it was in the past. It is not anything definite, but by continual self-appropriation of its intentional completed acts, which it claims as its own, and designates reflexively with the term "me," it presents a concrete ego. Indeed, consciousness is always tempted to take itself for such an objective unity. It alienates itself in such self-deception or "bad faith."

The difficulty of this position of self-creation becomes obvious when one considers Sartre's neglect of realizing structures, habits, attitudes, and historical and socioeconomic systems, established values, and destinies of man within a structured world. The world, both nature and society, it must be assumed, is not devoid of structures and their implicit, already existent meanings; the world is not such that it would only be waiting for the will that "puts every man in possession of himself as he is" and imposes a sense to specific phenomena and to life in general. Certain phenomena in our life-world present themselves in an immediacy of clearness and distinctiveness as if standing out and calling for our meaning, bestowing awareness. We are talking not only about trees, mountains, clouds, the sky, the sun, and the moon. Not only physical phenomena are structured, or at least prestructured; all our experiences are. In a sense, one must say that physical and ideal structures and values do not exist because they are perceived or thought, but rather because of their being they are capable of being comprehended.

SELF-DETERMINATION OR THE IDEA OF DOMINATIVE FREEDOM

Another of the most prevalent manifestations of the desire for absolute freedom is the wish to perform actions determined exclusively by one's own conscious decisions, that is, as little as possible controlled or even influenced by the will of others or by impersonal forces of the environment. One wants to determine his own destiny by acting through preferring and choosing in the full power of consciousness. Such an activity of self-determination or of autonomous being revives in our days the old ideas of the Stoics, Spinoza's theory of happiness, Kant's doctrine of the autonomous man, and similar classical images of freedom. Man chooses to construct his own course of conduct as he deems fit. The new version of the idea of self-determination intends also to liberate man from the tyranny of his own unconscious impulses. Like self-creation, self-determination is self-constitutive; but unlike self-realization, it is more patient with both structures and norms.

I shall term the idea of self-determination "dominative" or the "idea of dominative freedom." In distinction from "constitutive" freedom, which will be discussed in the next section, dominative freedom intends to be more than a freedom of particular preferences or choices, according to gratifying transitory wishes and desires. It presupposes a unity of an identical being consonant with its basic nature, in spite of a multitude of wishes and desires. Beyond a plurality of preferences and choices, the idea of freedom of self-determination presupposes a dominative, unique power of selfhood. This dominative power is determined to exercise its freedom through the media of individual preferences and choices. Freedom of self-determination does not make man's activities predictable and controllable. Only certain preferences and choices can be predicted. Dominative freedom manifests a will to master one's destiny, but it does not imply that man can write his autobiography in advance, even if he has decided to terminate it by suicide. On the contrary, the dominative power of selfhood is the very essence of freedom as self-determination.

The idea of dominative freedom of self-determination does not necessarily result easily in the notion of absolute freedom but can accept its own limitations. According to Hobbes, for instance, the will is freely executed when "a man throws his goods into the sea for fear the ship may sink," or, in a similarly desperate case, "when a man sometimes faces death only for fear of imprisonment." Fear and liberty are not inconsistent, and "generally all actions which men do in commonwealth for fear of the law are actions which the doers have liberty to omit."[4]

The central point of self-determination is not the execution of any desire that happens to arise at the moment with some strength to determine man's will, but rather the execution of those desires that are consistent with a conscious deliberation of prefereces, born by the understanding of alternatives and of their consistency with intelligent choices. Self-determination, then, is possible when the will of the individual, executed according to preferences and choices, does not express mere momentary whims or passions or wishes imposed by coercive conditions without the possibility of a deliberated decision. Self-determination, thus, can be understood as consistent with imposed necessities. However, it must represent the deliberate dominative will in its way of coping with fear or necessity, or, as Mortimer J. Adler formulates it, "not merely the realization of desires, but the fulfillment of the aspirations or purposes that constitute an individual's own estimation of what is good."[5]

Historically, the idea of dominative freedom of self-determination in its modern patterns can be traced back at least to the Humanists of the Renaissance.

The Renaissance message of the *Oratio de dignitate hominis* of Giovanni Pico della Mirandola foreshadows the existentialist concept of man's freedom of self-creation and the high evaluation of the category of possibility in man's self-determination.

In this message, which Ernst Cassirer described as a "summary of the whole intent of the Renaissance,"[6] it was proclaimed that it is man's dignity to stand at the center of the universe, capable of realizing his possibilities in whatever way he chooses. Man's position in the hierarchy of beings is thus determined only by his own deeds; he can"grow downward" or "grow upward": both the "lower natures" and the "higher natures" are within his reach. No stars, no fate, not even gods will of themselves dominate man's capability for self-determination.

The concept of human self-determination, namely, that man is capable of shaping his own destiny, was molded by Renaissance thinkers in their struggle against a tradition-bound destiny, as symbolized by the wheel of chances and the arbitrary, blind *Fortuna*. The notion of self-determination was affirming the power of *Virtu*, which meant the power of being, talents, charisma, and, foremost, of the capability of controlling *Fortuna*.

It seems that with Hegel and Marx the notion of self-determination of man has been extended to the material field of economic conditions and technological improvements.

As far as I can tell, no one before Hegel, and, in a sense, no one before Marx, ever claimed that man can transform himself by transforming the *material* world. But as soon as this idea emerges, the role traditionally played by practice, in the sense of ethico-political doing, will decrease until in Marx it completely gives way to the notion of *homo faber creans se ipsum.*[7]

Indeed, it has been noted that when Condorcet talks about progress, he still means merely moral perfection and improvement in the field of intellectual endeavors; his concept of progress evokes also the notion of sociopolitical reforms. But ostensibly absent is the idea of technological progress in harnessing nature. That man makes himself by mastering his natural and social environment through science and technology is an extension of Pico's idea of self-determination, as elaborated by Hegel and Marx and their followers, and later by an existentialist like Sartre.

CONSTITUTIVE, DOMINATIVE, AND REGULATIVE FREEDOM

So much for the two most prominent varieties of the concept of self-realization. We are now able to define in more detail this complex concept. At least three distinct aspects have to be considered. The first is what is commonly understood as self-realization, namely, the freedom of the individual to realize his wishes and to act out his purposes, in short, to translate his will into action whenever circumstances permit it. This basic meaning of self-realization I shall call the idea of constitutive freedom or constitutive self-realization, using the Kantian notion of a *constitutive idea*.

This constitutive aspect of self-realization as fulfilling those desires of man that he deems good, in a manner that he determines, still does not consider the adequacy of the desires, purposes, and will in general, to a continuous and unique selfhood. There is also a second concern that must be articulated in a full definition of self-realization. By this definition, self-realization means the fulfillment of desires and purposes of man as he deems them good and as expressing the continuous and unique structure of his self—the idea of *dominative* freedom of self-determination. The third aspect of self-realization I shall term, again in the Kantian tradition, the *regulative idea*. It is a regulative idea of freedom in the sense of the intention of the agent to emendate the activities of the empirical ego and even to do away with the empirical ego altogether for the sake of a noumenal perfect being.

The notion of what constitutes a self is, of course, decisive for the idea of self-realization. Is the self a monolithic entity, or is it composed of diverse elements, and, if so, which element is or should be the dominant one in the process of self-realization? The notion of a composed self implies a dichotomy between the "real" self and the "peripheral," "transitional," or "accidental," the disturbing powers within the self. The real self has to become the master; the accidental powers, like desires, illusions, and ignorance are conceived as enslaving external forces that have penetrated into the self after the manner of illegitimate usurpers. Self-mastery calls for control or expulsion of these uninvited strangers. The autonomous person who aspires to be the ultimate authority of acts and notions, the only master in his house, cannot tolerate these heteronomous opponents, the creatures of casual, external influences. We have already encountered this idea in the notion of dominative freedom.

The real self or the essence of man has been described in the intellectualistic tradition, beginning with ancient philosophy down to the Age of Enlightenment and the various schools of Idealism, as man's *reason*, and it has been argued in this tradition that reason is identical in all persons, though in different degrees, and expresses characteristic features of the structure of the universe itself. Passions and fears encroach on the power of reason and distort its functions. In order to free the self from its internal and external enemies, it has been advised either to retreat into its own noumenal world, as in Kant's theory of freedom, or to emancipate itself by transforming the power of passions into an active energy of reason, as in Spinoza's. In both ways, as well as through many other devices suggested to the self, the purpose was always to become autonomous and to escape bondage, to be conscious of oneself, as the responsible author of one's acts by free choice. This self-comprehension was always linked with the concept of positive freedom. The concept of negative freedom or "freedom from," meant not being prevented by others from choosing, the limiting or even the full elimination of any coercion, or not being subject to the deliberate interference of others within one's area. Positive freedom indicates the self-determining of one's acts by one's real nature. The concept of self-determination almost unintentionally implies the notion of something significant, essential or ideal for self-fulfillment, that is, of some higher value that is considered ultimately "real" and attached to the power of one's self.

This third aspect of self-realization led many to the path of ascetic self-denial and others to libertine hedonism. In the name of self-realization, monasteries of strict orders were built, and Stoic slaves, like Epictetus, felt more free than their masters. Others, like the ancient Cynics and Epicureans, pursued all pleasures of life available to them in the very same name of self-relaxation.

The difficulties in grasping this complex phenomenon of self-realization can be envisaged in each of these three aspects. I shall mention a few difficulties inherent in each aspect. On the constitutive aspect of realizing one's desires: must the conditions and circumstances be favorable to the desires, or is fear and coercion consistent with free self-realization, as Hobbes emphasized in his concept of free will?

The fulfillment of desires is conditioned by the absence of external impediments and obstacles. This is a common concept of freedom made popular by Hobbes when he asserted that freedom is the absence of external impediments to movement or activity of the body. It is obvious that this concept of freedom does not specify the characteristics peculiar to the freedom of human beings. Beasts and birds can also enjoy this sort of freedom. Moreover, external impediments and obstacles are of various types, some of them most needed for the preservation of the specific human freedom—for instance, the obstacles to murdering or robbing others. Freedom of fulfillment of passions and desires is probably the lowest type of freedom in the sense that in it selfhood is expressed only inadequately if the only condition is the absence of external impediments and obstacles.

The real self, then, can be interpreted in an individualistic and anarchic way: since men differ in their desires, the content of their desired happiness varies. "Each person's happiness is a good to that person alone" (J. S. Mill).[9] However, it can also be interpreted in a way that emphasizes the "true self" of the individual as sharing the goods within a community or a whole state, limited by the conditions of the possibility of actualizing purposes in harmony with others and according to common moral standards. Self-realization in this case means the fulfillment of one's desires only under these conditions of an integration of purposes, regulated by norms that the individual recognizes and imposes upon himself. For John Dewey, for example, who taught this interpretation of self-realization: a favorable social environment that allows the continuing process of growth is indispensable for the development of the power of creative intelligence to share his desires with those of others. Although each man must be free to pursue happiness as he perceives it for himself, the realization of his desires depends both on the favorable environment and upon the state of one's growth and power to judge wisely and to evaluate desires by the consequences that will result from acting upon them, by the power to select and order means, and to carry chosen ends into operation.

In this sense, the experience of self-realization is always a matter of degree. No man can actualize all the requirements of this complex concept fully and continuously. Only an omnipotent being could always enjoy self-realization. Indeed, this is the state characteristically attributed to God, and only by God's deeds can we learn what purposes constitute His own estimation of what is good for Him or for the world with which He is concerned.

ABSOLUTE FREEDOM AND THE INCREASE OF LIBERTIES

The idea of absolute freedom, as I hope we have validly demonstrated, is both disproportionately pretentious and impractical. However, it can be considered an inspiring claim for justifying particular sociopolitical freedoms, or better-termed, liberties. Liberties are specific freedoms that often are postulated on grounds of "absolute rights." Freedom must be specified in liberties, that is, in accepted relationships between concrete agents. One is free to act to the extent that somebody else does not have control over one's conduct with regard to these acts. I am free to do something, provided nobody prevents me from doing it or makes it punishable for me to do it, or, of course, provided nobody makes it necessary or mandatory for me to do so. This is the central sense of constitutive freedom in the classical liberal movement.

Liberties are plural in the sense of rights of an agent to do or forbid any particular actions. Freedom conceived abstractly, protects these basic rights, generally considered as "natural" rights, namely, the right of life, the right to own and dispose of property, the right of religious choice, the rights of press, speech, and assembly. To the classical theory of liberalism, freedom was synonymous with certain sociopolitical relations that served as sufficient protection of these basic rights. Neoliberalism defines freedom as the implementation of a certain range of possible choices, for example, to earn an adequate income without working more than a certain number of hours, and, in general, the implementation of guarantees for certain standards of life and social welfare. Another liberty is the establishment of government by consent or "representative" government.

Liberties are compromises in the struggle between the conditioning interests of individuals and groups in the sociopolitical marketplace, and the radical, "pure" ideas conceived as legitimate timeless postulates. Liberties bear the scars of this struggle both in the history of their development and in their actual performances. They were born on crossroads and carry within themselves the inconvenience of mediators closely bound to a variety of interests, thus bowing to private and public necessities, but also lifting their eyes to brighter and more universal and independent claims. Liberties express precisely the precarious, transitory equilibrium that can always be overrun by radical demands in the name of unconditioned freedom, or decreased, or even be totally abolished, in the name of the inevitable necessities. As participants of the two worlds, they represent the experience of the risks of complex sociopolitical structures and the transitory stabilities of public constellations. They derive their pathos from the claims of radical freedom and their sobriety from the prosaic necessities of compromise.

It is certainly a characteristic of our time that more and more liberties are demanded both as indispensable foundations of the democratic way of living, and in order to preserve and protect the individual's well-being. The platform of the Democratic party in the election of 1960, for instance, already declared among the liberties, recognized as indispensable, the following rights: the right to earn enough to provide adequate food and clothing and recreation; the right of every family to a decent home; the right to adequate medical care and the opportunity to achieve and enjoy good health; the right to adequate protection from the economic fears of old age, sickness, accidents, and unemployment; the right to a good education.

With the increasing erosion of self-determination in the United States in the 1970s, there is an apparent increase in the desire to do certain things for the American people that might have been done otherwise by the individuals themselves.

However, the main problem, both in the metaphysics of freedom and in the sociopolitical realm, seems to be the relation between the claim to absolute freedom and the balance of the diverse liberties.

Each of the three aspects of the concept of self-realization is characterized by a specific affinity to a sociopolitical theory of freedom. The moderate form of constitutive self-realization, namely, self-creation, is clearly affiliated with anarchic and totalitarian concepts of freedom. The dominative concept of freedom can accommodate various forms of regimes, but will be most decisive in internal struggles for power, tending always toward a political ideology. The regulative aspect of self-realization is easily expressed in its moderate form in terms of social democracy, and in its radical form in terms of totalitarianism.

Let me describe briefly these affinities. Those who base themselves on the theory of Locke adhere to a modified concept of constitutive self-realization: man is free when he acts according to his own judgment in a society in which he is not subject to the arbitrary will of others. But he is not unfree when he obeys laws created by legislators whose authority binds the individual's desires to make possible his freedom. Complying with laws made with general consent is consistent with the freedom of citizens. Without law, there is no freedom. The law of the state aims at preserving and enlarging freedom. It is understood, however, that these laws must be in accord with reason. Freedom without restraints of rational laws is license or "unrestrained liberty." Ultimately, Locke maintains that the law directs man to his "proper interest" and prescribes no further than what is needed "for the general good."[10] It is the precondition for regulative self-realization in a civil society.

The constitutive concept of self-realization is probably best expressed by radical liberal writers of the nineteenth century. Their main ideal is that every man has the right to full self-realization and that laws only "take away something from liberty." Consequently, "every law is contrary to liberty." Certainly even Bentham does not deny that laws protect the rights of the citizen, but he holds that laws, rights, and obligations imposed to protect the person and his liberty itself are basically "at the expense of liberty." One gains liberty only by sacrificing liberty. Nineteenth-century liberalism strictly adhered to the idea that liberty is to be measured "by the relative paucity of the restraints it imposes," and if the restraints are increased beyond the needs to prevent mutual harm, "it is not the proper kind of Liberalism."[11]

Those who conceive self-realization in the radical constitutive sense of freedom to do what one pleases, see obligations to the law of the state and to the rules of other legal institutions as curtailments of individual freedom. For them, freedom would exist only in those spheres that are not regulated by law, since being subject to law always means being subject to coercive regulations, or, at best, to regulations that do not interfere with individual desires. The realm of self-realization must be kept outside laws and regulations. According to the radical line of constitutive self-realization, one is led to philosophical anarchism: No man has an obligation to obey the law of the state. Under no circumstances can a state demand the obedience of its subjects on good grounds. Each man has freedom to determine the purposes and principles of his activities. He is autonomous and does not accept authority of the state to "monopolize force" (as Max Weber defines the main characteristic of the state). Even the democratic principle of majority rule is not compatible with the moral autonomy of the individual. He may not often be able to conform to decisions and laws that he thinks are immoral.

Anarchism, or the idea of self-creation, transposed into the sociopolitical realm, causes violent reactions, as Plato already indicated. "So the only outcome of too much freedom is likely to be excessive subjection, in the state or in the individual; which means that the culmination of liberty in democracy is precisely what prepares the way for the cruelest extreme of servitude under a despot."[12] When the idea of self-creation joins the regulative idea of collective self-realization, its results are all sorts of tyranny.

Those who believe that self-realization has its genuine meaning only in the actualization of one's dominative self or the best part of the self would not necessarily experience laws and rules of state and other legal institutions as an infringement on the possibility of self-realization. Since they reject the idea that self-realization implies the freedom of doing as one pleases without concurrent notion of the actualization of the dominative, best part of the self, obedience to law, when law is conceived as the articulation of the best possible insights in a certain kind of a state, would be accepted. Moreover, it would even be considered a high virtue.

The dominative idea of freedom takes a decisively conservative bend when it accepts uncritically the notion that freedom is nothing but the knowledge of necessity in the sense of adjustment to the necessities of sociopolitical and economic structures and situations. The idea that freedom is only the knowledge of necessity cannot be consistent with itself. This has been often argued; such an idea assumes that, although everything, in our case every sociopolitical or economic structure or situation, is necessary, man can know these necessities or fail to know them. In other words, if the idea of freedom as knowledge of necessity were consistent, everybody would necessarily know the necessities, and there would be no place for failing to know them. In the particular case of sociopolitical or economic adjustment to the necessities, the individual is or is not adjusted, and however he behaves, his behavior is of necessity. It is obvious that on such a ground one cannot master a sociopolitical situation by knowledge of its necessity. It remains only to accept it. Any change is presumptuous.

Hegel was often interpreted on these lines of a conservative ideology. But even Marx's revolutionary theory, as far as it has acknowledged the very same Hegelian idea of freedom as knowledge of necessity, could only result in a blind belief that the activity of the revolutionary is an integral part of the sociopolitical and economic developments as they necessarily happen. Although fighting alienation, a revolutionary theory, based on such an idea of freedom, ("freedom is appreciation of necessity," Engels), constitutes in itself a form of alienation. It gains the power of fanaticism, and may have a broad appeal by invoking the support of "nature" itself, of the "necessity of the historical process": and of the "objectively inevitable conditions" that allegedly "must" lead to the radical saving change, but it loses the power of critical examination and reflection, the very essence of freedom as a manifestation of selfhood.

In summary, the idea of self-realization can be envisaged either as compatible with the law of the state and even assisted by it, or as incompatible with the law of the state. Both conceptions obviously carry sociopolitical consequences. The one is pleased with freedom under government, and the other fights for freedom from government.

This more or less clear-cut theoretical division does not mean that in actuality the constitutive concept of self-realization necessarily denies the possibility of constraining and coercing laws, or that legal restrictions are needed, and that some laws express the very needs for self-realization. In other words, the idea of self-realization under law and government does not necessarily justify all laws and government, and self-realization that seeks freedom from law and government is not necessarily based on the belief that they are evils and should be abolished for the sake of self-realization. However, a clear distinction must be made between the prolaw and contralaw, if not antilaw, positions.

THE DANGERS IN SELF-REALIZATION OF THE "COLLECTIVE SELF"

If self-realization concerns not merely an individual but a whole group, a nation, or a coalition of nations, and if a "collective self" is willed in the name of some higher value or ultimate concern, such a collective self will try to remove all obstacles to the realization of its desires in the name of its value-ideology. Such sociopolitical self-realization, even more than a sovereign "self-determination of nations," opened wide doors to doctrines of self-righteousness, to intolerance, and to violent politics. Wars have been waged in the name of supreme values—to make man and world more rational, more God-fearing, more communal, happier and freer. Thus were many methods of compulsion sanctified. Liberty, equality, and fraternity, idolized in cults of political self-realization, became Molochs to whom hosts of worshipers themselves were sacrificed. Whenever liberty was conceived in the regulative concept of self-realization, to the neglect of the moderate constitutive sense of liberty, one finds groups of people wanting to enact their specific concepts of freedom, even at the cost of severe oppression. Rousseau, for instance, regarded by many as the philosopher of "positive liberty," taught a doctrine that was implemented by violence and oppression. Some activists, and even radical political theorists, believe that violent acts can prove or at least support the claim of certain political ends to absolute validity. However, it must be argued with Isaiah Berlin, that "to say that in some ultimate, all-reconciling, yet realizable synthesis, duty *is* interest, or individual freedom *is* pure democracy or an authoritarian state, is to throw a metaphysical blanket over either self-deceit or deliberate hypocrisy."[13] The cult of political self-realization, in its regulative aspect, seems to be inherently linked with a deep and incurable metaphysical need to guarantee the eternal validity of sanctified values in a harmonious sociopolitical system.

The idea of self-realization can be extended, in the political realm as mentioned above, to a collective self (a people, state, or class) that is considered an ideal society, either to be established or already in existence. Many political varieties of this concept of collective self-realization appear on the contemporary scene, as dominating totalitarian regimes, or as movements of protest and revolution in opposition to the dominating regimes. The individual self becomes enlarged in the state and absorbed by it, as in Plato's *Republic*. The sinful desires and destructive impulses, represented by chaotic, capitalistic individualism, economic competition, political rebelliousness, or "false consciousness" (Marx), have to be eliminated. By participating in the "general will" in "obedience to a law which we prescribe to ourselves" we gain our true liberty (Rousseau). Modern fascism and communism use the concept of liberty in the sense that a citizen has the duty to conform to the interests of society as a whole, even when his own interests have to be sacrificed. Hitler proclaimed that he acted in the name of freedom while suppressing all liberties: "Providence has ordained that I should be the greatest liberator of humanity. I am freeing men from the demands of freedom and personal independence which only a few can sustain."

The proponents of the idea of collective self-realization believe, or at least proclaim, that within the frame of the new sociopolitical and economic structure, the full development of the individual will be made possible to the highest extent. Only the ideal community guarantees the full enjoyment of self-realization. As long as this stage has not yet been achieved, the individual may suffer. As a matter of fact, he is called upon to sacrifice his welfare and liberties, if necessary, for the sake of the promised happy turn of human affairs at a future stage of the sociopolitical development. The books of Solzhenitsyn describe in unforgettable stories and scenes what happened to these promises, many years after the messianic revolution. They show how the Orwell "big brother" slogans, "Service to the State is freedom" and "War is peace" and Herbert Marcuse's statements, "Toleration is oppression," and "Freedom of opinion, of assembly and of speech becomes an instrument for absolving servitude," contrast in real and concrete conditions.

The Marxian idea of an individual self-realization, which can be fulfilled only in a collective framework of revolution-changed conditions that enable humanity to leap "from the realm of necessity into the realm of freedom," leads to the concept of an ideal society where freedom of desire and obligations will be reconciled in a full attainment of human perfection. Marx's idea invokes a vision of a changed human nature.[14] In this radical sense, the absolute freedom of collective self-realization is a projection of the dream of personal absolute freedom on a macrohistoric scene.

The modern conception of self-realization calls for respect for persons and entitles them to specific benefits as testified by the growing list of human rights. This conception, however, manifests a variety of forms of freedom and of their consequent "liberties," some of which produce aggressive interpersonal and intergroup relationships, as described above.

The endeavors to enhance human rights in our times can be justified by considerations of practical reason only when clearly designed to restrain conflict and violence (so often produced by a low degree of existing self-realization). Dispositions, motives, and springs of action of self-realizing individuals and groups must be channeled by normative directions on both sides of the iron curtain, by all participants of the Helsinki agreement.[15]

NOTES

1. This chapter on self-realization and human rights is a part of a larger study of freedom that aims at grounding the concept of human rights in the unique ontological structure of selfhood and its dialectical unfoldings in the sociopolitical realm. Another part of this study was published in *Idealistic Studies* 7 (1977).

2. In a letter to Lou Salomé, November 1, 1882, quoted by Karl Jaspers in *Nietzsche* (Chicago: Henry Regnery Company, 1969), p. 159. *See* the whole chapter, pp. 139ff., on "Man as His Own Creator," which portrays Nietzsche's concept of morality in relation to creativity as a manifestation of man's absolute freedom, or in Jaspers's terms, "freedom without transcendence." The notion of absolute freedom as self-creation was revived by Sartre, as correctly observed by Mortimer J. Adler in his *The Idea of Freedom, A Dialectical Examination of the Conception of Freedom* (Garden City, N.Y.: Doubleday & Co., 1958). This volume provides indispensable information and insights.

3. Jean-Paul Sartre, "Existentialism as Humanism," *Existentialism from Dostoevsky to Sartre*, selected and introduced by Walter Kaufmann (New York: The World Publishing Company, 1956), p. 291; and "Being and Nothingness," in *The Idea of Freedom*, Adler, pp.555-56. *See* also the "Conclusion," and "Ethical Implications." For my criticism of Sartre's position, in addition to the brief remarks here, *see* "Self and Reality," *Philosophy in Context*, Supplement to Vol. 1 (Cleveland: The Cleveland State University, 1972), p. 19.

4. Thomas Hobbes, *Leviathan*, quoted in *The Idea of Freedom*, Adler, p. 173.

5. Ibid.

6. Ernst Cassirer, *The Individual and the Cosmos in Renaissance Philosophy*, trans. Mario Domandi (Philadelphia: University of Pennsylvania Press, 1972), p. 86: "*Burckhardt* called Pico's oration one of the most noble bequests of the culture of the Renaissance. And indeed, it summarizes with grand simplicity and in pregnant form the whole intent of the Renaissance and its entire concept of knowledge. In this oration, we can clearly see the polarity upon which is based the moral and intellectual tension so characteristic of the Renaissance. What is required of man's will and knowledge is that they be completely *turned towards* the world and yet completely *distinguish* themselves from it. Will and knowledge may, or rather, must devote themselves to every part of the universe; for only by going through the entire universe can man traverse the circle of his own possibilities. But this complete *openness* towards the world must never signify a *dissolution* in it, a mystical-pantheistic losing of oneself. For the human will possesses itself only inasmuch as it is conscious that no single goal will fulfill it; and human knowledge possesses itself only inasmuch as it knows that no single object of knowledge can suffice for it."

7. Nicholas Lobkowicz, *Theory and Practice, History of a Concept from Aristotle to Marx* (London: University of Notre Dame Press, 1967), p. 139. The novelty was the extension of the concept of human self-determination from the realm of ethics and politics (the Greek idea) and the epistemological realm (the discovery of Kant's) to economics and technology. This turn is most decisive for the change of the whole notion of human existence in our times.

8. Efraim Shmueli, "Modern Hippies and Ancient Cynics: A Comparison of Philosophical and Political Developments and Its Lessons," *Journal of World History* (Paris: UNESCO, Fall 1970). It is obvious that each aspect of self-realization, like each of the three mentioned forms of freedom, can be destructive. For instance, when the entire being of man acts, in the dominative type of self-realization, freedom in its proper sense, based on "sympathetic appreciation," as I described in the paper mentioned in note 1, may still be distorted and negated. Man as an integral being can still be the slave of destructive impulses, commit criminal acts or indulge in a continuous inhumane behavior.

9. Or in a more famous formulation: "The only freedom which deserves the name, is that of pursuing our own good *in our own way* . . . ." J. S. Mill, *On Liberty,* ch. 1. Felix E. Oppenheim, *Dimensions of Freedom* (New York: St. Martin's Press, 1961), p. 153, describes Mill's concept of freedom as "a dispositional property of an individual, his capacity to perform actions not controlled—not even influenced—by others, but determined exclusively by his own decisions." In other words, what is termed here "dominative freedom." This being correct, I emphasize in the text the highly individualistic aspect of Mill's concept where the happiness of the person is not immediately related to a life of a community.

10. John Locke, *Civil Government* (New York: Barnes and Noble, 1966), Ch. 6, sec. 57 and ch. 6, sec. 59.

11. Herbert Spencer, *The Man Versus the State.* Quoted by Adler, *The Idea of Freedom,* p. 26.

12. Plato, *The Republic,* Bk. 8, p. 564. I would like to venture that Sartre's notion of absolute responsibility, discussed above, can be explained in the sense of Plato's remark, first as a grand philosophic attack on the totalitarian banishment of responsibility from the realm of the autonomous citizen. Hitler, for example, proclaimed that by suppressing freedom he promoted the general feeling of freedom. "Providence has ordained that I should be the greatest liberator of humanity. I am freeing men from the demands of freedom and personal independence which only a few can sustain." (Quoted in Oppenheim, *Dimensions of Freedom,* p. 171.) Second, however, Sartre's concept reflects ironically, I feel, the very notion of absolute freedom as usurped in practice by the dictators, namely the notion of freedom as absolute self-creation—the difference being that every citizen, not only the few ruling supermen, are called upon to exercise their freedom.

13. Isaiah Berlin, *Four Essays on Liberty* (London: Oxford University Press, 1969), p. 171.

14. Herbert Marcuse, *One-Dimensional Man* (Boston: Beacon Press, 1967), ch. 1.

15. On those "normative directions" at both sides of the so-called Iron Curtain, *see* the paper mentioned in note 1.

PART 4

The Applications
of Human Rights

D. P. CHATTOPADHYAYA ——— 10

Human Rights, Justice, and Social Context

In his defense of a contextualist thesis for the philosophy of human rights, Professor D. P. Chattopadhyaya argues that due consideration should be given to relevant social and historical conditions in the enforcement of human rights. His discussion centers on the close link between justice and human rights in matters of practical application. The underlying assumption of his argument is that a society is required to respect the various human rights depending upon its having attained a corresponding level of political justice and material well-being.

In this chapter I propose to show that (natural) human rights and justice have to be understood in their proper social context and that any attempt to decontextualize and thus *universalize* them is bound to prove more or less meaningless. However, this is *not* to deny their extracontextual relevance and *general* character.

Can one have any right in the state of nature? If the answer to the question is "yes," we must then admit that natural rights are inalienable and to that extent universal. The idea of natural rights is inseparable from the concept of the "state of nature," and the latter is by no means dead today. Of the historically influential ideas of natural rights, Hobbes' and Locke's are perhaps the best known. The relevance of their ideas today is said to be primarily negative, thus suggesting what to avoid in formulating a modern and desirable concept of human rights; but I think there are positive aspects in their views that merit attention and review.

The natural condition of man is a state of every man being against every man. And this in turn results from what Hobbes calls appetitive, passionate, and self-preserving traits of the human nature. Man is a passionate creature, only secondarily a rational creature.[1] Given a situation in which the available resources are limited in relation to the self-preserving desires of such creatures, a state of perpetual conflict is bound to follow. Hobbes' main doctrine is that it is only through an organized political authority, setting up an artificial condition under government, that this unbearable state of affairs can be ended.

"The right of nature," according to Hobbes, "is the liberty each man hath to use his own power as he will himself for for the preservation of his own nature."[2] This liberty is the only right one can have in the absence of a political authority to govern. But its worth is not of much consequence, since in the state of nature there is no authority to defend that liberty or, in other words, to enforce that natural right. Unless "the natural right of every man to every thing" is defined and regulated by enforceable law, nobody is under any obligation to respect others' natural rights. It is the surrender of natural rights to some supreme authority that explains the origin of political obligation. Every man must act or refrain from acting as if he were a party to an agreement to obey that supreme authority unconditionally. However, this authority is limited in one respect: it cannot order a man to take his own life or others to kill him.

Hobbes draws a careful distinction between a right of nature and a law of nature.[3] A law of nature (*lex naturalis*) is a general rule ascertained through reason, by which a man is forbidden to do what is destructive of his life or takes away the means necessary for self-preservation and to omit that by which he thinks his life may be best preserved. His right (*jus naturalis*) consists in liberty to do or to forbear something necessary for the preservation of his own life. The question has been raised whether Hobbes' concept of the law of nature and the right of nature are consistent. If, to quote him, "right consisteth in liberty to do or to forbear whereas law determineth and bindeth to one of them," one wonders how there can be both a law and a right to the same thing. An element of discretion is associated with the concept of right, but law leaves no room for that. Obligation knows no exception, but the same is not true in exercising one's right. On this interpretation, right and law are not only distinguishable but also mutually exclusive.

Even while I have the right to preserve my life, it is true, I may not exercise it. But since natural law, a rule of reason, enjoins me that I should use my power to preserve my life, my decision, an exercise of my discretion, not to use it only betrays my irrationality. Whether I betray irrationality or not, the matter of exercising my right is of secondary importance to Hobbes. What he is primarily interested in showing is that in his model state of nature we do have natural rights. Then by the concept of natural law, a rule of reason, he goes on to show that we agree to transfer our rights to the sovereign political authority and thus to put the state of perpetual warfare to an end. The question of transference of rights makes no sense unless the existence of such rights is first postulated or established.

Hobbes is often referred to as one of the chief exponents of the doctrine of absolute sovereignty and Locke as that of the constitutional doctrine. The implied contention is that the former is almost exclusively concerned with the unlimited power of the sovereign and that his defense of the individual's rights and liberties is deliberately of a secondary nature, as if it were left to the latter to defend the same. I do not totally deny that there is a point in this contention, but one must not overemphasize it. Rather, what is more important is the necessity of trying to understand their views on the matter against their different and definite historical backgrounds. The connection of Locke's ideas with Hobbes' has often been "distorted and exaggerated."[4] What Locke really intended is an effective refutation of Filmer's Tory defense of absolute monarchy. One is advised to recall in this connection Filmer's criticism of Hobbes on the alleged ground that the latter's consistent pleas in support of man's natural rights objectively limits the power of the sovereign and encourages rebellious activities. Being the liberal he is, Locke earnestly tries to prove equality and liberty of all men. In this important respect, his difference from Hobbes is unmistakable.

Locke's model of the natural state of society is God-ordained. In God's scheme of things, all men are equal and free, or, at any rate, destined to be equally free. If man cannot reach his moral destiny of equal freedom, it is either his own or civil society's fault. The power that could enable him to develop his moral potentiality, reason, fully is given to him from the time of birth. The same power, rightly realized, can ensure good governance of the civil society. The law of nature is an expression of God's will and, therefore, intrinsically consistent with freedom and equality of all men. "Law of nature . . . is the law of reason."[5] Reason reveals to men the law that forms the basis of their equality and also informs them that they are not subject to any external compulsion or to others' will. Those who violate the law of nature ensuring equality between and freedom of men are liable to be injured or punished by the victims of the violation. Wild beasts and despotic rulers are in different ways impervious to the influences of the law of reason, violate the law of nature, and thus threaten the security of life and tend to destroy the very "common bond whereby humankind is united into one fellowship and society."

Whereas in Hobbes natural rights take precedence over the laws of nature, Locke accords primacy to the latter. Man is bound to the universal order of things by the laws of nature that *oblige* him to become effectively a moral being, a free and reasonable being. Hobbes' accent is on self-preserving rights. In developing his concept of the law of nature, Locke points out that it *obliges* him to preserve not only his own life, limb, liberty, and other possessions but also, and *equally* so, those of others.

Liberty and law-based obligation are inseparable. Liberty is native to human nature. The law of nature has put man under the obligation to live freely, to make use of this freedom to develop a concrete moral life and at the same time a cooperative social life. This very obligation accounts for his "right of freedom"—"freedom of will and liberty of acting." *"The end of law* is not to abolish or restrain, but *to preserve and enlarge* freedom."[6] Both freedom of will and liberty of action are grounded in reason. Any authority, individual or collective, that is not grounded in reason and is not, therefore, itself capable of understanding and following law does not command or deserve its subjects' obedience, because the relation between the former and the latter are law-governed, decided by reason.[7] Man's freedom finds its best expression in freedom of judgment subject to the law of reason.

Locke's is not a purely intellectual conception of natural rights. Property is an external and a concrete expression of man's liberty. It is a right that is capable of being exercised on things, and its existence is prior to any explicit agreement or contract between men. Liberty is also a natural property. Locke uses "liberty" and "freedom" interchangeably. He would prefer the proposition, "Man *has* liberty," to the proposition, "Man *is* free." Although he says "man is born free and rational," what he means is that "man has in him the potentiality of being free and rational," and it depends on the character of natural law and civil laws to which he is subject. Liberty, a natural right, is a sort of property that can be *owned* and, therefore, encroached upon or even taken away, *unjustly.* Liberty qua property, like other natural rights, is given by God to *men in common* for their self-preservation and self-development.[8]

To account for the origin of the community ownership of property, the concept of law of nature is enough; but to preserve and enlarge private ownership, men do need civil society and civil laws. For the defense and undisturbed enjoyment of private property, civil society must be brought into being by "compact" and consent and vested with due executive and legislative powers. Offenses against liberty and proprietary rights defined by the laws of civil or political society must be punished according to law. Government comes into existence simultaneously with civil society, but its end (the preservation of the rights and liberties of the people) is somewhat limited in comparison with that of the latter, and in the event of its failure to act in conformity with its end it is dissolved.

The natural rights of Hobbes and Locke, with their focus on the equal right of all men to be free, constitute the moral foundation of human rights as recognized (at least in principle) in our time. But, also, if the equality of all men to be free is recognized as a right, justice naturally demands its protection. The concept of justice applies to men, actions, attitudes, and states of affairs. Equality of freedom (of all adult rational human beings) is a state of affairs, with both subjective and objective connotations, and as such is a good, perhaps primary, subject of justice. In order to pass a judgment of justice on a state of affairs, what we are called upon to look into are the qualities and relationships of the concerned human beings, and the transactions they enter into. Justice may be considered under two heads, *aggregative* and *distributive*.[9] An aggregative principle of justice is concerned with the total amount of goods and services enjoyed by a group, and a distributive one with the share of goods and services that different members of the group can enjoy. The distributive principle may refer to *valued mental states* such as happiness and want-fulfillment or to *material resources* such as income and education. The distributive principle itself may be *egalitarian* ("divide the cake equally among the children") or *differential* ("give the hungriest more than the rest"). The egalitarian principle simply lays down the mode of distribution, whereas the differential principle specifies the ground of difference in distribution; the ground may be *need, desert,* or *right*. The most basic character of justice seems to be embodied in the definition: render each his due. Of course, what one's due is cannot be decided in a general or an abstract manner; to arrive at a just decision, one's qualities or lack thereof and socioeconomic circumstances have to be taken into account.

This general definition of justice seems adequately to take care of the well-known contrast between *legal justice* and *social justice* and that between *private justice* and *social justice*.[10] Legal justice in its substantive aspect deals with the punishment of offenses and the compensation of injury by means of enacting and enforcing appropriate laws, and in its procedural aspect states the principles of fair trial, rights of appeal, among others. Social justice refers to the distribution of benefits and burdens among the individual members and between the groups of members of society through regulation and by setting up appropriate social institutions—property system, taxation system, public distribution system, restriction of monopoly trade practices, old-age pension, unemployment allowance, and others.

Broadly speaking, there are three different, not necessarily conflicting, interpretations or theories of justice: *right-based, desert-based,* and *need-based*. First, rights may be legal or positive, and moral or ideal. The former is recognized and enforceable, the latter may or may not be recognized and, even if recognized, not enforceable by the lawful authority. This distinction, in effect, is not as clear-cut as it is generally supposed to be in the abstract level of juristic thinking. For the rules of positive law, the accepted basis of legal rights, are not free from practical ambiguity, often need interpretation before application, and the cases, especially the hard ones, in which the rules are sought to be applied have to be clearly identified. Moreover, in time, ideal rights often ripen into positive right through propaganda and public discussion. The claims which appear unjust and are unacceptable as right today may appear just and be statutorily recognized as right tomorrow.

Social consensus acting as a natural force hastens the process of ripening of a moral right into a legal one.

Justice is a part of morality. J. S. Mill thinks that the concepts of justice and right are coextensive. "Just claims" are also "right claims"; when they are denied, the right-holder is wronged and therefore deserves some law-sanctioned protection.[11] Of course, just claims in most cases turn out to be weaker than right claims unless they have some independent strong *social* justification. The time lag between just claims and right claims is indicative of what is called the forward-looking, as distinguished from the conservative, backward-looking, character of justice. Because of their moral force or other social compulsion when just claims are accorded legal recognition, the persons related to the rightholder in respect of those rights are put under corresponding duties. The rightholder, in the sphere of civil law, may or may not press his rights, that is demand that the duty be performed or waived. In other words, there is a basic connection between rights and *free choice.* In addition, rights provide *security,* and the rightholder rationally expects others to respect his right to something. The main advantages that flow out of positive rights are freedom and security. Obviously this does not hold in the case of ideal rights that are not legally recognized and enforced. The question of *content* or subject does not *ordinarily* arise in the case of positive rights, because their *forms* themselves are the object of recognized contract or agreement, and that ensures both secure enjoyment and respect of others concerned. Content is the essence of ideal right, and its moral undertone is unmistakable. Like the rights to life, liberty, and property, natural rights constitute a very important part of ideal rights, with many assuming the dignity of positive rights through the legal recognition of various types in different societies.

Ideal rights in some societies occupy an intermediate position between positive rights and pure moral rights. For example, "directive principles" of the constitution of India recognize "the right to work, to education, and to public assistance in certain cases" (Article 41) and explicitly state that these principles "shall not be enforceable by any court . . . [but] . . . are nevertheless fundamental in the governance of the country and it shall be the duty of the state to apply these principles in making laws" (Article 37). Some of these principles (in the nature of prescription) have indeed been followed up by appropriate legislation. But many are yet to get the backing of positive laws. What are still ideal rights in developing countries like India have long been recognized as positive rights in the developed countries of Europe and the United States. To understand the true content of rights, what is most important to look into is neither the constitution nor individual pieces of legislation of the state but its existing sociological conditions: how the laws are actually interpreted by the judiciary, followed by the executive, and made practically available to the common man.

The theory of desert-based justice is also beset with numerous practical difficulties. For this is an area in which theory and practice interpenetrate deeply, and the line of demarcation between the two is badly blurred by sociological considerations. It is easy to say "somebody deserves something" or "something is due to somebody," but it is not at all easy to decide how a particular person or group deserves a particular thing (income, reward, or title). Sometimes desert is defined in terms of right (the man who paid the premiums regularly deserves the insured sum at the end of the maturity period), sometimes in terms of need (the poor farmers of the drought-affected area deserve to be exempted from the payment of annual land revenue). Taking advantage of a loose definition of desert, one may put forward an unjust claim and demand that it be recognized as one's right. The underlying moral tone (though often very misleading) of the concept of desert has to be recognized first; when we say, for example, "X deserves reward" or "Y deserves punishment," what we leave unsaid (but implied) is the *reason* or *basis* of X's reward and Y's punishment. The reason may be an *action* or *quality of character* of the concerned person. Besides, the question of *social evaluation* of the said action or quality is also there. Again the sociological considerations enter into the matter by the backdoor (in the good sense). Social evaluation and recognition of what one deserves may be prompted by utilitarian considerations, such as "This will induce others to follow his good examples in the services of society,"[12] or contractarian considerations, such as "This is likely to yield a fair distributive outcome" in the nonmoral and nonsubstantive, procedural sense of the term.[13]

Doubts have been expressed on the question whether *needs* constitute an independent criterion of justice and suggestions made that needs are either disguised desert or camouflaged right. If need without the support of right, need *simpliciter*, cannot be accepted as the criterion of justice, then one has to concede by implication that the needs discussed by social reformers and political revolutionaries that have not yet been recognized by the concerned authority are of no significance or consequence at all. Even in a predominantly feudal society not committed to a welfare state, people do speak of the needs of land reforms, of ensuring minimum wages to the agricultural laborer, of rural banks and cheap credit facilities for the poor farmers, of rural health service centers, and the like. Although these needs cannot be brought under the category of rights, they can hardly be dismissed as frivolous and unjust, unless of course the financial and other implications of the needs are quite beyond the capacity of the concerned society. Besides, the need for equal distribution of the available resources of a society, such as national income, between the different sections cannot be disputed either, at least not on the ground of justice. At this stage, one may like to intervene and say that the question of equal distribution or even that of equitable distribution cannot be justly settled unless we bring in the concept of desert. Need claims, according to this view, are likely to be made in an arbitrary and self-centered manner, in total or partial disregard of others' needs. It is clear that it would land us in a near-anarchic and unjust state of society. To remedy the situation, it has been suggested, need claims have to be backed up or justified by desert. Otherwise, if there are two individuals or groups in a society, one privileged and the other underprivileged, how can we think of distributing something equally between them without sacrificing the principle of justice. In no case should goods be *equally* distributed between the two unless they deserve the same equally. Even for the purpose of equitable, in a sense nonequal, distribution of goods, some rules of desert determination should be followed.

To talk of desert-based needs is not particularly illuminating. For in addition to the difficulties involved in determining one's desert, we have to face here the problems attending the determination of one's needs. Neither looks nor words nor social position of a person, certainly not others' certificates about him, provide any definite basis for the determination of his needs. Needs may be classified under different headings: substantive and *procedural; intrinsic* and *extrinsic; original* and *imitative.* They may be illustrated by corresponding need statements in the same order: "Travelers need passports to visit foreign countries," and "The applicant for a passport needs information regarding how and to whom to apply for it"; "Ram needs music and poetry to live his life," and "Rahim needs colormatched curtains and cutglass flower vases for his drawing room"; "We need food, a house, and clothes to live as human beings," and "My children need a color TV set."

In the case of the need statements of ordinary language, the possibility of cross-classification cannot be entirely ruled out. As Brian Barry[14] has quite rightly pointed out, every need statement of the form "A needs X" is incomplete, and must be completed in the form "A needs X in order to do (or have) Y." Even what I call "intrinsic" and "original" need statements are not quite free from this inarticulate or hidden (form-) condition. Somewhat like ordinary language, needs are society-bound and also bear the stamp of time. Luxuries of the last generation are regarded as bare necessities of life by the present generation. Certain needs, such as those of food and drink, are grounded in our body system; certain needs are borrowed from others' (contemporary peoples') value schedules, such as those of enjoying a particular level of consumption and of performing particular types of productive work (to the exclusion of others). To make the characterization of needs more concrete, one may try to relate them to "human nature" and refer to the Marxist or the Freudian theories on the matter. But in all cases, we come across one genuine difficulty: needs are self-exceeding or dynamic both in relation to the individual and society. Even one's bodily needs, especially the quality of the goods which can satisfy those needs, undergo change and are not static.

Advancement of technology and exposure to modern communication systems have a silent but continuing influence on our needs and values, one influencing and being influenced by the other.

All these considerations highlight the difficulties involved in the precise determination of both desert and needs, especially the latter. But this is not to deny the relevance of the concept of need to arrive at a rational criterion of justice. Relativity of needs might lead one to believe that inequality is perhaps bound to be an element of a just decision. However, that is not the case. Justice does not command that all needs of all men should be given equal weight. If some men, because of their education or imagination, can transcend the bounds of their time (history) and place (society) and present a unique value schedule, listing the goods and services that they sincerely feel should be recognized by a concerned society, I think it would not be just on the part of society to oblige them, even if it can. What justice demands is the *equality of concern*: needs of all men deserve the earnest and rational attention of society. When it comes to the question of recognition of needs, a stratified society (marked by inequality) would be well-advised to accord priority to original needs (of food and house) over imitative needs (of a color TV set) and to original needs of the worst-off group over better-off. This judgment, though not precisely formulated, seems to be quite consistent with the principle of justice. In other words, *equality of concern* and *inequality of recognition* are both consistent components of a just decision. In fact, it is in-depth judgment marked by the equality of concern that enables one to realize the rationality and advisability of the inequality of recognition.

That neither the theory of social contract nor that of natural rights is out of fashion is evident from John Rawls' careful and comprehensive work, *A Theory of Justice.*[15] Instead of "the natural state of society," he uses the term "original position" to denote a hypothetical social situation in which the persons, the contracting parties, who are ordinary human beings (neither Hobbesian savages nor Rousseauist angels), are characterized by rational self-interest and concerned only with their (family's) share of the primary social goods, such as wealth, income, powers, self-respect, and liberty. Moreover, they are aware of each others' capacities and limitations, of the general laws of contemporary society and ethics, are "mutually disinterested," accept their position of equality, and operate behind a veil of ignorance. The original position is a status quo and, therefore, it is claimed, "the fundamental agreements reached in it are fair."

The concept of original position is used by Rawls in two related ways, *expository* and *justificatory*. He analyzes and defines the contracting parties and conditions of the original position in such a way that he first feels justified in asserting that it is the ideal initial choice situation, and then he comes forward with the claim that the choice of the principles of justice made therein are indeed most rational and justifiable. Before we point out the weakness of this logic of choice, let us look into his formulations of the principles chosen:

(1) Each person is to have an equal right to the most extensive total system of equal basic liberties compatible with a similar system of liberty for all. (2) Social and economic inequalities are to be arranged so that they are both: (a) to the greatest benefit of the least advantaged, consistent with the just savings principle, and (b) attached to offices and positions open to all under the conditions of fair equality of opportunity.[16]

Rawls also refers to two priority rules: Liberty can be restricted only for the sake of liberty; "the second principle of justice is lexically prior to the principle of efficiency and to that of maximizing the sum of advantages; and fair opportunity is prior to the difference principle." Lexical or serial ordering is intended to ensure that "a principle does not come into play until those previous to it are either fully met or do not apply." The object of the priority rules is to protect the interests of the least favored, as recipients of all primary goods, liberty and opportunity, income and wealth, and the bases of self-respect. And by implication, priority rules both presuppose and recognize the continued existence of hierarchical society.

Rawls' is a natural right-based theory of justice. In the original position, the basic liberties of the contracting parties are taken for granted and their rights are not subject to political bargaining or to the utilitarian calculus of social welfare. Unlike the utilitarian, he is not prepared to consider natural rights as of secondary importance, for these are inviolably based on justice and not on utility. Satisfaction of desire, as such, is of no value to the contractarian; he relates satisfaction to the question of right and also to what flows out of it. In justice as fairness, the question of good is subordinate to that of right; whatever offends or turns out to be inconsistent with the principles of justice would be disallowed. Since the contracting parties are supposed to be operating under a veil of ignorance, one does not know others' motives, propensities, and attitudes, and the consequences thereof. And that provides an additional reason for the contractarian to assert that nothing should be allowed at the initial stage that proves inconsistent with the first principles of ethics, the basis of justice as fairness. The difference between the contractarian and the utilitarian is claimed to be basic by the former; one thinks of a well-ordered society as a scheme of cooperation for mutual benefit governed by the principle of justice as fairness, the other as the efficient management of the material and human resources of society to ensure maximum aggregative satisfaction of desires as aggregated by a hypothetical *impartial spectator* on the basis of given individual systems of desires.

Rawls is not ready to compromise on the matter of principles like liberty and equality on the dubious utilitarian ground that it would result in aggregative benefit unless, of course, his priority rules are satisfied. Once the contracting parties agree to submit to the priority rules, that proves not only mutually advantageous to *all* concerned in their cooperative venture, but also those, who voluntarily restrict their liberties, acquire a *right* to a similar acquiescence on the part of those who have benefited from their submission. This is how the principles of fairness put both the benefactors and beneficiaries under reciprocal *obligations* individually. In addition, as equal moral persons, the contracting parties are required to do certain *natural duties* to support and to comply with just institutions that exist and apply to them; and since this requirement is unconditional and not concerned with voluntary acts, the related duties are called natural and thus distinguished from *obligations*.

From our limited context, Rawls' theory appears to suffer from at least one main defect. In spite of its admirable comprehensiveness, the concealed sociological assumptions and ideological leanings of Rawls' theory, when disclosed, make its application very restrictive and its claim to generality spurious.

Rawls claims that by assuming certain general desires, such as the desire for primary social goods, suitably defining the original position, and accepting the agreements arrived at that position as a basis, he has succeeded in showing how his theory of justice is independent of circumstantial relativity.[17] Again, this claim seems to me untenable.

The contractarian theory of justice is individualistic in its formulation of both the original position and the principles of justice. To minimize the effects of individualism, diverse psychological propensities, value- and preference-schedules, reference has been made to an Archimedean point from which the institutional arrangement necessary for distributive justice is appraised and also to the ideal of a person whose rational plan of life and demands for goods are accepted as typical of others' and as the basis for agreements between all leading to the principles of justice. In spite of Rawls' protestations to the contrary, it is clear that his concept of the ideal of a person is a priori, and his reference to Kant on this point has not proved very helpful, for Kant's concept of the rational self itself is open to the charge of a priorism. Unevenly open to the influences of social institutions, the demands for goods of different individuals are not really alike.

The ideal of a person is an oversimplifying methodological assumption. It is the concept of the good of such a person and his demands for goods that the Rawlsian theory of justice presupposes. To ensure the unanimity of choice of the individuals in the original position, Rawls substitutes for the real individual of flesh and blood an ideal, Kantian-type person. Individualism is compromised for the sake of unanimity. Then it is to be justified on the ground of justice, the priority of justice over efficiency and that of liberty over social and economic advantages. On scrutiny, the justification turns out to be more imaginary than real; for in the real-life situation, the individuals are organized in different groups or classes and, as such, their demands for goods and plans of life prove considerably different, if not conflicting. Elements of difference and conflict are, in fact, accommodated or tolerated in the institutional arrangement and recognized from the Archimedean standpoint. That means that the scheme of cooperation envisaged in the original position seeks to legitimize social conflict and economic competition.

To meet the criticism against legitimized conflict and competition, the contractarian argues that they follow from the original agreements and are in accord with the principles of justice. One can be sure that individualism and unanimity do not go together. When it is claimed that they do, what is meant is either that individualism is sustained by a hidden universalism or that the unanimity principle is spurious. Basically, this claim dilutes the value of the principles of liberty and equality.

We may note how Rawls' rider to the principle of liberty, the unequal worth of it for the people concerned, takes away the substantial value of the principle and allows its distribution as a primary good among the intended beneficiaries to be unequal. Apparently this idea does not disturb Rawls very much, for he seems to believe that *if* the basic (political) liberties of the citizens (the right to vote and to be eligible for public office, freedom of speech and association, freedom of the person and from arbitrary arrest, and the right to hold personal property) are established, the citizens would not be inclined to trade them off with socioeconomic advantages. If the citizens were so inclined, the assumption would be that the basic rights and liberties definitive of a just society had been effectively established.

I do not question these arguments (in the form of assumptions) as such. My difficulty lies elsewhere: the effective establishment of these rights and liberties itself is contingent upon the attainment of a certain level of economic well-being. I do appreciate Rawls' giving priority to the liberty principle over the inequality principle in his *theory* of justice; but when it comes to the question of its *practice*, I do not quite see in the context of developing countries how the socioeconomically worse-off people could be benefited by it in the intended manner. It seems that the developed democratic and capitalist countries of West Europe and North America, especially the United States, provide the sociological and ideological backdrop for Rawls' principles and their lexical priority. According to Rawls, the primacy of the liberty principle is nonnegotiable, except for the sake of liberty itself, because "a departure from the institutions of equal liberty...cannot be justified by, or compensated for, by greater social and economic advantages." My experience of the developing countries is that the very "institutions of equal liberty" are in many cases nonexistent and the question of any departure from them does not arise at all. What is more important to note here is that the said nonexistence is mainly due to the wide social and economic gap and conflict between different classes and groups. Obviously Rawls would try to meet this point of criticism by pointing out the distinction he draws between the liberty principles from the standpoint of the original position and the stage when the basic liberties have been effectively established. I note Rawls' defense of the denial of equal liberty "to raise the level of civilization so that in due course these freedoms can be enjoyed."[18]

Several questions remain to be answered. Why does Rawls propose to impose restrictions only on fundamental liberties to the exclusion of other, nonfundamental, liberties, and then on the condition that the former must be legally recognized? We may note that legal recognition of what are and are not fundamental is a very shifting affair, and often the shift is brought about by and in the interests of the ruling groups. Why does Rawls propose to make unequal distribution of liberties conditional on its acceptability to those with the lesser liberty? I raise this question because the people with the lesser liberty have nothing to lose by objecting to the proposed unequal distribution of liberties unless, of course, they believe that it would further reduce their share of liberties. In the Rawlsian scheme of justice principles, this belief has hardly any place, for one must assume that the lexically prior rule, "a less extensive liberty must strengthen the total system of liberty shared by all," has already been applied. The fact that this belief has no place in the scheme does not mean that it has not been entertained. A system consisting of different and partially conflicting groups, I suspect, cannot satisfy these requirements and seems too unrealistic to be accepted by "those with the lesser liberty."

The Rawlsian scheme of social cooperation in the pursuit of justice is still unworkable in many parts of the world. This, however, is not to deny the imagination and ingenuity underlying the scheme itself. Rawls' principles of justice and the priority rules are basically *conservative* in their inspiration, designed to conserve the existing liberties of the groups and at the same time to reflect an awareness of the necessity for a just redistribution of the primary goods. The scheme of cooperation he envisages for the purpose rests on the *practical* compatibility of the first principle (of equal right of all to equal basic liberties) with the second principle (of social and economic inequalities weighted somewhat in favor of the least advantaged but qualified by the rule of unequal worth of liberties). Rawls' arguments and examples give one the distinct impression that his primary interest is to show the *theoretical* compatibility of the two principles. When facts threaten the first principle, he compromises his egalitarian position by making the worth of liberty unequal, apparently forgetting in the process the fact that inequalities in the worth of liberty are primarily due to significant second principle inequalities. No pain is spared to show that significant inequalities resulting from private ownership of the means of production are compatible with justice as fairness.

It seems to be that natural rights are not as natural as Hobbes, Locke, and Rawls try to make us believe, nor are human rights as universal as their protagonists preach. These theorists are motivated by a noble consideration—to provide a moral and an egalitarian basis for the definition and enlargement of human rights and liberties. They share an antipathy toward legal positivism, the view advocating, among other things, that the substance and scope of human rights and liberties should be determined by the laws of the land enacted by the competent authority and not left to speculative or controversial ethical principles. As we have seen, they operate at two levels: first they construct their models of the state of nature or of the original position, and then derive from these the substance and scope of natural rights. Outwardly, the models appear abstract and unrelated to the sociohistorical contexts in which they were conceived and constructed, but careful analysis of their elements and assumptions reveals their concealed, intended, and true character. These models are somewhat like legal fictions and serve a heuristic or an *expository* purpose. One might ask "why they resort to model construction technique instead of description of appropriate sociohistorical contexts for the purpose of derivation and definition of natural rights. Perhaps it is because of the well-known difficulty that from the *description* of an existing situation nothing very *general*, certainly not the *ideal* principles of justice, liberty, and human rights, could be derived, and one suspects—is almost sure—that the natural right theorists had deliberately imagined the *natural* in such a way that the *ideal* could be derived from it. Whether this derivation is defensible or not is a separate question; its motivation at least is clear, and that is *justificatory*.

Justification in this type of theory is designed to work in two (often very related) ways: *direct deductive* and *inverse deductive*. In the former case, the elements and assumptions of the model of the natural state or the original position are formulated in such a manner that the intended rights and liberties could be directly deduced from them. In the latter case, first an existing state of affairs is described, and then in order to justify it an inverse deductive reference is made to the model embodying the ideal. Any of these two methods could be used for both conservative or progressive purposes. Whereas Hobbes uses an inverse deductive method to defend a relatively conservative theory of rights, Rawls follows a direct deductive method to defend a relatively egalitarian one. Neither of them seems to be interested in using a *critical deductive*[19] method, which can bring about a creative match between existing facts and ideal principles without forcing one into another and into a sort of dogmatism, or without resorting to open-ended ad hoc-ism.

As we have observed, Hobbes defends only a narrow set of rights and liberties of the person, the right to live and the liberty to refuse to give self-incriminating evidence. Locke argues for a relatively broader set of rights and liberties. Mill defends equal liberties of thought, action, and expression primarily along the lines of individualism and strongly advises the state not to intervene in matters that can be managed by the citizens unless, of course, intervention becomes unavoidable in the public interest. Although these liberal thinkers—liberal in varying degrees—stand for more or less equality in the political sphere and try to justify it by contractarian or utilitarian arguments, they find nothing wrong in the socioeconomic inequalities entailed by their justificatory arguments. The theoretical framework of liberalism has been designed so that political equality and socioeconomic inequalities can coexist. One wonders to what extent this theoretically contemplated coexistence can be effected in practice and assuming it can be, whether it proves peaceful. This query is very relevant, for the underlying assumption of the liberal thinkers is very questionable—that political institutions, their structure, and function can be considered in isolation from the socioeconomic conditions.

Even Rawls' theory does not appear to be entirely free from this assumption. As we have observed, the *special* conception of justice, which, given priority over equality of liberty, applies only when a society has attained a certain level of material well-being. Otherwise, in the underdeveloped material conditions of a society, the *general* conception applies and the difference (inequality) principle governs the distribution of all social goods, including liberty. It has, however, to be admitted in fairness to Rawls that in his theory at least an attempt has been made to establish a weak connection between the socioeconomic conditions and the realizability of equal liberty. If this attempt has not yielded a sufficiently encouraging and concrete result, it is because of the author's scheme of work itself, which has made it impossible for him to take adequate note of the diverse sociological perspectives of enactment and administration of law ensuring peace. In his understandable eagerness to construct a "moral geometry" around the concept of justice, he has resorted to an abstractionist strategy without looking into diverse, puzzling, and interesting sociological contexts of justice that perhaps might threaten his "clear and coherent" geometry. The only real society which apparently has weighed on his mind (should I say "from behind the veil of strategic ignorance"?) is the American one.

I have already mentioned that to understand correctly the import of the principles of justice, and particularly those of social and economic justice, we are required to look into the sociological context in which they are discussed. The context may be considered diachronically or synchronically. To my mind, the major diachronic or historical contexts are the primitive (egalitarian) society, the feudal (hierarchical) society, the market (competitive capitalist) society, and the socialist (cooperative-conflict) society; and the major synchronic ones are the First World (one can take the United States as its paradigm), the Second World (USSR), and the Third World (India). Typological classification is bound to be approximate and therefore inexact. The resulting methodological defect can be substantially overcome by perceptive placement and measurement of the individual cases within the type. In each of the context-types there are bound to be mixed and marginal cases. For example, in the First World there are Second World and Third World characteristics; similarly in both the Second World and the Third World one can identify the characteristics of each. Partial heterogeneous and overlapping characteristics of the context-types suggest two apparently different, but basically consistent, phenomena: (1) principles of justice obtained in a context-type have to be lexically ordered and suitably qualified by appropriate rules so that they can prove perceptive to the diverse needs of the type; and (2) every set of principles, although characteristically useful in and applicable to a particular context-type, has extracontextual reference and significance. This is not my prescription regarding the nature and scope of the principles of justice. This is, in fact, what we do find in the (preenactment) "data" of law, public opinions regarding desert, need, and contribution of the different segments of the public, moral sentiments of the people, the existing rules of social conflict, and cooperation. In most cases social customs, conventions, and practices ripen into laws through legislative recognition and formulation. I hold this view because I find much substance in what sociological jurists like F. K. v. Savigny, as distinguished from positivist ones like Jeremy Bentham and John Austin, have to say on the nature of law and the principles of justice. This, however, does not mean an extreme form of cultural relativism advocated by anthropologists like E. A. Westermarck.

Admissibility of rights presupposes certain institutions and rules and also some criterion, such as desert or need, to evaluate the social goods for distribution. But the very concepts of desert, need, and social goods are differentially *used* in, say, primitive societies and market societies. In a market society, a man's ownership rights to hold, enjoy, and dispose of a given piece of land, are absolute and exclusive. But in a primitive society the rights of ownership of land may belong inclusively to several persons at the same time. One may lose one's right simply because one changes one's place of residence. In a feudal society, the ownership rights *notionally* belong to the king or, in some cases, the landlord, while the rights of possession and enjoyment *actually* belong to the tenant subject to his fulfillment of certain conditions. What happens in a hierarchical feudal society almost as a matter of rule is that different types of rights for different sets of people are simultaneously valid in respect to the same property. This can be found occasionally also in a primitive society. The Samoan tribal chief, for example, retains his residual right of ownership over a piece of land, which in fact is used by another person; but if the latter changes his place of residence, the right to dispose of the property reverts to the village headman.[20] This sort of hierarchical rights has outgrown both the tribal and the feudal societies and can be observed in the modern market societies as well. An owner of real estate can lease out his property to the lessee who, in turn, if not otherwise prohibited, can rent it out to the tenant; so, in relation to the same property three different rights (ownership, leasehold, and tenancy) become simultaneously valid and enjoyable. The point is what I have already said before: the analogies of a particular sort of rights found in one context-type may be discovered in other context-types, but on close examination of the contents and conditions of these rights it would be found that they are indeed analogous and not identical.

In primitive societies one's property rights may be overridden by others' individual needs or by social need in general. If one is not using one's means and instruments of gathering food, others in need are free to use them as their properties. The exercise of this right is not contingent upon the owner's consent (as in the case of market societies), kindness (as in the case of feudal societies), or comradery (as in the case of socialist societies). In fact, to be helpful, kind, and even generous to the needy is a duty of a primitive man and; the former has a right to draw upon the latter's kindness or generosity. Thus in a primitive context-type it is very *natural* for the needy to tell his fellow beings, "You are bound to be kind and generous to me." But then "kind" and "generous" are being used in a different sense than ours. The "benefactor's" duties and the "beneficiary's" rights in these cases are primarily reflective of *social needs* (needs of a people living almost at a subsistence level) and *not* of a moral *ideal of equality* as it is ordinarily understood in a market society. Consequently, one would be advised to use such neutral expressions as the "recipient's rights" and the "giver's duties." Obviously this game of translation of society(language)-bound words and expressions cannot be played fruitfully beyond a point.

The same point can be illustrated with reference to the issue of distribution. Primitive people follow an egalitarian *practice* in the distribution or divisions of the spoils of hunting and fishing expeditions. The rules governing the distribution are widely different; for example, one can deserve and get one's equal share by joining the expedition, by lending one's canoe or weapon for the purpose, by waiting to receive the returning expedition party on the seashore or at the outskirt of village, or simply on the ground that one needs it. This shows that the rules of distribution are not only egalitarian but also liberal. And it is very natural for tribal people haunted by constant scarcities to frame and follow the rules of desert and needs with a liberal and distinct egalitarian bias. But, I think it would be wrong to give a utilitarian interpretation to the whole thing, for the necessary moral motivation, on which Mill would have insisted, is not there. Nor is it a matter of following the *principle* of distributive justice as fairness: from the primitive's point of view perhaps it is nothing more than a case of following the rule of social *practice.*

Perhaps it can be better understood in terms of face-to-face or dominantly personalized (as distinguished from dominantly institutionalized) human relationships. In this context-type familiarity, kinship, and emotional involvement mark the interpersonal relationships, whereas in the market context-type these relationships mediated by a large number of conflicting institutions tends to become more and more impersonal and anonymous. In a society that is not well institutionalized, people's rights are neither clearly defined nor easily enforceable. Endless diversity of rules, lack of definition, and codification of those customary rules help the authority to settle disputes overnight, but they render the administration of justice (in the modern sense) very difficult. When a primitive man is kind or generous to a fellow man in need, it is a sort of customary or habitual response, and therefore one can characterize it as natural. When customary and habitual practices can substantially take care of disputes and conflicts, judicial authority has minimal responsibility to discharge and society is relatively homogenous. However, this does not mean that within the primitive society one cannot draw any distinction between moral right and customary right or between customary right and legal right. Perhaps one can; but, I think, those distinctions would be quite different from our understanding. In primitive society the line of distinction between practice and principles is often very thin and unclear, the former seems to be imbued with the latter. The point made earlier that natural rights, however unrealistic they might sound, have a definite *moral* undertone, lends them an air of acceptability, even if they are not immediately accepted.

Both the direct human relationships and the homogeneity that mark primitive society are largely missing in feudal society. I am talking of the Indian feudal society that existed until the eighteenth century. The main characteristic of this type of society, hierarchical order, emanated from a series of contracts, explicit or implicit. Under the king, a large number of hierarchically arranged statuses formed the pyramid of the social structure; the intermediate statuses were held by various noblemen—*subadar* (the provincial governor), *zamidar* or *bhumidar* (the big landlord), *talukdar* or *jotdar* (the small landlord); and at the bottom were the *bargadar* (the tenant), the landless peasant, and the bonded laborer. The persons of the first four categories held their statuses and enjoyed their titles as the result of explicit contract; the statuses of the persons belonging to the lowest two categories were governed by implicit contract. Each piece of land was subject to several sets of property rights and owned by the corresponding right-holders, from the tenant who actually cultivated the land, through the landlord to whom he owed service, to the landlord of that landlord, and so on. Within this general structure, the rights of a person were largely determined by custom and partly by law, and justice consisted of the protection of the rights by means of both law and custom, especially the latter. Feudal justice meant preservation of the status quo and therefore inequality. Attempts have been made to justify this inequality referring to the caste system and such scriptures as *Manu-Saṁhitā* and *Dharma-śastra*, and by pointing out how the hierarchical order imparts stability to the social system, enabling it to withstand external shocks and to absorb or regulate internal convulsions. However, in spite of its inegalitarian and rigid characteristics, feudal society did allow the holders of the different statuses to establish personal relationships and to foster a sense of mutual obligations. To a limited extent status mobility was also observed. By rendering an extraordinary service, civil or war, to the king or a superior, one could improve one's rank, add to a landed estate, or get exemption from the payment of usual revenue. But by and large, feudal society was marked by its stable hierarchy of rights and duties and highly unequal liberty.

To understand the true nature of our rights, liberties, and what is meant by justice, one has to look into the complex structure of our social system, which consists of heterogeneous subsystems (primitive, feudal, and market) and their interaction. Since we are already familiar with the main characteristics of primitive and feudal societies, let us have a quick look at the market (early capitalist) society for our limited purpose. In a real-life situation, a market society starts operating against the background of the vertically divided classes of feudal society, disturbing and dislodging the people from their fixed place in feudal hierarchy, destroying obligations of primitive kinship and traditional status. All are theoretically equal in the eye of the law, and positions are determined by contracts and exchanges, by the market forces, and not by birth or the superior's desire. Gradual breakdown of the old hierarchical structure paves the way for the rise of liberalism and individualism. Individuals are free to choose between their professions, to buy and sell their produce (work and worth) in the market, to form associations and companies, to gain wealth and prestige. These market operations result in division of labor and unequal distribution of social goods, and further encourage individualism. Justification of individualism, a product of market society, was sought in Europe on the theory that men are born free and equal, possessing rights derived from their inherent natural capacities. Market culture and its associated ideas were brought into India and taken to the other parts of the world by the imperial powers. A new concept of justice is brought into operation by market society, and that is the requital of desert. Man makes himself, and the basis of his desert—abilities, efforts, and skills —is his own, self-formed character. Man makes himself mainly for others, and the worth of his abilities is determined by the market. The market is the ultimate desert-definer. The inequality of hierarchical society is gradually replaced by the equality of the marketplace. The process starts in the metropolitan towns, the centers of trade and industry. In the Indian context, the market society and its culture first appeared in the towns like Calcutta, Madras, and Bombay.

While the vanishing feudal features still exist in rural India, despite all land reform acts, a new form of society—a developed capitalistic form—is steadily emerging. The workers, professionals, and administrators are becoming more and more organized through their trade unions and service associations, and have considerably improved their bargaining capacity and, in many cases, pay scales and service conditions. In contrast, the unorganized workers, especially the agricultural laborers, are very poorly paid. In their case the minimum wage act provisions are hardly implemented; they have no leave provision; in the off-season they are literally unemployed; the talk of pensionary or old-age benefits does not make any sense for them; and, one must bear in mind, they are the single largest section of the Indian population. Of course, they *deserve* a better deal, higher wages, better service, and living conditions. Their *desert* has to be estimated in terms of the service they render to satisfy the *needs* of the society as a whole, especially those of the organized sector of the economy. When the social and economic conditions are very unequal, as they are in our society, which is in part highly organized and in part totally unorganized, equity demands that market forces should not be allowed to determine the desert of the worse-off. So in a complex society like ours, the principles of desert and need have to be suitably reconciled. But to achieve this objective, the path is beset with numerous difficulties: the desert claims of the better-off are seriously objected to and at times even bitterly opposed by the worse-off, and the needs of the latter are not ordinarily appreciated or agreed to by the former. Obviously, the criteria of their judgments are not the same. Despite this, the compulsion of market society keeps them tied together by a love-and-hate relationship and engaged in a conflict-and-cooperation situation.

In the process, the market society itself undergoes change and the subsocieties tend to regroup into different and less heterogeneous classes—the working class organized under trade unions, the middle class under service associations, and the owner-entrepreneurial class under chambers of commerce. Relatively better organized and stronger groups favor the idea that the market should determine everyone's desert and that the outcome would then be fair and just, whereas relatively weaker groups want desert to be socially estimated and feel they should not be asked to sacrifice or suffer for being disadvantageously placed in a highly unequal competitive situation.

The point that I am making diachronically, that is, by referring the questions of rights, duties, and justice to the developing and different historical types of society, can be made out synchronically as well, by referring the same questions to the different types of society of the contemporary world—developed and developing. Neither of these two types is homogenous; for example, developed countries like the USA and the USSR, differ in many important respects; developing countries like India and China also differ on such issues as the rights and duties of the people and the desiderata of a just society.

The contemporary societies of the world have often been classified under three headings—First World (represented by the United States), Second World (represented by the USSR), and the Third World (represented by India).[21] Making allowance for their internal unevenness, this appears to be the most satisfactory classification from our point of view.

It is very interesting to note how human rights and justice are recognized and followed in the three different worlds and at three different levels—academic, social, and legal. It would be equally instructive to note the gap between the profession and practice of the official policies on these matters. The gap is particularly evident in what the representative states of the three worlds profess to the outside world and what they practice within their own territory. Even after the UN Declaration of Human Rights (1948), which clearly recognizes the inherent dignity, equality, and inalienable rights of all members of the human family as the foundation of freedom, justice, and peace in the world, we have witnessed, apart from the cold war between the First World and the Second World, the tragic incidents of Hungary, Czechoslovakia, and Poland, and the hot wars of Korea, the Middle East, Algeria, Vietnam, Bangladesh, and Angola.

War means negation of all human rights. Even without war, human rights are often very seriously threatened. During the days of John Foster Dulles, the U.S. administration kept a suspicious eye on many leftist thinkers and activists, and some of them were harassed and persecuted. Even after the Helsinki Declaration, a number of dissident scientists and artists in the Second World have been harassed or jailed. Since the official charges against them are not open to public verification, one can hardly ascertain their substance, if any.

Although many of us are critical of the negative attitude of the rulers of the Second World toward the dissident defenders of human rights and liberties, and of the continued positive attitude of the rulers of the First World toward some dictatorial regimes, especially the military treaty allies, we cannot deny that the state of human rights in most Third World nations is indeed lamentable. In the name of national security and rapid economic development, one-party rule, suppression of the opposition, preventive detention, detention without trial, and denial of justice and civil liberties have become very common.

One might say that if we accept, as I do, the contextualist, the above distortions of human rights and denial of justice can hardly be criticized. But this is wrong. My attempt to understand and explain rights, including human rights and justice, in terms of their sociological context should not be taken as a sort of justification. *Explanation* may be, but is not necessarily, *justification.*When a political theorist of the First World says that traditional political and civil rights can be readily secured by legislation restraining the government's executive arm, he assumes uncritically that what is possible in a country like the United Kingdom or the United States is also possible in a country like Pakistan or the USSR. The difference in the levels of the political and civil rights actually available to the peoples of the three worlds first has to be understood and explained in terms of their different sociological contexts (including the economic, ideological, and morphological conditions). All things being equal, the countries where experiments with constitutional democratic government started in the seventeenth or eighteenth century and have struck roots are certainly placed in an advantageous position in the matter of granting civil rights to their citizens. But whether the countries of the Second World and the Third World should blindly follow the First World in this respect without assessing their own social needs and their order of priority is, of course, a separate question.

Why this question is separate becomes clear when one tries to settle the disputes between the people and the government of a developing country over such social and economic rights as "the right to work" and "the right to social security." In one sense, it seems obvious that by making suitable laws a government can secure for its citizens both civil and political rights and also social and economic rights. But before making such laws, the concerned government cannot afford to ignore practical conditions, such as social climate and executive ability, and economic resources. The government of China, for example, because of its present political system and perhaps the organized public opinion, cannot allow its citizens to enjoy "the right to freedom of opinion and expression...[including] freedom to hold opinions without interference and to seek, receive and impart information and ideas through any media" (Article 19, UN Human Rights Declaration, 1948). If the government of China fails in one respect (civil and political rights) for one reason, the government of India fails in another respect (genuinely universal moral rights) for another reason. The latter, for example, simply does not have the resources that could enable it to provide each of the 662 million people of India "a standard of living adequate for the health and well being of himself and of his family, including food, clothing, housing and medical care and necessary social services, and the right to security in the event of unemployment, sickness, disability, widowhood, old age or other lack of livelihood in circumstances beyond his control" (Article 25).

In these cases, contexts are being cited as explanatory reasons for the failure of the concerned countries to conform to "a common standard of achievement for all people and all nations." The failure is not confined to the nations of the Second World, marked by the rigors of proletarian dictatorship and one-party rule, and of the Third World, marked by poverty, low level of education and political consciousness, and different forms of authoritarianism; the failure exists also in the nations of the First World who are not only committed in principle to extend all forms of international cooperation as enjoined by several UN and UNCTAD declarations, but also are placed in the best position technologically and financially to implement the principle. The works of such economists as Raul Prebisch and Albert Hirschman have convincingly shown the untenability of the classic assumption that development following from technological innovation will *automatically* benefit industrialized and nonindustrialized nations alike through the mechanism of free trade and are also of the view that the cost factor of modernization through foreign capital might not prove increasingly differential. Under the circumstances, what is needed to establish a rational world order in which human rights can be realized and enjoyed is an economically *just form* of international cooperation; the *market form* of it will not do, for its effects are inherently differential. The existing world "order" is patently unjust in both the Rawlsian and the Marxist senses: its inegalitarian structure, the growing gap between the poor and rich nations, is not for the ultimate benefit of the former. Growing inequalities entail even more unequal distribution of primary social goods such as liberties and self-respect.

The structural conditions necessary for the realization of human rights are, in most nations of the world, minimal and in some cases almost absent. Even so we feel morally inclined to prescribe human rights for all people and all nations. Underlying this moral inclination there are two considerations.[22] First, when we make a moral judgment we make it *about* something, in this case human rights, and therefore cannot logically afford to ignore the *relevant* and *genuine* (as distinguished from spurious) facts constituting the context of realizing and enjoying the concerned human rights. When we prescribe that a course of action should be followed or that some rights should be enjoyed by some persons in a particular situation, we take into account both the *abilities and desires of the concerned persons* and also the *possible states of affairs* in the situation. The relation between the two is weak but operative. The former is influenced but not determined by the latter. Factual components of a context certainly have a bearing on what (for example, a range of primary goods) the persons in a given social situation can reasonably expect and enjoy, but, I agree, there is no strong logical relation between the two. The "elastic" character of this relation becomes clear when one recalls that the factual components of a context include, among other things, common psychological and behavioral traits, customs, conventions, and insituations of certain groups of persons. Second, the elastic character of this relation between the social context and human rights of the "context-bound" persons can be used as a ground for generalizing the principles governing the realization and enjoyment of those rights. Social context performs three roles: (1) it helps us to understand how certain human rights originated in it and can reasonably be enjoyed within its boundary, (2) how further human rights, together with the existing ones, can be realized and enjoyed, and (3) how the human rights, realizable and enjoyable within one social context can be gradually generalized beyond it.

To say human rights are gradually generalizable is not to say these rights are universal. A moral judgment involves a sort of evaluation of what the judgment is about: the principles used in evaluation are not the product of, but are influenced by, the context in which the moral judgment is made. Undoubtedly a significant part of our dispositions, ideas, and actions have been historically influenced by our society, and at the same time it has to be admitted to an equally significant extent that our ideas and ideals do exceed the boundary of the society we live in. It is from this perspective, one might say from the point of view of man as an ambiguous creature, that one has to understand the wide gap between the ideals of human rights embodied in different declarations of human rights and the actual state of affairs obtained in the highly uneven social contexts of the different nations of the three worlds; and yet one must not feel cynical about it. For our commitment to human rights is basically a moral one.[23] On the grounds that these rights remain substantially unrealized and that necessary national effort and international cooperation are not forthcoming, we must not retreat from our commitment: we should, however, review it in the light of the disappointing but instructive experience of the last three decades.

It is evident that both the theoretical and the practical architects of human rights are very conscious of the inherent difficulties of their task. The carefully chosen language and formulations of different declarations are in effect an earnest and a continuous exercise to find *"a common standard of achievement* for all peoples and all nations to *the end* that every individual and every organ of society . . . shall *strive* by teaching and education to promote respect for these rights and freedom and by progressive measures, national and international, to secure their universal and effective recognition and observance" (UN Declaration, 1948, author's emphasis). If previous strivings have not yet proved to be up to the standard and have not brought us nearer to the end, that does not mean either that the standard should be lowered or that the end should be given up. Like the natural rights of the classical and modern contractarians, human rights rest on some "transcendent" moral ideal that can only be partially realized in society; but, instructively, this ideal is becoming generally recognized (at least in principle) as a basic feature of a just world order. Gradually, this recognition of the ideal in principle is likely to percolate down to the level of practice, pointing toward positive legislation and executive implementation. But, then, by that time the ideal of human rights itself will be further broadened, deepened, and redefined. In the pursuit of human rights and justice, perhaps we are well advised to avoid the extremes of positivism and romanticism.

NOTES

1. Thomas Hobbes, *Leviathan*, introduction by A. D. Lindsay, (New York: E. P. Dutton, 1953), ch. 13, p. 66.
2. Ibid., ch. 14, p. 66.
3. Ibid., pp. 66-67.
4. John Locke, *Two Treatises of Government*, ed. Peter Laslett (New York: Cambridge University Press, 1960), p. 75.
5. Ibid., pp. 322-23.
6. Ibid., pp. 58-59 (author's italics).
7. Ibid., pp. 325-26.
8. Ibid., pp. 303-08.
9. Brian Barry, *Political Arguments* (London: Humanities Press, 1965), chap. 3.
10. David Miller, *Social Justice* (London: Clarendon Press, 1976), pp. 22-23.
11. John Stuart Mill, *Utilitarianism: On Liberty; Representative Government*, ed. A. D. Lindsay (London, 1964), p. 46.
12. Henry Sidgwick, *History of Ethics* (London: Macmillan & Co., 1967), p. 284.
13. John Rawls, *A Theory of Justice* (Cambridge, Mass.: Harvard University Press, 1973), sect. 48.
14. Barry, *Political Arguments*, chap. 5.
15. Rawls, *A Theory of Justice*, pp. 11, 28, 32.
16. Ibid., p. 302.
17. Ibid., p. 263.
18. Ibid., pp. 61ff, 542-43.
19. D. P. Chattopadhyaya, *Individuals and Societies: A Methodological Inquiry*, 2d ed. (Calcutta: Scientific Book Agency, 1975), chap. 5.
20. Margaret Mead, *Cooperation and Competition among Primitive Peoples* (Boston: Beacon Press, 1961), p. 292. *See* also A. S. Diamond, *Primitive Law, Past and Present* (London: Methuen, 1971); and M. Gluckman, *Politics Law, and Ritual in Tribal Society* (Oxford: Blackwell, 1965).
21. Irving Louis Horowitz, *Three Worlds of Development* (New York: Oxford University Press, 1972).
22. R. M. Hare, *Freedom and Reason* (New York: Oxford University Press, 1972); *see* also C. I. Lewis, *The Analysis of Knowledge and Valuation* (La Salle, Ill.: Open Court Publishing Co., 1946).
23. D. P. Chattopadhyaya, "Freedom and Human Unity: Ideal and Actual," in *History, Society and Polity* (Delhi: Macmillan Co., 1976), pp. 234-61.

LESLIE ARMOUR —— 11

Human Rights: A Canadian View

In recent years, it has become increasingly common for religious, ethnic, and racial minority groups to demand reparations from the larger society for injustices done to them and to their ancestors. In Canada and in other large pluralistic societies, some important philosophical difficulties have emerged in attempts to adjudicate such compensatory claims. In this chapter, Professor Leslie Armour identifies and clarifies some of these difficulties and proposes a way to help resolve them.

In many modern democracies, Canada among them, the concept of human rights has recently become enveloped in conundrum and enigma.

After more than 200 years in which, in most of Europe and North America, concern was focused on the rights of individuals, attention has turned to the rights of groups—the rights of French Canadians to their language, of Dukhobors to their communal culture, and of blacks to compensatory justice for wrongs done to their progenitors. Group rights and individual rights inevitably clash under our existing arrangements. Actions taken to protect the French language clash with the existing rights of those who prefer to be educated in English; the rights of the extremist fringe of the Dukhobor sect to express its contempt for the material culture through arson and nudity clash with settled notions of property and propriety; and, if black men are to have more room in the sun, someone may have to move over. Between rights of different kinds no ready principle settles disputes and, indeed, the very notion of "groups" poses problems.

In 1960 when Canadians decided to tidy up their constitutional affairs with a bill of rights, most issues seemed clear to the parliamentarians. The "Act for the Recognition and Protection of Human Rights and Fundamental Freedoms" turned out to be very brief.[1] Even with the necessary preambles and clauses repealing old legislation, it fits neatly onto three printed pages of ordinary book size. It may be summarized even more briefly. It guarantees "life, liberty, security of person and enjoyment of property"; promises due legal process and "equality before the law"; and specifies a list of freedoms: freedom of religion, speech, assembly, association, and the press.

This bill of rights was inspired by British tradition, the amended constitution of the United States, and nearly a century of Canadian practice, and it provoked, at the time of its passage, only two kinds of discussion. One dealt with incursions on the doctrine of the supremacy of parliament and the other with the doctrine, embedded in the Universal Declaration of Human Rights adopted by the United Nations General Assembly twelve years earlier, that certain economic rights form essential correlates of the political rights embodied in the Canadian act and its traditional counterparts.

The first of these problems was solved by a compromise: The act said that parliament could not override the Bill of Rights Act unless it expressly said it intended to do so. It was assumed that no government would really dare commit to writing its express intention to violate well-established human rights. But, just in case, the act went on to offer some procedural protections. No law of Canada, it said, shall be construed or applied in any way to authorize arbitrary detention, imprisonment, or exile, to impose cruel or unusual punishment, to deprive anyone of the right to retain and instruct counsel or remedy by way of habeas corpus, to deny protection against "self-incrimination," to abrogate other "constitutional safeguards," or to deny the right to a fair hearing, to be assumed innocent until proven guilty, or to have reasonable bail and the services of an interpreter.

The second issue was postponed. Eight years later, Pierre Trudeau, then the minister of justice, wrote that "the guarantee of such economic rights is desirable and should be an ultimate objective. There are, however, good reasons for putting aside the issue at this stage . . . .It might take considerable time to reach agreement on the rights to be guaranteed and on the feasibility of implementation."[2] In general, there was agreement that such rights must come and those who had agitated for them waited for an opportune time to exploit the real or imagined understanding.

During the debate, little attention was paid to the philosophical concept publicized by T. H. Green and well understood by his Canadian followers, including George Paxton Young and John Clark Murray—that the individual human rights specified in the Act are only abstractions unless they are backed by the capacity to act on them.[3] One must eat before one can think of self-expression. Nearly as obviously, freedom of speech is of limited use in a complicated society without access to the means of public communication. Neither right stands much chance of reasonable and effective exercise without an education.

Less obvious was the fact that debate over the limitation of the powers of parliament was itself, overtly and covertly, a debate about individual and group rights. Overtly, the question was whether or not the community, if it expressed itself through parliament, could override the claims of individuals *and* the claims of groups differently constituted. The issue involved a clash of both groups against individual and group against group. The resultant compromise reflected an obvious uncertainty. Parliament could do what it pleased; but the act made doing some things awkward. It was assumed that they would not be done.

But Trudeau's brief essay of 1968 did contain a hint of something else, for it included a brief reference to "language rights." The British North America Act, still Canada's constitution, specifies a very limited array of such rights. In the federal parliament and in the legislature of the Province of Quebec, the use of French and English is mandatory. But the act says nothing about the language of the workplace or the marketplace. Trudeau suggested a modest extension so that communications between citizens and governments and educational activities would be possible in either language, as a royal commission had recommended.

The British North America Act had made one other provision for "group rights," and other statements had been embodied in earlier legislation. The act had provided for denominational schools supported by public taxation and guaranteed their continuance for those groups that had rights at the time the constitution came into force. Later, those rights were extended. It had been widely thought that the provision guaranteed the continuance of such facilities in the form in which they existed at the material times—for example, that a group in a French Catholic school would be entitled to keep it just as it was. After the turn of the century, when the Ontario government reorganized its school system to the detriment of schools in which instruction was wholly in French, however, the privy council, sitting in London as Canada's final court of appeal, allowed the action in a decision that was far from clear.[4] The decision suggested that only the denominational character of the schools was protected by constitution, but it also held that the extent of the assault on French instruction was limited.

Languages tend to define at least some major and obvious cultural groups, and therefore, language rights have tended to form an increasing concern of French Canadians, Hispanic Americans, Flemings in Belgium, and innumerable other groups. Trudeau's suggestion reflected a widespread concern. But he did not give it clear definition.

Little action, in fact, was taken by the federal authorities, and the eventual result was legislation in the Province of Quebec in 1977, legislation grandly styled the Charter of the French Language.[5] What it did was to turn Quebec into a geographical region within which French is given extensive legal protection as the language of the workplace, the marketplace, and governmental communication outside the legislature. It maintains schools in which instruction is given in English, but one may enroll in them only if one's parents received their basic education in English and in the Province of Quebec. Immigrants of all sorts—numerous in the province—must be educated in French.

The claim is that French would disappear if open competition with English were permitted. Immigrants would tend (and have tended in the past) to seek an education in English for their children. Large corporations would seek to make English the language of the workplace, since their engineering manuals, advertising, and general policy statements are almost always in English if their businesses extend beyond the confines of a single province. The right of a majority in a specific place to defend its culture through its language, it is argued, extends to denying rights to one or more minorities (Quebec has a substantial Italian-speaking community, for instance). The minorities can move, if they wish, to another part of the country where *their* rights may be more likely to be recognized.

But, of course, language is only one of the actual or prospective group rights. Specific legislation originally granted exemption from military service to bodies of religious conscientious objectors. Those exemptions were maintained during the short periods during the two world wars when conscription for military service existed in Canada, though, in pursuit of a more orthodox theory of human rights, it was argued by John Diefenbaker (later the author of the Bill of Rights Act) that the original grants did not accrue to the *groups* in question but only to the individual immigrants who composed those groups.[6] If the Diefenbaker interpretation had stood, the protection would not have extended to World War II, because few if any of the original immigrants would by then have been members of the age group affected by the conscription acts. It should be remembered that, although the then Prime Minister William Lyon Mackenzie King appears to have held that the notion of group rights was quite intelligible and had been intended by the original grants, conscription was, in any case, widely opposed, and the prime minister has accepted it reluctantly himself and only after a national referendum.

Less popular causes did not always fare as well. The legislation under which land for homesteading was originally opened to immigrant claimants provides an example. The act limited the amount of land that an individual might claim and required that, in order to obtain final title to it, the claimant must work the land and make specified improvements. It provided however, that groups might acquire such title collectively and then might acquire title as *groups* by making improvements to the land in general though those improvements might not extend to every plot. This provision was intended apparently for the same groups as the exemption from military service—religious sects whose tenets extended to the communal ownership of land and other property.

When the Dukhobors attempted to make use of the provision, government authorities put various obstacles in the way and most of the Dukhobors migrated to another locale where they bought land and made use of the law of corporations to establish their communal objectives. "Communism," as the Dukhobor practice was called, lacked the popular appeal of pacifism.

These historical cases graphically raise moral principles, and they are connected to legal issues. The legal notion of a person is, after all, of a set of rights and duties as the law dictionaries suggest. One claims one's legal identity under the appropriate headings.

Beneath that legal identity is an experienced set of relations to a community. I know who I am because I know, partly through experience and theory and partly through social agreement, what I am responsible for and what I am not responsible for. I experience the correlations between my decisions and certain results, I theorize about other connections, and I accept still others as social understandings. I decide to press the keys of the typewriter and words appear. I theorize that I am responsible for the births of my children. But we accept this in a context of custom or conventions: I could hold that, when I throw something out the window, God is responsible for its landing on someone's head. He could have deflected the object, warned the victim, or prevented me from doing what I did. (Hobbes and Spinoza, indeed, were inclined to the view that we have a right to do what we do because God gave us the power to do it.) Custom has it, however, that *I* accept responsibility. Convention has it, too, that I accept responsibility for the birth of my children and, for a time, for their actions.

Since I cannot tell by observation *who* acts (do I act or does God act through me?), I cannot tell who I am by watching myself *act*. I must *ascribe* some events to myself, some to you, and some to nature. If I try to find myself inwardly, the self for which I search, of course, runs away: I think about myself but not about the self that is thinking about myself. And of the many things going on outside me, how am I to tell which belong to me, which to you, and which to nature? The option is always there: I can ascribe everything to nature or to God or to you or to blind chance or nothing to any of them. The sense of being myself comes when I adopt effective social conventions and achieve a sense of secure understanding through noticing that we all accept the same conventions, can act on them, and find one another.

My identity, therefore, is, importantly, parisitical on our joint sense of community. There will always be hard cases. We cannot find ourselves in all of our ascribed acts, and sometimes we cannot find *anyone* in a given event: If Smith owns a wharf and rents it to a man with a limited sense of duty, the tenant may, in turn, sublet portions of it to a company whose personnel policies are so bad that it hires a lunatic to drive a crane. The crane driver may kill someone. In life and in law we may not know who is responsible. The lunatic is a lunatic and is excused. The laxness of a personnel policy is far from murder and may not even amount to negligence. The original tenant took a narrow view of his duties but wide definitions are tyrannous. The owner is, apparently, too distant in the causal chain. This case *will* be "hard," for someone will have to pay damages or else the relatives of the victim will have to bear the whole burden of events, which they did not bring on their own heads. But such cases show just how rich our conventions are: We do identify people through the application of such notions as responsibility, negligence, laxness, duty, tyranny, and comprehensibility. But we do it through a set of social understandings.

Without those group understandings, we do not know who we are. It is because black men and white men do not always read the same meanings into the same acts—and because they differ *systematically* in some of those readings—that we think there is more than one culture involved. In a Dukhobor society, some acts that are praiseworthy in other cultures are signs of deep spiritual malaise, that the culture has its own direction, which may well lead to acts that their perpetrators admire and others regard as deeply reprehensible. (A Dukhobor of the Sons of Freedom subsect would, on occasion, regard the burning of his own or another's house as a mark of moral rectitude: the renunciation of the things of the world. He would also regard enlisting in the army to defend his country against a physical threat as profoundly reprehensible, the surrender of the spirit to mere physical force. His orthodox Dukhobor neighbors would support him in the second cause but not in the first, while his non-Dukhobor neighbors would think domestic arson as affront to the unhoused poor and military service an act of public responsibility.)

It is important to see that these moral differences involve actual differences in communal understandings that go into personal identity; a change in one's moral opinion about cases *like these* will involve an actual change in one's basic identity.

The Dukhobor who belonged to the Sons of Freedom sect at the time when it had considerable power and cohesion would have regarded God as responsible for the state of the world in general, including whatever features of it entered into the creation of groups of poor and unhoused people and whatever features of it entered into the making of wars. Men, he would have said, must learn to accept suffering and to transcend it. The notion that one should avoid suffering merely leaves one forever the victim of further oppressions. The Kingdom of Heaven is to be had by piercing the illusion. One's real or spiritual self, therefore, is not to be found in ordinary acts but in the acts, precisely, that are involved in the acceptance of suffering and of self-abnegation. Acts of arson and public nudity in search of the life of the sinless Adam are therefore essential to finding oneself. They are the very reverse of destructive. When such a man gives up these basic beliefs, he changes his identity in a profound way.

The relation of language to self-identity, to be sure, is more problematic than the relation of theology to culture and culture to self-identity. Yet the way in which one sees oneself and gets responses from others is crucial to the process. Some of the elements in this are simple: French and English have personal pronouns with very different implications for the relations which hold between their users. Others are subtle: Different value judgments have been attached to expressions that figure as translations of one another and everything is, therefore, subtly but significantly changed in the process of translation. (Indeed, the motto of the province of Quebec *Je me souviens* translates as "I remember," but the verb is not reflexive in English. Does it have the same meaning? In any case, the motto only makes sense in a deeply traditional society in which the past has metaphysical significance, which it usually does not have for English Canadians.)

If, then, one's identity depends on one's community and its social understandings and one's rights depend on one's identity, the rights are associated with one's community and must extend, somehow, to its protection.

Of course, there must be severe limits on such principles. The principle of individual rights has usually been limited by the need to establish equal rights for others, and the same consideration applies to group rights. That is a weak criterion but, given it, the rights of the Sons of Freedom to practice arson depend, I suppose, on the degree of their isolation and on the possibility that such practices can be rendered consistent with general concerns about human responsibility.

If groups must not impinge unfairly on other groups, what counts as a defensible group? The answer must have at least two parts. First, a bona fide group is one that is intimately involved with the personal identities of an existing and identifiable group of people. Second, such a group cannot be a community devoted to Naziism or a community whose central aim is to put into practice aims like those of the Ku Klux Klan, because such groups are not compatible with the survival of the groups whose claims are equally good.

As we know, the clash comes most frequently with individual rights. To be legitimate, the group must recognize individual rights. Indeed, the limitation must be that the group is willing to take part in a larger society that has as its aim the facilitation of the movement of individuals from one group to another and the protection of the general physical and moral integrity of the individual. If we protect groups and establish group rights, the individual's claims are meliorated and, ultimately, limited by the community, within which he finds himself.

But the claims of groups can only be compared to those of other groups unless we also protect the rights of individuals. We must add something to the general principle that one group may do what it pleases subject to its respect for the claims of other existing groups. For, by itself, this would give us the moral disadvantages of social individualism projected on the larger stage of the claims of groups. Most individualists hold that personal liberties are constrained only by the interests of other actual individuals. But they usually have forgotten possible individuals, the unborn, those who may in the future discern values that we overlook now, and beings outside our ken who may yet have a claim on us. The effect has been to permit the plunder and pillage of resources, for I may claim and exploit whatever has not been claimed by another, whatever belongs to no one, whatever is not needed by anyone now alive if the only limit is that provided by the claims of other existing individuals. Claims of the same kind have been made for nations, which are themselves, as a rule, groups of groups. The result, at that level, is obviously disastrous.

Individualism may be tempered by considering groups, since groups represent *kinds* of individuals and so extend to the possible as well as the actual. But then other limits must be prescribed for groups. There must be a minimum obligation to make possible a process of transfer from one group to another. (That means, among other things, that no group should be impossible to join.)

Groups, if they are to be regulated and to have responsibilities, will have to have resources but, in giving them resources, we may be able to cope with the most vexing questions of our time, the relation of group to individual rights and the question of economic rights. We may see this if we ask how these principles relate to such bitter disputes as those that lie behind such concerns of the American law as those experienced in the *Defunis* and *Bakke* cases. Each of these cases involved group claims to special rights of admission to schools that would train them for professional careers. Defunis and Bakke represent persons outside the claimant groups who, though more qualified than some members of the special groups, were denied admission as a more or less direct consequence of the assignment of group rights.

Suppose, however, we were to establish the rival groups as vested social and *economic* entities. We have usually allowed various public resources—the air and rain,[7] for instance—to go free to those who lowered their value to make a profit. But suppose we held that everyone had an interest in them as a community and that, therefore, every group deserving group rights was entitled to royalties on behalf of its members on the use of those resources and could spend them as a group with the consent of its members for group concerns. Then, for example, a disadvantaged group could contract with a professional school or establish a new one or otherwise use its resources as it saw fit without colliding head-on with the rights of others.

If we demanded that more equality between groups was needed, we could act as we do in analogous cases with respect to individuals. Royalty payments would be taxed. A group whose members averaged $25,000 a year in net earnings could pay more than one whose members averaged $5,000. A system of negative income taxes could transfer funds from one group to the other. Whether a group opted to start its own law school or to add to the endowments of an existing one on condition that its members were admitted would depend on the *group's* reading of the old dispute about "separate but equal." And if the groups to which Defunis and Bakke belong felt threatened by these moves, they could respond in kind, form new groups, or do whatever proved feasible.

How does this bear on such disputes as that in Quebec over the language law? I suppose such a law would be prohibited under such a code of rights.

For what it does is stand in the way of those who would move from one group to another. A condition of moving, say, from the French Catholic group to the English Protestant group is that one should be able to change not only one's religion but one's language as well. Thus, *one* means of protecting the French language would be ruled out. There would be nothing to stop the French language group—or groups in a complex culture like French Canada where one may be French and Catholic, French and Protestant, French and Jewish, and so forth—from offering great advantages, out of its resources, to those who would learn and use French. Indeed, if it were a flourishing society, investing and using its resources wisely, it could create very great advantages.

Such a scheme seems also better than simply stamping on another's apparent rights. The alternative, I fear, is a clash of claims about rights that could, at its very worst, be ultimately destructive to pluralistic societies in the United States and Canada.

In any event, such a proposal enables us to look a little more deeply into the structure of the problem of rights as it now appears. Rights are important, essentially, as the expression of an acceptable balance of power. They specify when and under what circumstances individuals who want to do something shall be protected from interference and under what circumstances it is a public and general duty to aid them in doing so. Most rights codes fall short of specifying the conditions under which the rights in question would actually obtain. Do I have the same "freedom of speech" as the director of the Canadian Broadcasting Corporation or the president of the Columbia Broadcasting System? If not, why not? Do I have the freedom to move from one social group to another? If not, why not?

The answers usually have to do with one of two situations. The first is economic, and the second involves social acceptability. The current method of vesting property assigns broadcasting rights in Canada to a public corporation and to a number of private license holders. Those license holders have a different kind of access to the facilities than do the rest of us. And it does not follow that I have more access to the publicly owned system than to the privately owned one: The "public" in this sense is a political corporation to which access, after all, is also influenced by affluence and, where political influence is effectively prohibited, by the right social connections.

One may alter the balance in these cases only by altering the system of vesting. If we assume that there is a general public interest in the resources we all share, we can vest that interest in a combination of individuals, cities, and cultural groups, and that may be the only way to alter the balance. Such groups, to be sure, would become powerful new "vested interests," capable of trampling on the interests of individuals and of other groups, including the whole human public.

The solution, however, seems to be to vest the group in such a way that would be to their advantage to seek to accommodate individuals rather than to trample on them. Substantially, if the vested royalty income of a group were to depend upon its membership, such groups would find it to their advantage to make membership open as widely as possible. Is it not possible that it would be better for French Canadians to offer advantages to those who chose to speak French than to impose penalties upon those who declined to?

The second problem is not necessarily solved by this means, however much it may be ameliorated. If you are not black, you may not mind being excluded from that cultural group now, but, if it is vested in a certain way, invests its funds wisely, and becomes more powerful, you may mind more and more. The real difficulty is that such a system would require a way of determining which groups are entitled to be vested. The obvious way is to find out if there are a reasonable number of people who want to make their primary identification in a given way. And identifications, as I suggested, run across various lines. In Canada, for instance, the historical lines of distinction have been mainly by language and religion. Although most French Canadians are Roman Catholics and most English Canadians are Protestant, there are many people who do not fall into either group and many for whom the predominant combination does not hold.

Most likely, the result would be that there would be many attempts to launch, and find recruits for, vestable groups, and eventually laws would be necessary to govern the tactics used in recruiting. The test would be effectiveness in promoting some kind of group life; in general, members would find themselves in demand, especially if allowed to split assignable royalty several ways. Surely, "exclusive" groups would develop who declined to invite the general public, and who sought to use their resources to create arenas of special privilege for their members. Perhaps we should put up with them, bearing in mind that we can always use the vesting rules to make it as likely as possible that everyone is in demand from some group. One must notice the dialectic at work here.

The traditional method of vesting had two general properties: Directly or indirectly, vesting was to individuals. (Corporations could be dissolved, in principle, into their shareholders.) And vestment did not generally include the most basic resources, even space itself. It was thus generally acceptable to convert public resources into private gain, and since the system rewarded those who transformed through the application of labor and not those who conserved such resources, the system had a natural expansionist tendency. The effect was virtually certain that there was always more wealth in any given year than there had been the year before so long as wealth was calculated in vestable disposable goods. However, the enrichment was not necessarily of individuals but of something usually called the "economic system" and was expressed often as an increase in the gross national product. The result was to enrich a fictional group represented by "the system," although the individuals in that system might fare very badly or extremely well according to whether or not they were winners or losers in a not very well-established game. A system intended to champion the individual succeeded, in short, very often in championing either fictional groups or unintended real groups.

The alternative, the vesting of groups, tends, in theory at least, to have the reverse effect. Since it creates a demand for individuals as members of those groups, it gives the advantage to those who court individuals; and since it taxes basic resources through a royalty system, it at least gives an advantage to those who conserve such resources. In general, one would expect a better outcome for individuals' rights where the advantage goes to concern for individuals.

NOTES

1. Canada, *An Act for the Establishment and Protection of Human Rights and Fundamental Freedoms*, Statutes of Canada, 1960, ch. 44. For a description *see*, W. S. Tarnapolsky, *The Canadian Bill of Rights*, 2d ed. (Toronto: McClelland and Stewart, 1975).

2. P. E. Trudeau, *A Canadian Charter of Human Rights* (Ottawa: Information Canada, 1963).

3. *See Principles of Political Obligation* (Ann Arbor: University of Michigan, 1967). The point was commonplace in much philosophical writing in Canada in the late nineteenth century.

4. *Roman Catholic Separate Schools of Ottawa* v. *Mackreel* 1917 A.C. 62.

5. Charter of the French Language, *Quebec Official Gazette*, September 1977, pp. 4615-35.

6. It is important to notice that the question of group rights is likely to become more important in time. When promises of exemption from military service were made to the Dukhobors it did not matter whether they were made to them as individuals or as a group. To the next generation, however, the point was obviously crucial. Similarly, in the United States at the time when slaves were maltreated, it did not matter if one considered that the maltreatment applied to individuals or to the group. Now, when compensatory justice is demanded by the heirs to those maltreated then and later, the point is obviously crucial. For an account of the arguments, *see* George Woodcock and Ivan Avakumovic, *The Doukhobors*, (Toronto: McClelland and Stewart, 1977).

7. Contemporary climate control techniques have already made rain merchandising a reality.

TIBOR R. MACHAN* —— 12

On Human Rights, Feudalism and Political Change

Professor Tibor Machan's theory of human rights is a modern development of the traditional natural rights view that originated in the writings of John Locke. In his rights-related defense of private property and of foreign intervention in certain cases of domestic rights violations, he adapts the concept of natural human rights to a discussion of specific feudalistic features of Hungarian society. This analysis offers an illuminating test of the consistency of his theory when its application is made in practical affairs.

Although one of the credentials leading me to write this essay is that I was born and raised in Hungary, there is something paradoxical in expecting human rights to be discussed from a national or ethnic perspective. The simple truth is that a sensible conception of human rights is inherently universalist, transcending all human groupings so as to capture exactly what is required by human nature. As Professor Martin Golding noted some time ago:

For someone to ask me to concede something to him as a human right is implicitly to ask whether I admit the notion of a human community at large, which transcends the various special communities of which I am a member; whether I admit him as a member of this larger community; and whether I admit a conception of a good life for this community.[1]

It may be true, as Richard P. Claude argues, that "preliminary to any movement toward human rights development, the framework of an operative legal system must be securely established."[2] It seems just as correct, however, at least if there are human rights and they are not simply fancy

*I wish to thank the Earhart Foundation, Ann Arbor, Michigan, for supporting my work on this paper and the Reason Foundation for providing me with facilities to carry out my work. The views expressed here are not necessarily reflective of the orientations of these organizations.

ideals we have invented, that no legal system can be regarded as binding upon the citizens within its jurisdiction unless it respects human rights or what amounts to human rights considerations (framed in different language). Claude's point may, of course, be simply than an effective enforcement of the principles of human rights requires an organized government and framework of law. Even this can be disputed on grounds that some people and groups may be competent at protecting and preserving the rights of their members and wise enough to do so justly, without elaborate written legal codes and forces of state. History provides a few examples of this from Ireland in the Middle Ages.[3] But something like adequate force, organized to observe something like due process, would be required to implement the principles and provisions of human rights in any large human community. Without such force, violators could go about with impunity and the system would be no more than a gleam in the eyes of political idealists.

These points are directly relevant to the only sense I can make of a regional or national or ethnic concern with human rights. This is that in different human communities, with their varied social, political, economic, climatic, geographical, and related circumstances, the question about how to establish a system that protects and preserves human rights will have to be answered differently. We might use as an analogy the case of sickness versus health. It depends on what ails a person, how severely, and how well-informed one is of available remedies, whether this or that approach should be taken to alleviate the condition. The principle that one should not do what one cannot do applies here as well as in all realms of human conduct.

Now one of the circumstances that Hungary shares with virtually all nations on the globe is that its legal system, if one can call it that, does not serve to protect and preserve human rights in a consistent, sustained fashion. What Hungary does not share with most other nations is its peculiar history of feudalism and virtual constant foreign intervention into its national affairs, combined with the great confusion of its people and leaders as to what kind of community Hungary should be. Although over 1,000 years old as an identifiable distinct human community, Hungary has rarely been a powerful nation on the model of, for example, Rome, Spain, or Great Britain. In combination with Austria, as the Austro-Hungarian Empire, the same cannot be said, but there is little disagreement among historians over the fact that in this combination it has been the Austrians, largely, and not the Magyars, who have taken the leadership. The Magyars would have if they had had the opportunity; prior to the emergence of the Austro-Hungarian Empire there were numerous "pure bred" Hungarian monarchs who did not shy from imperialist conduct toward those nations that lay in Hungary's vicinity.

After the demise of the Austro-Hungarian Empire Hungary once again came under foreign rule, first by the Third Reich and then by the Soviet Union. In both cases, the relationship between the Hungarian nation and the others has, in formal legal terms, been that of equal partners, allies, voluntary associates, although Hungary first came under Soviet occupation after the decision at Yalta in punishment for its alliance with Hitler. Now, however, Hungary is legally regarded as an independent nation, although, in terms of the real-politiks of the situation this is nonsense.

What is relevant in the Hungarian situation that might provide a fruitful exploration of some aspect of the human rights issue? Its foreign-supported feudalism could be an interesting test case for how human rights might be given greater respect and protection, and, eventually, official preservation in a complex social system. What should those who uphold the principles of human rights do given Hungary's history of feudalism, foreign intervention, and foreign rule that has been supported by portions of the national population?

I shall explore the problems of transforming a community from one in which human rights are systematically violated or evaded to one in which they are given official acknowledgment, protection, and support, I shall speak in general terms that deal with some pervasive topics surrounding human rights and shed light on some of the problems human rights advocates in Hungary have faced and still are facing. Some of the problems I will discuss concern the justifiability of violent revolution and consider such conduct within the framework of a perspective that takes human rights seriously. I will also consider when the admonition to work "within the system" should be heeded, and whether all those with human rights complaints should embark on a similar path in their efforts to remedy the situation. Finally, I will consider briefly the possible relationship between those in a country striving to establish respect for human rights, with or without revolutionary means, and those in other countries, including perhaps governments, who share these ideals and may have the option of lending a hand.

My major task, however, will be to sketch a characterization of human rights and to indicate, briefly, the reasons I consider their existence a well-established and vital feature of our moral universe.[4] First, I will provide a brief historical background.

A BRIEF GENEALOGY OF THE IDEA

There is a lot of talk about human rights but not a great deal of clarity about what human rights are. Historically the concept that eventually brought human rights to the fore was natural rights. The Declaration of Independence, written mainly by Thomas Jefferson, refers to *unalienable rights* that all men are endowed with by their Creator. The philosophical or theoretical foundation for such a view came from the English philosopher John Locke (1632-1714), who advanced an argument for natural rights in his *Second Treatise on Civil Government*.[5] Before Locke, the idea made its appearance in the works of Thomas Hobbes (1558-1679) in a different form. And there have been discussions of basic rights before that, for example in William of Ockham's (c.1290-1349) *Opus Nonaginta Dierum* where we are told that "Natural [divine?] right is nothing other than a power to conform to right reason, without an agreement or pact; civil right is a power, deriving from an agreement, and sometimes conforms to right reason and sometimes discords with it."[6] The first reference to rights in this sense seems to have occurred in Aristotle's (384-322 B.C.) *Politics,* where the sophist Lykophron is said to be advocating a conception of law as "a guarantee (or guarantor) of mutual rights *(dikaion)."*[7] Still, it was Locke's position that exerted the decisive influence,[8] and he advocated the idea of natural rights.[9]

Natural rights are so called because the rights in question—to life, liberty, and the pursuit of happiness—are supposed to be derivable from an understanding of human nature and the requirements of human community life. Human nature, in turn, is supposed to mean something quite specific. The nature of something consists, in this framework or perspective, of certain factors that are evident about every human being and make every human being a member of the human species. Human beings are characterized by innumerable factors that they may or may not share with others. Much of what we are many other human beings are not; but some factors about us that can be found in the case of every other person serve to differentiate us from other living beings who are not human, and these factors constitute our human nature, our essence as human beings. The idea underlying natural rights theory is that there are some rights we all possess solely because of our human nature.

The idea of rights is so widely used today that we need not spend much time defining it. When someone has a right to something, such as the use of a car, a pension at age 65, or an education up to high school level, others must not prevent him from exercising the option to enjoy or refuse what he has a right to. If someone has a right to use a car, it does not mean that that he will use the car, or should do so, or will be well off if he does so. It means only that others must not—may be prevented if they try to—interfere with his exercising the choice to use the car. Having a right places an obligation on others to refrain from interference. Others must refrain from the kind of interference that the person who has the right cannot resist without effort. (Thus, to give someone the advice that he should not use the car that he has a right to use is not really the sort of interference at issue here, because he can simply reject the advice and move on.) It is really preventive or obstructive interference that must be avoided, usually physical coercion or its threat, to impose a decision upon someone who has the right to do something.

There are many sources of rights, most of them contractual or institutional. Being a child in a family may establish the right to receive food or the needed and available care from the adults of that family. Having contracted for the building of a house on one's property, one has the right to have this house built by the contracting party. As a member of a university faculty one may have the right to use the faculty club. And as an employee of a firm, one may have the right to be paid a given wage at a certain time. Clearly, these sorts of rights are not natural, since *as a human being* one might or might not have them depending on special circumstances. In the philosophical literature such rights have thus acquired the name of special rights.

The question is whether we have any rights as human beings and what they are. A right is a social condition that human beings are required to uphold by refraining from interference with some range of conduct on the part of someone. And a natural right is a social condition that human beings are required to uphold by refraining from interfering with some range of conduct on the part of some *in virtue of someone's being a human being.*[10]

The only confusion that may be generated from this characterization of natural (human) rights is that in our day it is widely believed that there are certain natural or human rights that require not simply the abstention by others from interference but also certain productive activities by others. On the one hand, if each of us has the natural right to life, others could be required not to act to deprive us of life. No productive activity is required of others in this case. Sometimes, however, having the right to life could require others to produce what another's life requires, for example, food, shelter, education, health care, jobs, possibly vacations.[11] But in strict terms, this would not be correct, because one would then have the right to what those people produce, not simply to their abstention from interference with one's life. There are complicated reasons why the right to life concept has been extended to rights such as that to life supports, the view that human beings are really incapable of furnishing their own life supports if they are not interfered with and must, instead, have these life supports supplied by others, society, or the government—even when others forced to supply those supports may have some of their rights violated.[12] On the other hand, if each of us has the natural right to education, health care, or employment, others could be required to furnish us with these provisions, and we would have the option to exercise our right and choose between utilizing or not utilizing these provisions.

Historically, the natural rights theoretical tradition has laid exclusive stress on those rights that involve other's mere abstinence, leaving the production of life supports, for example, to considerations other than those having to do with the protection and preservation of our natural rights. This is well exemplified in the wording of the Declaration of Independence. It lists among the rights all men have the rights to "life, liberty and the pursuit of happiness." As Ayn Rand notes:

Observe . . . the intellectual precision of the Founding Fathers: they spoke of the right
to *the pursuit* of happiness—*not* of the right to happiness. It means that a man has the
right to take the actions he deems necessary to achieve his happiness; it does *not* mean
that others must make him happy.[13]

The situation has changed considerably in our time. The United Nations
Universal Declaration of Human Rights, adopted on December 10, 1948, by
the General Assembly of the United Nations at the Palais de Chaillot, Paris,
France, includes "the right to social security" (Article 22), "the right to work,
to free choice of employment, to just and favorable conditions of work and
to protection against unemployment" (Article 23), "the right to rest and leisure" (Article 24), "the right to education" (Article 26), and, oddly enough,
"everyone has duties to the community" (Article 29).[14]

A great many reasons may be cited for this change. Some observers, including A. I. Melden, believe that the change in the conception of human
rights came about "because of the radical changes in the circumstances of human life, which have occurred since Locke's own time, as the result of which
neither the moral judgments he expressed nor the very moral concepts he employed have remained unaffected."[15] Vladimir Kudryavtsev of the Soviet
Union also wishes to dispense with "anarchistic discourses on 'universal
human rights,'" and maintains that "a right is an opportunity guaranteed by
the state to enjoy the social benefits and values existing in the given society."
And he concludes that "the same right [for instance, the right to education]
has an entirely different content in different historical and social circumstances."[16]

But there is one question of special interest to the philosopher. Why is
there today hardly any sign of unquestioned advocacy of natural rights that
were previously taken to be unalienable, universal, basic to all human beings, and commanding respect, protection, and preservation in all human
communities? Certainly this is a difficult issue, but one reason stands out, at
least for purposes of philosophical scrutiny. This is the very idea of the nature of man, of human nature, of the view that for each human being there
are certain essential factors that warrants his or her being classed among
human beings, has lost both philosophical and popular respectability.

Let me mention some of the evidence for its loss of popular respectability.
Two centuries ago the idea that human beings are radically different from the
rest of the living beings on earth had been both a theological and philosophical conviction. Today, with the widely proclaimed success of getting chimps
to "think" or at least make signs for purposes of communication, with the
demise of the dominance of theological ideas, with the speculation about ex-
traterrestrial life, and so forth, the idea that a distinct human species exists of
which we are members is on shaky foundations. In ordinary thought and

action, of course, most people are quite sure that some factors render certain beings human, so for ordinary practical purposes the idea of human nature prevails. As Laszlo Versenyi notes, "Barring all knowledge of human nature—that which makes man a man—the word man would mean nothing and we could not even conceive of man as a definite being distinguishable from all other beings." And, as he further points out, "Consequently anything we might say about man would be necessarily meaningless, including the statement that human nature as such is unknowable to man."[17] But our ordinary, popular thinking is permeated with what we learn in colleges, through magazines, and television specials, and while in practice we might cling to an idea of human nature, in our thinking great confusion has resulted. Some of this confusion has led to serious proposals about the "rights" of animals, even trees and mountains, not simply in philosophical speculation but in the chambers of various legislatures.[18] Since even our current popular discussions about human rights occur mostly at a complex theoretical level—since very few people believe that anything like full adherence to human rights (never mind how this is used) exists anywhere in the world—the confidence of the Founding Fathers of the United States is long gone concerning what man should be conceived as in theoretical, philosophical, and legal terms.

The philosophical respectability of natural rights started to wane almost as soon as John Locke gave the idea credibility. Many philosophers, and in some curious fashion even John Locke, found flaws in the idea of something having an essence. Thereafter the idea of stable, lasting principles of human community life came under severe fire. Jeremy Bentham, who made a special project of ridiculing natural rights,[20] thought that the belief in such rights would prevent governments from instituting progressive legislation and would thus hamper social progress. John Stuart Mill held to a watered-down version of natural rights, based not on considerations of the nature of man but on the utility of upholding certain principles since this would promote "general utility."[21]

Other influential thinkers, such as Georg W. Friedrich Hegel and Karl Marx, regarded the entire worldview out of which they claimed the natural rights tradition emerged as flawed, or, at best, as a mere stage in history's inevitable progress toward humanity's full emancipation. For example, Marx was hostile to the very idea of the right to freedom, because, he thought, it "is not based on the union of man with man, but on the separation of man from man."[22] The individualist tradition, within which natural rights formed the political ingredient and constituted a bulwark against the idea that human beings may be used, against their will, as resources or pawns by others, especially by government, had gradually lost its philosophical support not only among outright foes but also among those who willy-nilly considered it still a fruitful, albeit seriously deficient, system. Even in the United States, where individualism has mostly been considered paramount for two centuries, the support for natural rights and the political and legal principles it fostered, has been lost, at least, among the intellectuals, especially the philosophers.

By the turn of the century, the dominant philosophical atmosphere in the English-speaking world was very different from the perspective that gave natural rights its earlier philosophical support. The idea that we could know right from wrong in ethics or politics was disputed increasingly. Most professional philosophers came to believe that judgments as to what is right, good, wrong, bad, decent, evil, and so forth really amounted to exclamations of preference, emotional disposition, and sentiment. And by the time World War II ended, just when the UN Declaration was being signed, the English philosopher Margaret Macdonald wrote:

"'Man' equals 'rational animal' Df." is the fossil preserved in logic text books since Aristotle. . . . And men's rights depend upon this common nature and end by which they are subject to the natural or "unwritten" law. But this seems to me a complete mistake. . . . Men do not share a fixed nature, nor, therefore, are there any ends which they must necessarily pursue in fulfillment of such nature.[23]

Macdonald was saying this in reply to Jacques Maritain, who suggested, at about the same time, that "there is a human nature and this human nature is the same in all men. . . ."[24] But Maritain was a thinker closely aligned with a theological tradition, and his views did not convince the mostly secular Anglo-American academic philosophical community. The bulk of them accepted the view Macdonald advocated. This view was, in its essentials, that "To assert that 'Freedom is better than slavery,' or 'All men are of equal worth' is not to state a fact but to *choose a side*. It announces, *This is where I stand*."[25]

Yet the idea that there is little more to human rights than some people preferring it while others prefer something else, did not meet with wholehearted approval. For several decades the view Macdonald advocated held sway among academic philosophers, especially in England and America. This community generally abandoned the entire field of political philosophy, and theorizing was left largely to behavioral political scientists who expunged value judgments. A new discussion of rights, including human rights, surfaced in the 1960s in connection with the civil rights movement. And about the time that the U. S. entered the war in southeast Asia, interest in political matters reemerged among students of philosophy.

The idea of human rights that became the subject of new attention is not the same idea as natural rights in the Lockean tradition. The very method of thinking about these rights is different. Today's method generally involves examining the common, ordinary usage of such words as "human" and "rights" and drawing inferences from what emerges as a reasonably consistent use of such terms. Observing Ludwig Wittgenstein's dictum, that "the meaning of a word is its use in the language,"[26] the method of examining human rights—of discovering what it means to be a human right, to have one, and what human rights are—involved, to put it roughly, seeing whether certain expressions employing the idea "human rights" came naturally, were "happy" in the language, and then seeing what followed from that collage of uses that were found acceptable and consistent. Remember also that, aside from the widespread acceptance of this method of philosophizing, there had been a widespread rejection of the idea of essences. As Wittgenstein observed, and his influence on this period of philosophical scholarship cannot be overstated, "there is not always a sharp distinction between essential and inessential."[27] So the view of human rights that emerged, under the influence of these ideas, was almost self-consciously antiessentialist, a rejection of the natural rights tradition.

In our own times there is no longer a discernible orthodoxy in philosophical politics. Several natural and human rights theories are making their way into the philosophical literature. And the theory of natural rights that shaped the American political system and, in a way, still holds the attention of the public and the professional theorists, even if in an oblique way, is being reexamined as well.

But the political arena is mostly under the influence of the much looser, less demanding thinking surrounding the theories of human rights. These theories have clearly lacked the (at least implicit) depth of the Lockean natural rights tradition. Their conclusions give rise to innumerable, very often mutually exclusive, human rights. And they make possible something that seems quite perplexing, namely, that official spokesmen from countries with as divergent political histories as those of the United States of America, the Soviet Union, the Democratic Republic of Germany, Chile, and Uganda can all claim to be upholding the principles of human rights within their legal systems.

It seems worthwhile, then, to explore whether or not the older suggestions, with possible needed modifications, might not still be the best. Alexis de Tocqueville noted almost a century ago that there is something remarkable about human rights:

There is nothing which, generally speaking, elevates and sustains the human spirit more than the idea of rights. There is something great and virile in the idea of right which removes from any request its suppliant character, and places the one who claims it on the same level as the one who grants it.[28]

But Tocqueville also suggested something that may indeed have proven to be the Achilles' heel of contemporary human rights theory: "But the right of the poor to obtain society's help is unique in that instead of elevating the heart of the man who exercises it, it lowers him."[29]

There are today many putative human rights—to virtually anything someone has found he wants very badly and believes should be given him. It may be that some of these wants should be satisfied; it may be that some of these wishes are a fine thing to attain. But it is doubtful, as I will try to show, that such things belong in the list of those rights human beings possess simply because they are human beings.

THE NATURE AND EXISTENCE OF HUMAN RIGHTS

In familiar popular contexts, human rights are discussed very loosely. A cynic might say that this is diplomatically inevitable, but the cynic would be wrong. There have been, and still are, times when in the highest of diplomatic circles ideals are spelled out clearly and uncompromisingly. One need but reflect on the substance of the Lincoln-Douglas debates to confirm this. No, the central reason for the looseness of political discourse, the ambiguity of the concepts involved, and their ultimate shallowness is the lack of a philosophical base for what is being discussed. For almost a century the intellectual community in America has tended to give support to pragmatism, the philosophy in which the very idea of firm principles is regarded as unsound and tantamount to dogmatism. And pragmatism explicitly eschews systematic philosophical and political thinking. It treats human rights as rules of thumb, with ample room for compromise.[30]

In the last few decades the main focus in discussions of human rights has been on the right to free expression and political participation, roughly, what people refer to as civil rights. When individuals are forbidden to speak and write about their society, culture, and government, it is admitted by even the most pragmatic of American intellectuals that human rights are being violated.

But even this admission gives us a clue to the broader meaning of human rights, what source they have, and even whether they exist at all. And in the next few paragraphs I will aim to provide an answer to the main question we need to confront—whether there are human rights at all—from a natural rights approach and in language that is accessible to most people.

Human beings are thinkers. Other living beings exist either by responding to environmental stimuli with preset or instinctual behavior, or by following innate drives, usually a combination of the two. Human beings may rely on this drive at first, but are *distinct* because of their dependence on their own chosen thinking operations. Unlike other animals, human beings must learn to behave rightly and for this purpose they need to activate their minds.

Of course, these are controversial points and need extensive argument.[31] Just let me point out one main reason why it makes extremely good sense to regard human beings as essentially and distinctively thinking beings. This has to do with the enormous importance ideas have for us. Ideas are always general, they are principles by which we confront the world. There are no ideas out there, in existence, other than what we formulate by our thinking. Ideas are, therefore, something created by us, but we can create faulty ideas as well as sound or valid ones. However, if we had no choice about whether we would pay attention to reality and think about it or evade it, there would be no way to tell the difference between faulty and sound ideas, they would all follow automatic mental processes. Faulty thinking follows sloppy mental processes, when the person is inattentive, when he or she pays no heed, whereas sound ideas are usually the result of careful thought. Thinking does not happen automatically but must be done through choice and effort.

Still, though thinking is a matter of choice, thinking should not be confused with intellectualizing or being members of the profession of theorists, artists, scientists, writers, and so forth. These professionals are not necessarily better at thinking than carpenters, taxi drivers, advertising executives, toy manufacturers, or circus masters. The possibility of leading a thoughtful life exists, regardless of one's profession.

Nevertheless, to deny freedom of thought, which goes directly against those who specialize in expressing their thoughts in print or orally and not by their machines, hands, organization charts, and travel plans, is perceived by most people as a direct attack on humanity. In any cursory concern about human rights, attacks on the right to free expression in voice or print can appear to be more serious than anything else.

Singling out such specialists is quite unfair. Long before Andrei Sakharov and Aleksandre Solzhenitsyn began to make their revulsion at the Soviet regime public, millions who are and were less expressive had their human rights violated every minute of the day. To single out the dissidents, the artists, the political opponents of the regime, as is done by Amnesty International,[32] for instance, is a form of discrimination.

However, this focus on the right of free expression gives us a clue as to the deeper source of human rights. If as thinking beings we are forbidden to choose what we think is right, we are forced to be passive participants in our lives, this is so evident and clear that it can be widely protested. To deny our right to live by our minds is to deny our humanity. With dissidents and artists, this denial is easy to perceive—with carpenters and farmers it is not. The crucial clue is that any denial of the conditions for living a human life, for flourishing as a human being, is the denial of the existence of human rights.

The denial and systematic violation of numerous basic conditions are just as horrible as are the denial and systematic violation of the right to free verbal and written expression for artists and scientists.[33] It is these basic conditions that John Locke identified as our natural (fundamental, basic, essential) human rights. They refer to what we are essentially as thinking animals. We single them out, and they are rights because it is wrong to violate them, to interfere with our choosing within the area designated by these rights.

The objection that human rights cannot be very specific because they depend on a nonexistent human nature can be answered by first considering that only because human nature had been conceived of as fixed did it *appear* not to exist. In fact, there is a human nature we all have, and it consists in our being the only animals that depend primarily upon thinking for survival and success in life. That some exceptions can be found, people who are parasites or lifetime dependents, and some other animals that exercise some thought, makes no difference. Human nature is *not* some *fixed* mold with geometrically sharp edges. To so conceive of it leads to skepticism, but one can improve on that idea. Any scheme of categorization—whether in astronomy, geometry, mathematics, physics, sociology, ethics, or politics—will involve some gray areas,[34] but that is no ground for denying the soundness of the scheme or the implications that may be drawn from having placed something in this or that category, for example, in the study of politics.

What of the objections that the belief in natural human rights places an unwarranted restriction on law and social policy? The answer is that principles always imply some definite scope and, provided the principles are well thought out and warranted, the definition of the scope involved should be followed. Bentham was wrong to object to some limits on social progress. After all, even those of us who find population increases dangerous would not simply wish to kill off a certain number of people to make advances toward population control. The means of enhancing social progress—what Bentham was concerned about—are not unlimited, and natural human rights do place certain limits on what is permitted in human interactions. We might indeed further political stability, as the Soviet Union is trying to do, by punishing criticism of the government.[35] This would perhaps further something that is of value to us, but at what price?

So, yes, Bentham was right that if we accepted the view that there are natural human rights this places limits on social policy. But the objection is irrelevant, because such limits are indispensable to any conception of community life. Even anarchists want to limit community life to entirely peaceful and equal human relations. To those who wish to abolish the limits to social control or engineering, the limiting function of human rights will appear objectionable, but they see human community life in the wrong light. Society is not the highest good. It is one of many human goods.[36]

Human beings are social, but society is not an entity over and above individuals. Every society is, instead, an elaborate network or set of complex human relationships among individuals, their many groups, families, professions, clubs, institutions, and multifaceted undertakings (in art, science, entertainment, education, law). In the final analysis, it is individuals who are the real beings of society: mankind, countries, nations, races, religions, and the other special networks of people in various association with each other. For all to exist as valuable aspects of human life, certain basic principles called human rights have to be respected. That is why all the fuss, outcries, complaints, and protests, why even wars permeate the globe in the name of human rights.

The fact is that some people, many of whom are in official and powerful positions, refuse to respect others' human rights. This is evident in the governmental suppression of free speech. Yet beyond this widely agreed-upon violation of human rights, there are many more, less often noted offenses.

What would result from a serious regard for human rights? First, we must answer on a general, abstract level. Human rights are general principles of social conduct. Unlike most scientific theories, the principles of social conduct apply to entities that can exercise choice. Recognizing this, John Locke knew that although we all possess basic rights, it does not follow that we will all respect these rights. Some of us simply will not listen to reason; some will refuse even to think about what principles apply to our social conduct. And Locke, in particular, explained the existence of governments as answering the need for protection and preservation of our human rights. So establishing governments might be an initial result of respect for such rights.

Yet governments can be the greatest threat to our rights. Unless officials of government abide by the principles of human rights, not only will they fail to protect their citizens' rights, but they will be instrumental in violating these rights.

In the case of the United States, the government was established with considerable concern about human rights. Those who believed that the U.S. Constitution needed even greater direction along those lines amended it so that some of the basic rights already implied in the Declaration of Independence were mentioned explicitly in the Bill of Rights. Yet the debate about the need for the first ten amendments is still raging among constitutional scholars.

The first amendment declared that Congress cannot control speech, religion, and peaceful assembly. Other amendments declared that government may not violate people's property rights, nor control people in their efforts to arm themselves for purposes of self-defense. Certain procedural implications were spelled out, so that we have in our Constitution the famous due process clause that directs government to fully respect human rights even when dealing with those suspected of crimes.[37]

However perfectly or imperfectly the U.S. legal system gave expression to the theory of human rights, there is ample reason to consider that theory a good answer to our concern with how a civilized community is structured best in order to give full official recognition to each person's natural human rights and to provide effective means by which either private citizens or government itself can combat violations of those rights.

Of course, no written document can guarantee full adherence to an idea. Subsequent generations of interpreters and enforcers of a legal system that gives full expression to human rights can still default on the responsibility to uphold the importance and integrity of the principles of a decent, civilized human community. Indeed, this has occurred in the United States from the outset of its history.[38] Despite this need to keep the spirit and letter of a legal system based on human rights theory alive, without first establishing that system, it is very difficult if not impossible to take human rights seriously in the community. The customary or common laws that have grown out of people's efforts to answer the crucial questions and solve the problems of social life are powerful, but they are easily subverted. An explicit legal system with the appropriate foundations can delay the decline, but there is no substitute for the active public attention to what a human community requires for a decent chance to make a peaceful, hopeful, and just setting for people's lives.

To enhance this possibility, let us look briefly at the implications of a human rights theory. What basic rights do we all have? How do they relate to our practical, day-to-day activities and concerns?

Thinking and choosing are our characteristically human means of existence, and existence is the first requirement for pursuing a successful life.[39] Thus the concern with the right to freedom of expression points clearly toward our most basic human right, the right to life. The right to life means that no one may prevent our efforts to sustain ourselves and carry out the actions that will make it possible to live. The right to life does not mean that we must be given our livelihood (except by our parents during our state of dependency on those who brought us into this existence). The right to life, for adults, is the fact that none may interfere with our actions, because each of us must take actions in order to live and flourish.

Although this is not difficult to understand, the full impact of the idea on actual social life is often not detected. That is one reason why, after this most basic human right has been spelled out, other *implied* rights are also mentioned by human rights theorists. For example, the right to liberty is implied by the right to life; mentioning it makes it clearer what the right to life means: that no one should trample on our freedom to act, to judge, and to behave as we see fit. Since each of us possesses the right to liberty, it is clear that this freedom involves only those actions that do not negate another's rights.

Human rights must be consistently applicable to *all* who live in human communities. If the freedom to act included acting in ways that would obstruct other people's freedom to act, the right of everyone to this freedom could not be respected consistently, and the resulting clashes between people could not be resolved by reference to the right in question. Thus the freedom to take any actions whatsoever is not a human right. A theory cannot lead to contradictions, or else it is unsound and, when it comes to applying it to human life, worthless. Thus, theories of politics that develop principles leading to irreconcilable conflicts are inherently flawed. Some try to escape this by making their principles relevant to different, future ages, even to more "advanced " people. For example, one of Karl Marx's basic political principles, "from each according to his abilities, to each according to his needs," does not apply to human beings alive today, or even in the next decade. This principle, like others he developed, was to apply to a "new man," some group of beings like humans but very different, and to a social situation in which virtually infinite abundance would prevail (after, as Marx believed, capitalism created enough for everyone to have whatever he or she needed).

Human rights theories for actual human communities are not sound if the principles involved can not be applied to all without inherent conflict. The human rights theory I am sketching would be consistent and applicable here today. It is for this reason that another crucial implication of the human right to life has to be spelled out. I am referring to that most controversial of human rights, the right to own things, property rights, or the institution of private property.[40]

Most people with some awareness of ideological conflicts around the world, even here in the United States, know that the belief in the institution of private property is controversial. The fear is widespread that protection of the right to own things will lead to great wealth for a few and poverty for a great many. The fear is also that wealth will yield extraordinary leverage in political and legal matters, so that the law cannot be used to secure justice for all because the wealthy will subvert it. Moreover, in the capitalistic system that supports property rights the wealthy, it is feared, will gain enormous economic power by forming monopolies.

This view has been refuted many times, and I am not going to try to do this here. Economists have argued for a century that the only way great monopolies come into being is when the law is already subverted, when some people in an industry gain special privilege.[41] Then, and only then, will some people be able to exclude others from competing in a productive enterprise. Without such special privileges, some may indeed become wealthy, but only if they produce what people want. In short, defenders of the right to property argue that the economic realm is not similar to a boxing ring where, if one participant wins, someone else must be flattened. It is similar to an endless marathon race, with positions changing constantly, some leaving the race, others joining it, many succeeding with very good progress, and only a few being completely wiped out under the strain of competition. Aside from this general fear of the idea of the right to property, we could consider many other objections. But most people will think of them on their own. What we need to do instead is show why property ownership is something each person has a right to.

What we are talking about is not having property, but having the right to work for things and keep them if earned or received from others by their own free will (*not* by theft, fraud, or extortion). Often a theory of property rights starts by envisioning unrealistically a situation in which there are unclaimed resources, untouched land that people make their own. It is misleading to think along these lines. There never has been an easy way to obtain what one wants, even when no prior claimants stand in the way. Acquiring resources like gold, water, wood, sand, and salt has always taken hard work. Acquiring land requires going to where it is available. Today it is actually much easier to obtain what one wants. Today there are relatively free markets, even in highly regulated economies. Again, efforts are required to obtain them. It is necessary to exchange the products or services one can create for those others create and are willing to part with for a price. Money is the medium, but once one has chosen a field of production desired in the community, money can be obtained. And that enables one to exercise the right to liberty, namely, acting to obtain what one wants (in *this* expression of that right).

The human right to own things, property rights, means that no one may interfere with them—and calls for economic liberty. It is no accident that in the United States, where human rights have had greater influence in the workings of the legal and political system than anywhere else, there has been a relatively free economy. In a system that would fully adhere to the principles of human rights, a free market would continue to prevail. Everyone could own, and exchange what he or she owns, without anyone permitted to interfere. The government's job in this regard would be to protect and preserve freedom of production and trade, nothing more.

Of course, some will immediately raise objections. What if someone starts with very little or makes a few big mistakes? What chance does such a person have to acquire more than enough to get by in life, let alone flourish?[42]

To this the human rights theorist must honestly reply that in a legal system based on human rights there is no stress on economic equality (although there is a great deal of emphasis on equal *rights*). Economic well-being is not primarily for human life, or so a human rights theory would maintain. People could aspire to be economically well off, artistically excellent, educationally proficient, scientifically accomplished, but there is no requirement that they be equal in these measurements. For some people, increasing their wealth may be good; for others it may be a waste. For me, a teacher of philosophy, great wealth would usher in undesired troubles. For others embarking on jobs for which they are unsuited would not permit them to lead fulfilling lives. Exactly what will make a person's life flourish is sometimes difficult if not impossible to tell. However, a seven-foot-tall person obviously should not try to be a jockey, while a five-foot sports enthusiast should not try to play professional basketball.

In general, a human rights theory refuses to assimilate what is good for individuals into one goal, purpose, or mission. Each must find his or her own way. What is crucial is that none try to subvert the efforts of others but that each make the best of his own situation. Only by assigning enormous, unwarranted significance to certain kinds of success—fame, wealth, power, particular skills, particular enjoyments—will one expect a good political system to do more than respect everyone's human right to act freely and to attempt to make material progress. The possession of human rights, including the right to own and retain possession of things, is imperative for creating a civilized, decent society. That this does not achieve all that people might want to achieve individually, that it might indeed be right for them to achieve, is beside the point. It is only maintained in human rights theory that this kind of human community should open up the opportunity for those individual achievements far more than any other system does.

In the Soviet Union, for example, the artists, intellectuals, and scientists who strive to succeed in their lives are prevented from doing so. And they are prevented partly by the government's refusal to recognize the human right to own things. In socialist societies, the state owns the major, sometimes the entire, means of production. The state owns the means by which people may advance their own lives. An artist requires tools; a writer needs paper, a typewriter, a printing press. If what he writes is opposed by the state, and the state owns these things, the writer is left without materials. In a free country, no one is guaranteed that the tools of his trade will be available to him, but in the marketplace it is likely that individuals and groups (businesses) will want to sell these items, without ideological strings attached. Of course, ideological strings can enter even the free market, but then those who favor one's ideology will help. In the United States, for instance, publishing firms usually publish what will sell, and enough Marxists buy books so that many publishers publish books by Marxists. And even racists, bigots, and other objectionable writers get published, because the diversity of human beings makes this more likely where no centralized property ownership and regulation dominate.

Perhaps this discussion has been somewhat abstract, but we are dealing with general ideas, and political principles are never really concrete. Only the decisions based on them bring home their concrete implications. Thus, why is theft considered wrong? Why are those who commit fraud punished? Why are embezzlers jailed or fined? Because, insofar as a legal system respects the human right to own things, it also responds firmly to those who violate this right. Prosecutors take action when a charge of theft is leveled against someone. If the grounds of the charge are proven in court, within the framework of the adversary process of defense versus prosecution, the accused is found guilty and is punished (unless a powerful excuse can be found, such as mental incapacitation).

Sometimes governments do not abide by the system of property rights, themselves engaging in theft. They appropriate people's belongings for purposes they decide are warranted. We have become accustomed to this, calling it redistribution of wealth, taxation, or serving the national purpose. Wherever the government serves goals not designed to protect and preserve the human rights people have, their activities are not in principle different from the thief's. A drastic charge? No more so than the charge that the Soviet state is violating the human rights of those whom it jails for speaking out against the government's policies or ideology. That, indeed, is the most overt, unconcealed manifestation of the violation of human rights, something everyone can recognize as such.

So far we have specified the rights to life, liberty, and property as basic human rights. And this is in keeping with the pertinent tradition, in spite of recurring debates about the right to property. But what about the now widespread idea that people have a right to a certain level of income, to housing, to medical care, and so on? Notice that these are not simply more detailed specifications of the right to property, as the right to liberty is implied by the right to life. For the right to property is the right to acquire things in freely undertaken creation and exchange. Rather, when rights to income and medical care are spoken of, it is meant that human beings have a right to have (at least some amounts of) these things provided for them. But someone must produce these items or fork over the funds to buy them! Originally, human rights would be violated if people interfered with each other's lives, liberty, and property. But according to the UN document, it is a violation of human rights not to do things for everyone, not to let oneself be enslaved.

There are, of course, popular and widely argued political and moral systems that give support to certain ideas about how we are all obligated to serve our fellow human beings. Many such systems exist, and, indeed, most philosophers even now defend them.[43] The human rights theory outlined in these pages is hardly supported by prominent thinkers.[44]

But it is nonsense to regard the claims of the UN Declaration of Human Rights, or similar claims, as valid. They lead to contradictions and to impossible demands made by some people on other people. Moreover, the UN document actually affirms human rights outlined earlier, too, because there is no effort to be integrated and theoretically clean in principle. It is a political document produced by people with inherently conflicting political ideas and ideals. In effect, all that is left of human rights theory is the words, nothing more.

But in the present discussion we are examining human rights theory realistically, in a form that does not engender inherent conflicts; that could be implemented, even if it is unlikely that it would be soon. There are plenty of works advocating opposite or different doctrines. For a time we might simply give some thought to the theory of human rights that gave the very idea of human rights its appeal, its inspiration, and its political and moral force. The fact that the idea, consistently worked out, is not popular does not matter essentially. The question is whether the theory makes good sense (I believe it does.) today, when hardly anyone understands precisely what human rights are, and when even fewer people would claim to know that such rights really exist. Outcries about the violation of human rights manage to make an impression on us, even to move us to join the protest.

It has been my claim here that human rights are real. In other words, there really exist certain normative principles derivable from an understanding of human nature and communities, placing certain limits on what one person may do to another, including what governments may do to their citizens. Each of us is a living being who should aspire to live a good and prosperous life, and each of us must choose to do so because the activity of thought, which underlies all achievement of values and prosperity, must be initiated or chosen by the individual who is the thinker. In the company of other human beings, their basic idea needs to be respected in order for all to be able to pursue their own good and prosperity. The principles or standards that will, when observed, enable everyone to pursue his or her own good and prosperity—to pursue his or her happiness—are the natural human rights of each individual. These rights have their point in a human community, for it is only other human beings who can interfere with one's chosen way of life or refrain from such interference. Only human beings have a say about whether they will be good or evil, and in each other's community the most categorical evidence for interpersonal evil is the violation of others' rights to life, liberty, and property, that is, the destruction of others' moral nature and human dignity.

TOWARD A CONSTITUTION OF HUMAN RIGHTS

Early in this chapter I quoted Richard P. Claude's claim that "preliminary to any movement toward human rights development, the framework of an operative legal system must be securely established." Yet if, as implied in the foregoing analysis, a commitment to the principles of natural rights, the only consistent version of human rights, must be the very foundations of a scheme of justice[45] of a human community, how could "an operative legal system . . . be securely established" before human rights have been developed?

There is, of course, much debate about whether any system of rules or edicts or statutes constitutes a legal system proper.[46] As an example, can we really accept that the system of rules operative during the Third Reich or in Stalin's Russia or in Idi Amin's Uganda constitutes a legal system? From the perspective of normative political science, such systems cannot be accepted as bona fide legal systems. They have to be regarded as aberrations or corruptions of lawfulness; otherwise no sensible distinction between the mere imposition of arbitrary edicts by might and the establishment of the rule of law is possible. The rule of law is precisely to be distinguished from the imposition of might. As ancient a thinker as Alcibiades (450-404 B.C.) observed this. Law, as distinct from arbitrary force, consists in principles of human conduct appropriate to human social existence. A community ruled by law is a community that is *primarily* subject to principles suitable to human community life. Some deviation is always to be expected, inasmuch as in human communities perfect adherence to such suitable principles is unlikely, due to human fallibility. However, it is one thing to admit to the imperfection of law, and quite another to claim that no distinction between lawless and lawful codes and regimes can be identified.

Legal theorists have debated this matter since the time of the early sophists, who believed in conventionalism, to the contemporary positivists, who think, in essence, that the existence of officialdom suffices for the presence of law. In the present framework law properly understood exists only when the principles (constitution) on which it rests are in accord with human nature and the nature of community life.

For the next stage of our discussion, the main task is how one might and should go about transforming one's community from a lawless to a lawful one. Specifically, we want to differentiate between a community that has no or minimal respect for its reigning system of edicts and for natural human rights and a community that manifests real respect. The issue is not simple, when applying political principles to situations in which a community is reasonably near to being in accord with a constitution of human rights. However, we are concerned with communities in which men and women interact without the guidance of written and sound constitutional principles.

How would those who understand the imperative of striving to establish a constitution of human rights undertake this task? Is there anything about feudalistic systems, for example, that requires special methods for this task? Can force be employed, and why? Would different circumstances faced by individuals seeking justice on grounds of ethics require different approaches? And, is it possible, in the last analysis, to ascertain universal principles of conduct for all citizens for purposes of striving for the establishment of a legal system that respects human rights? It is to these matters that I will devote the remaining portion of the chapter.

Let me stress that this is not a historical inquiry, as the questions above should indicate. We are concerned with what human beings *should* do with the *imperative* of establishing a system respectful of human rights as their guide. The reason I emphasize this is that in the field of political science the preponderance of research has dealt with the *behavioral regularities* that might be identified in periods of major political change. Under the formidable influence of studying human communities *scientifically*, conceptually known as positivism or behavioralism, many political scientists regard their task as one of describing and analyzing what actually happens and producing predictions on the basis of their findings.[47] But this whole approach is called into question from the point of view of the present discussion. The idea that human beings can be understood as if they behave in regular patterns under similar circumstances is based on the extrapolation of studies of pigeons or laboratory rodents to the human sphere. The idea has strong appeal, of course, because it promises to simplify matters. And once the view that man contains a divine, ergo, ineffable element (that is central to his humanity) lost its influence, the alternative appeared to be that man is really nothing but a complex animal with nothing *fundamentally* distinctive about him. Since we have found that, in biology, zoology, and other fields that study animals, certain regularities concerning the behavior of animals are usually present, this view appeared sensible vis-à-vis the study of human affairs. Moreover, if one is concerned with behavioral control, the promise of finding regularities in behavior is considerable. Once the significant variables are identified, their manipulation promises changed behavior. Social engineering is clearly based on the prospect of this approach to understanding the life of all social beings.[48]

But there is a serious flaw in this line of thought. There are innumerable aspects of human life that are clearly quite different from well-known animal characteristics. For example, animals are believed not to study themselves and lack the capacity for self-reflection, especially at the abstract, theoretical level. There is no evidence that any other animal besides man engages in the study of political science, physics, biology, or aesthetics. This kind of evidence is impossible to integrate with the view that human behavior is only a more complex form of the behavior evident in chimps. The numerous efforts at fitting such evidence in with the behaviorist approach have failed. And alternative theories of human behavior have shown far greater theoretical, though not necessarily predictive, power.[49]

Although political thinkers since the time of Machiavelli have tended to eschew theoretical work along normative lines,[50] this is no proof of the adequacy of that sort of approach. (Some have suggested that many of the problems we now face in our social and political existence in part result from the scholarly and practical reluctance to come to terms with the *essentially* normative character of human life.)[51]

In terms of our concern, feudalism is not very different from the numerous political and social systems we find around the world today. Ideological preconceptions have led us to apply different names to these systems,[52] of course, but that is not crucial. The following remarks, applied to feudalism, could just as well be applied to other systems, although the specifics would vary considerably:

The essence of feudalism [is] the personal tie of protection and service, military at the core, which can be seen proliferating throughout western Europe from about the ninth century on. In its way, feudalism [is] as personal a relationship as kinship.[53]

Considering that personal relationships in the Middle Ages were not particularly warm and loving when peasants were mostly serfs and children mostly slaves, the relationship in question is not very different from ones we find in modern bureaucratic systems. In these it is officials who relate to subjects in protective and caretaking ways.[54] The world of social workers, welfare state relations, testifies to that with some differences worth pointing out, lest I be misunderstood. In hindsight, the stability of status and general economics in feudalism appear unique. In feudalist communities human beings enjoyed a feeling of continuity, a sense of knowing that they had their place and status within an orderly world, but this feeling was probably the only stable aspect of feudalist communities at best, the only aspect that could be found present universally. The feeling of responsibility on the part of the most noble of nobles, the feeling of protectiveness on the part of the most conscientious of monarchs, the feeling of duty on the part of the most humble of peasants—these feelings (now regarded as the great advantage of feudalist eras)[55] were and still are the makings of a very uneven human social system. And whenever these feelings are even slightly corrupted, leading nobles to be masters, leading the peasants to be aggrieved serfs, and leading the monarch to be either a tyrant or a puppet, the system no longer presents itself to the observers as the image of harmony and tranquility that Marx observed about feudalist lands.[56]

For us to grasp the significance of a feudalist society, it is necessary to consider some features that are in sharp contrast to distinctive features of the contemporary liberal democratic societies familiar to Westerners. The idea of feudalism, in contrast to liberalism, is that all land and all status depend on the will (supreme by virtue of divine right) of the head of state. All offices are held as titles bestowed by the monarch. All lands are the property of the state, and all its users and tenants enjoy privileges granted in return for loyalty and service. The head of state is sovereign and may act by decree. No private ownership is recognized as a matter of right; no due process of law is adhered to; no participation in the decisions affecting the realm is permitted except by invitation.

The purest form of feudalism would be a version of monarchy combined with patriarchy. Most Western feudal states began to be transformed into parliamentary or constitutional monarchies at the end of the Middle Ages, and the few nominal monarchies of our day—England and Sweden, for example—are worthy of the name only by the most legalistic definition. Still, there is a residual monarchism in many parliamentary and constitutional systems that has important implications for the evolution of the law of such societies. For example, even in the United States of America the doctrine of police power, invoked by state legislatures and courts in justifying various caretaking activities by government, harks back to the time when the head of the realm was regarded as responsible for the health, morals, and other benefits of his (or her) subjects. The royal police power now has the aura of "arbitrary and despotic methods of inquiry and punishment in consequence of the political struggles in which the Crown found itself engaged in the seventeenth century." Yet, as Ernst Freund continues, "for a long period of its existence the Star Chamber [as an example of the executor of royal police power] exercised what was at the time considered a normal and legitimate function of state, namely, an inherent executive police power."[57]

Although modernized considerably, with innumerable elements of law interposed between the monarchs (or, in the case of Hungary between the two great wars, the regent Miklos Horthy von Nagybanya), the feudalistic elements of the essentially monarchist Hungary of the pre-World War II period could not be denied. The particulars would require extensive historical description, of course, but it is sufficient for our purposes to realize that prior to the transformation of Hungary into a one-party (Communist) dictatorship mainly subject to Soviet rule (through various puppet regimes until after 1962 and to some extent still), the system was *essentially* feudalistic. Some qualifications are important, however; once a feudalist system begins to undergo modification in the direction of constitutional or even parliamentary restraints (on the theoretically final power of the monarch), it is possible to consider nonrevolutionary methods for purposes of instituting a human rights oriented legal order.

Suppose that under an essentially feudalist system it is beginning to be understood that feudalism constitutes a drastic violation of the principles of a good human community. Through reflection and education, through common sense or theoretical inquiry, there is no doubt that this realization can occur in an essentially feudalist setting. Moreover, it is quite clear that even during the Middle Ages some theorists, such as William of Ockham and Thomas Aquinas, advocated views that called attention, if only indirectly, to the inhuman characteristics of feudalism.[58] (Moreover, earlier systems of government paid closer attention to the equal dignity of all members of society than did most Western feudal societies. Thus, history itself could teach one what to aim for.)

One of the most neglected principles of ethics, one that transcends the content of any ethical system, is that one should do only what is actually possible to do, and indeed, that it is necessarily false, even meaningless, to consider something that is impossible an object of responsible conduct. This may appear incongruous when we consider it in the light of some of the most prominent ethical systems in human history, because the reaching for the impossible dream and the striving for the perfection of one's soul have been aspects of moral systems throughout human history.[59] That is one of the tragedies, of course, and it has left its mark on many areas of human endeavor, not the least of which are the various efforts toward political change.

I am making this point because I wish to consider the ethics that apply to making the effort to change the political conditions of a society. Although one might have a very clear understanding of the rights of individual human beings, there may not be a case simply calling for a physical attack upon the existing regime.[60] The context of one's situation is decisive in guiding one's plans and actions.

For example, there are different qualities in all human beings within a society, including loyal feudalists (the nobility, the members of the court). Men and women are often born into circumstances whose understanding can lead them, if they are persons of essential virtue, to work for changing those circumstances *even when this may imply eventual loss of power.*[61] If one can discover the existence of "benign rulers" in one's community, the actions one should take would be different from actions taken when faced with real scoundrels.

The effective communication of revolutionary ideas, involving the careful and advantageous selection of those to whom the ideas will be communicated, may make violent revolutionary action inappropriate. In the process of striving for political change, one must give careful thought to the basic principles of human relations. Without such principles, the method by which political change is to be brought about can be either wholly ineffective or wholly out of accord with the aims at hand.

For example, if one advocates the principle that the government is not permitted to condemn a suspected criminal without first demonstrating beyond reasonable doubt the guilt of the suspect, one might undermine that purpose by reckless attacks upon members of one's community in the name of political change. When one embarks on political change to further the respect for individual natural human rights, the ensuing conduct toward others must be a model for what one is attempting to institute. This is because the basic laws to which a recognition of human rights would give rise are precisely applicable to how one must act toward other human beings, namely, by not punishing them for wrongdoing unless such wrongdoing has been proven. There can be extraordinary circumstances in which a political adversary might be cut down even though he would not be found culpable. For example, if in one's own defense a soldier of an aggressive power, who has been conscripted, must be killed, there might appear to be an exception to the principle of the onus of proof lying with the punishing party. But in such a case one is compelled to destroy another by a third party who is culpable, both for launching the attack and for coercing someone to carry it out.

It must be evident by now that, as in the case of any ethical discussion, the ethics of political change are conducive only to general characterization, with the implementation of principles necessarily left to individual instantiation. The basic task can involve only the explanation of the central ethical principles of human life and some of their direct implications for conditions met during circumstances of political change.

Are there central ethical principles that apply universally, to human beings as such, regardless of special circumstances (age, epoch, nationality, geography)? From the point of view of the present discussion, it is evident that there are. For the argument that demonstrates human rights exist, presupposes a general ethical framework applicable to all human beings. This ethical framework is rational individualism or egoism, the view that each human being should, first and foremost, strive to achieve happiness in life. And happiness for human beings is the process of living successfully as human beings. To live successfully as human beings, it is necessary for everyone to actualize one's distinctive human capacity in the circumstances of his or her individual existence. In short, the ethical or moral life constitutes the application of the essence of a rational being to the circumstances of an individual's life.[62]

Since this is a life that must be lived as a matter of individual choice—that is, each human being must, as a matter of human nature, initiate the thinking process that leads to rational conduct, which, in turn, leads to human happiness in one's own case (although it does not guarantee a fully satisfactory outcome, since accidents can always obstruct this result)—the results, or what each person should actually do, cannot be spelled out in a general theory. In this respect, ethics is like engineering: one can teach general principles, but their implementation is left to be discovered when some task is at hand. Our understanding of human nature is, as it were, the science of ethics, while the virtues are the engineering principles. And the central virtue is the act of choosing to think about one's life. This thinking will result in some general principles whose acceptance and practice are the substance of the life of human excellence or virtue.

For example, we can learn from thinking about human existence that we *should* be honest, since this means, plainly put, that we take full cognizance of what exists and act accordingly. We can learn, also, that we should be productive, because to live requires the satisfaction of various needs and wants. We can learn that we need to integrate our goals and values and principles, because otherwise we would be acting in discordance with ourselves, or at cross purposes. We need, also, to understand that we must value ourselves; otherwise we will not prevail during times of difficulty. We must, in short, have self-pride. Regarding our fellow human beings, we must realize (and will, if we think carefully) that they too share these basic, general requirements for a successful life. So we must cherish both our own success and the possibility of others' success—indeed, this is the very foundation of the principle of natural human rights.

The circumstances in which we find ourselves will have to be integrated by us with these general principles of conduct. For example, when we deal with our fellow human beings who are respectful of human rights, including ours, we will have to make sure that we accord them similar treatment. Should we, however, be in the company of violators of our rights, we will need to act defensively, depending on our capacities and opportunities. And this kind of situation can produce some of the most trying tests of human integrity for us.

Which brings me back to the consideration of acting for purposes of political change. For the bulk of ethical and political theories, instituting political change has meant doing something for mankind, for humanity, for our race, for our nation.[63] But in the individualist, human rights framework, this is not the purpose of acting for political change. That purpose is, first and foremost, the enhancement of our own happiness as human beings. The rationale for establishing a legal system based on respect for human rights is that this will further our own proper goals in life, as well as those of others.

This change from feudalism to a constitution of human rights must be understood as an important personal and social goal. As such, all the pomp and nobility associated with liberation movements must be understood as both self-serving and humanitarian. There is no conflict between these motives; indeed, the self one is serving is that part of humanity over which one has some understanding and possible control, so it *should* be the prime candidate for enhancement.[64]

Once this concept is appreciated, the central difference can be identified between the proper justification of revolutionary or evolutionary political action and the justification most frequently sounded by revolutionaries. The former is tied to enhancing one's life, whereas the latter customarily stresses the altruistic aspects of protesting tyranny, oppression, or the simple stagnancy of decadent systems. If the history of efforts to change social systems has been a disaster, it is probably explainable by the doctrine that one should change a political system for the sake of mankind and not for one's own sake. For, if this doctrine is accepted, the methods one will accept as means for instituting change will very probably (though not necessarily) include self-destruction, martyrdom,[65] and self-sacrifice. Yet a worthwhile goal cannot at once require that one simply give up one's life unless it is so essential to one's life to gain this goal that risking life is worth it. But for revolutionaries the self-destructive actions required from the victims of oppression are usually regarded as duties to some "higher cause" than self.[66]

This is a not too complicated theoretical account of the futility of such approaches to human liberation that has to do with the relationship between ends and means. In order to pursue a certain end efficiently, with the greatest likelihood of success, not every course of action will do. There are rational and irrational approaches. The goal of liberation is to be considered as requiring pretty specific means for its attainment. To understand these means, one must consider just what the goal involves. Liberation means the institutionalization of full respect for the individual natural human rights of everyone involved, all members of a community. The function of this liberation is expected, though not guaranteed (since men have free will), to be the unleashing of creative efforts in directions conceived by the individuals themselves, not by those who have kept them in bondage. Why is this important? Because individuals are, on the average, in a better position to assess what will enhance their own welfare than are those who might command them. Not all of them will be better equipped, to be sure. There are men and women who, while quite free, completely neglect their well-being.[67] But this is a risk worth taking, for in a free system such neglect, unlike in an unfree one, cannot be legally transferred to or distributed over others.

It seems, therefore, that the fundamental underlying motive of liberation movements is a sort of broad-minded self-interest, namely, the pursuit of happiness. But if the method of liberation negates this idea, it is self-defeating in its approach to gaining its end. There cannot be a compromise on this principle: the end determines the principles of the means by which to achieve it. Any attempt to escape this fact simply undermines the goal in sight.

The history of liberation movements is replete with such self-defeating efforts. And the central reason for this is that while in political terms many people have realized that principles of community life should benefit the members, they have not realized that in personal terms the principles of private conduct must also benefit the agent, first and foremost (but not exclusively). Even the so-called bourgeois liberation movements suffered under the misconception that theirs were national or class or even humanitarian struggles, with personal prosperity only a side benefit.[68] Theorists of liberation movements, such as Adam Smith, David Hume, John Locke, refused to name the central objective of liberation: the achievement of individual good. Instead, many of them smuggled in self-interest through the back door, as a mere intermediary tool to further the public good.

This is all very unfortunate and it accounts, in part, for why liberation movements have lacked prudence by which to temper fervor and violence. For the crucial ethical principle to recall in the process of fighting for the good political order is the same as that which is central to all, namely, that *each person should strive for the best life for himself as a human being.* This very general principle immediately informs us that reason and temperance and moderation and prudence must all play crucial roles in the assessment of what one should do. Although in times of social and political upheaval the application of virtues may not be a matter of habit, as one hopes is the case in normal times, the test of a human being of quality and excellence is to make his virtue govern his conduct even when times are confusing and difficult.

Consider, for example, that although a feudal society is host to numerous injustices, something close to a sense of justice does find itself part of the idea of a feudal order. As Munroe Smith notes:

The whole system may be regarded as a system by which all the land of the realm was drawn into the service of the realm, or as a system by which those who render service to the community receive, in the form of the yield or produce of land, payment or salary for their services.[69]

As Sabine observes, "Feudalism, then, in its legal principles, was a system of land tenure in which ownership was displaced by something like leasehold."[70] To put the matter plainly, not all of this is entirely askew as far as the system of justice of a constitution of human rights is concerned. In politics, as in all normative areas, there are gradations, and some aspects of feudalism could by no means be placed on a par with, say, tyranny or totalitarianism. Of course, in a feudal order "if the land-system were logically worked out, the king would be the sole landowner." And, as such, for the purest conception of the relationship between feudalism and human rights, there is no question that the feudal system, qua system, has to be regarded as corrupt—the human right to acquire, own, and trade items of value, including (and especially) land, was not recognized.

But under the feudal system, especially with the illogical or inconsistent modifications that had been brought about through various trends and the ultimate incoherence of the system (and, therefore, its impracticality in pure form), the opportunity for advancing the cause of liberation exists without universal violence. For any individual who would understand the imperative of the human rights idea, even if put into different terms, the possibility of taking meaningful steps toward liberation could exist on certain fronts. Among those parts of the feudal elite, there are usually numerous decent human beings who would not recoil at cooperation with an effort to make advances toward universal liberty. Granted, much persuading and agitation is necessary under such circumstances, as is well known from history. But there is a marked difference between the sort of efforts that permeated the semifeudal society of the American British colonies—involving education, pamphleteering, political action, petition, boycotts—and the sort characterized by the effort to liberalize feudal France. If anything gives liberation movements a bad record and leads them toward failure in the end, it is the forgetting of the ends to be attained while the effort is being made to attain them. That is just what differentiates, in large part, the American and the French revolutions.

Interestingly enough, the Hungarian revolution of 1848 had closely resembled the revolution in America, at least in form. Its demise, too, resembled more one that America might have experienced had the British been able to muster help from outsiders, for the Hungarian revolutionaries were scholars, poets, businessmen, and landowners who worked, primarily (at first) by means of mass meetings, education, and pamphleteering, and were finally subdued by the Russian army, not their actual adversaries, the feudal state of Austria.

This is not to claim that the 1848 Hungarian effort was peaceful, but peacefulness is not the issue here. What is at issue is that defending human rights requires the most careful use of force. For one, only the force that constitutes retaliation against equal (previous or present) force is justifiable as a general policy in liberation movements. Terrorism, for example, is in essential violation of this general policy. Terrorism is differentiated by its use of force against those in no way connected with the enemy—for example, children. There are circumstances in which the killing of the innocent by freedom fighters is justified, namely, when the innocent are being used by oppressors to set up a shield against retaliation, but only if no other alternative is available. But the deliberate and unprovoked introduction of innocent parties, for purposes of attaining some goal through the sense of restraint against these innocents by the oppressors, is unjustifiable. Indeed, terrorists are, contrary to Marxist and related rhetoric, not freedom fighters. For another, even if force is justified, as in retaliation, the presence of peaceful alternatives may well introduce facts that render its use unjustifiable. Moreover, if the use of retaliatory force is justified merely on grounds of just punishment, if there are more pressing goals to be pursued, the alternative of punitive action should be avoided.

All this generality may appear academic, but in fact it is precisely this sort of careful assessment of what one should do in order to pursue one's proper goals that should precede at least all organized liberation efforts. If one is serious about one's attempt to achieve liberty through the institution of a constitution of human rights, then one is justified in rejecting the significance of these sorts of considerations in the context of examining what one should do.

One of the most serious shortcomings of liberation movements has been alluded to above. I am referring to the fact that mature theorizing concerning human rights had not been accompanied frequently enough by mature theorizing on morality. The major philosophical supporters of natural rights, most notably John Locke, focused their attention upon political matters. Although there had been some discussion of morality, its extent was meager compared to the detailed analysis provided about various political issues. In this regard, Adam Smith provided a very valuable insight about the bulk of modern moral philosophy, and what he said is largely true in our day.

In the ancient philosophy the perfection of virtue was represented as necessarily productive, to the person who possessed it, of the most perfect happiness in this life. In
the modern philosophy it was frequently represented as generally, or rather as almost
always inconsistent with any degree of happiness in this life; and heaven was to be
earned only by penance and mortification, by the austerities and abasement of a
monk; not by the liberal, generous, and spirited conduct of a man.[71]

Although on the political front, philosophers were eager to spell out
what's right and what's wrong, which in many cases (Locke, Hume, Kant,
Mill) amounted to giving support to movements of liberation (even if not
always in the framework of natural rights), on the ethical front nothing so
detailed had been produced, at least not until after liberation movements
had gotten well under way.

But politics, although a distinctive aspect of human life by virtue of its
focus on the organized and just use of might, is but a small portion of the
tasks with which human beings must cope in their lives. And unless there is a
fairly clear idea about the general principles of personal conduct, the rights
and wrongs of what one should do in one's life, and why, the most elementary principles for carrying out even the initial stages of political action
will be lacking. These initial stages are not themselves subject to the guidance
of civil law; for it is precisely against the corrupted versions of law that
movements of liberation must be directed; and law, therefore, is not yet
available to provide the standards of right and wrong. Outside of law it is
ethics, in its myriad applications (in family relations, friendship, professional life, commerce, and so forth), that provides the guidelines for conduct.
And although ethics can make clear only the very general principles or virtues of human existence, without those general principles the individual has
no compass. As a compass, ethics needs to be interpreted in one's individual
situation. And one can fail to do this well, of course, even if the general principles are available. But without the general principles it is only good
common sense that exists. Common sense is fine when faced with the familiar problems of life, but liberation movements give rise to crises, emergencies,
peculiarities, and nuances. It is in such cases that elaborate care must be applied so as to make progress a real possibility.

My efforts have been to stress the indispensability of ethics for purposes of
proper political action and for instituting appropriate political change. I
have stayed at the level of generality appropriate to a philosopher. As a person who was himself part of a liberation movement when living in Budapest
(1939-1953) and who is still part of such a movement in the United States,
there are innumerable (but largely anecdotal) episodes in my life that bear
directly on what I have been discussing in such general terms.[72] My entire
family has had to cope with the tasks I have been discussing, although not all

have worked with the institution of a constitution of human rights as their major political task. And this fact, though very particularized in the lives of the millions who are involved in living with the violation of their rights, does raise a further general point that bears considering.

First of all, it is not always possible to strive for political change, since such change necessarily involves other people who may hold reactionary political positions. If one is alone in the conviction that a constitution of human rights is imperative, it may be true but irrelevant for present purposes when no one else agrees. Among others who have freely chosen to reject moral and political imperatives, it is impossible to follow political imperatives. One is *forced* to confine himself to focusing on the moral ones.

This is one reason that escape from a tyrannical society is perfectly justified. If there is an insufficient consensus about the need for liberation, then one is not at home with those ideas. A sense of nationalism or ethnic loyalty or familial attachment or a state of sickness, ignorance, or poverty, may make escape undesirable or unwise. But rational human beings, who make the effort to improve their lot in realistic ways, should not sit by stoically and tolerate oppression and tyranny simply because their fellows do so. They should try to lead a prosperous, spirited life elsewhere.

Second, if emigration and escape are impossible and life is totally dehumanizing, the alternatives of defiant protest and resistance become valid options. This is the only case where something on the order of martyrdom is compatible with liberation movements. In this kind of case, the alternative of living as a serf or slave is recognized as so self-debasing, so intolerable for any person of self-respect, that making, as it were, a final stand is very likely the only alternative left. This should not be confused with self-sacrifice, for one must consider what is meant by "self" here. And if one reflects that the self at hand is the self of someone who has ambition and pride, and that the alternatives are death or total submission to evil, death is indeed an act of self-assertion, even of selfishness.

None of what I have said in support of a code of self-liberation should be understood as implying that success is ever guaranteed. I used the analogy of engineering, but, although even engineering will not guarantee success with the best principles guiding the engineer, in human affairs, especially involving matters of community concern, there is always the problem that others might disagree. The freedom that all human beings are born with,[73] to attend to the world (always) or to evade it (frequently), besets community life with the problem of unpredictability. One can only speak firmly about hypothetical prospects, namely, what would occur *if* all would aspire to reach their proper ends. And one must always keep that in mind as the ideal prospect. But in the bulk of cases, the chance for consensus is highly variable. The permutations of a code of self-liberation must take into account this variability. Options must be kept open. What if my comrades desert the cause? What if my opponents change for the better? What if I abandon my own principles and fall behind?

Throughout the last section of this chapter I have discussed the ethics of change, using the system of feudalism as a springboard. One can find a fairly clear answer to the questions I posed for myself when I began this discussion. I have indicated why seeking the establishment of a constitution of human rights must not involve violation of human rights. I have indicated that feudalism is at best a very loose system of law; it is better understood as a system of practices and customs, which may have more or fewer beneficial elements from the point of view of human rights theory. (For example, if the feudal system is monarchical with constitutional restraints, and the actual feudal membership tends to favor liberalization, the movement toward liberation must take this into consideration.) Thus, force is only one option for those moving toward liberation. I have indicated why liberation movements, and freedom fighters, must be eclectic—why there is no one set of steps to be taken by all. I should mention that personal temperament is not a negligible factor here, something that statist revolutionary movements systematically repress, very much in line with their statist aims. Finally, I emphasized that the only general principles available concerning efforts to institute a constitution of human rights are the general principles that are proper guidelines for human conduct as such. These, applied with care and deliberation, will point the way toward a proper interpretation of circumstances and what one should do when faced with them.

It should be clear that the mention of feudalism is virtually ornamental in this essay. The main issue has been the way to cope with human community life that involves the systematic (regimented, institutionalized) violation of human rights. In contemporary Hungary we find the situation somewhat similar to the feudal circumstances that have served as my background. What has changed is: whereas in feudal systems the centralized state is relatively weak, with the monarch requiring the loyalty of his nobles who, in turn, receive fee, in the semisocialist society of Hungary today the central state has its own armies and police and prisons, with the capacity of national surveillance.

But in some respects the situation is not very different. And I am personally acquainted with individuals in Hungary today who are adhering precisely to the sort of principled pursuit of liberation I have outlined in this paper. They are a diverse group, some posing as state agents, others in open opposition to the state, others working "through the system" by teaching, writing, and translating. And there are also those who are rash and haphazard in their opposition to the state. And this is causing much worry to those in the former group.

Put in these terms, the situation is not difficult to recognize. As an individualist movement, liberation movements are pluralist, decentralized, adjusted to the needs and priorities of the individuals involved. This may appear to some as a weakness, compared to the Leninist method of the cadre, for example. But that method, it must be recalled, was aimed at establishing a powerful totalitarian regime, not a free society. And it completely rejected the notion that ethics plays a role in the guidance of revolutionary movements; Lenin regarded ethics as a bourgeois prejudice and adhered to unqualified pragmatism when it came to pursuing the goals of the revolution. The price to be paid for the importation of Leninist efforts into liberation movements is the disintegration of the movement, that is, the placing of the means into conflict with the goals. The reward of the more patient and deliberate approach outlined here is that a clear chance exists for instituting a constitution of human rights. Without a doubt, this is a considerable prospect and worth every bit of the restraint that it requires of those who seriously aim for human liberation.

HUMAN RIGHTS AND FOREIGN AFFAIRS

The final concern of this chapter is what members of other communities, with more or less proper legal systems, might and should do when aware of the systematic violation of human rights in some neighboring community. I am concerned here mainly with official or governmental relations. As to private assistance, there is no ground for prohibiting the aid members of a free society might give to those in other societies who are working toward the establishment of a constitution of human rights. (Cases involving the aiding and abetting of tyrannies or other lawless regimes are not at issue here. In some cases, of course, private help to civilians might pose a threat to the community whose members provide this help, in which case the government might have to appraise the matter on the model of aiding aggression, inadvertently.)

Issues arise because victims need to know what they may expect and neighbors need to know what they are justified to do in support of victims. Regarding another kind of community, lawlessness may appear to invite intervention. This seems to be the reason why the recent concern with "human rights" has produced worries abroad. The reason is that in the Western political tradition of the last three centuries the concept of human (natural) rights has played a crucial role with reference to the fundamental legitimacy of a given system and regime. Failure to protect and preserve the rights of individuals in a country would call into serious question the lawfulness of the regime and system of statutes in force. Admitting for our purposes the controversial nature of such a supposition, the impact of this Western political tradition is great enough to make the suggestion about the concerns of the Soviet regime quite plausible.

Yet, is there any rational ground for supposing that even if the government of the United States concluded that failure to respect, protect, and preserve the human rights of citizens of the Soviet Union seriously suggests the lawlessness of the Soviet regime, the policy of the United States government vis-a-vis the Soviet Union would *have to* become hostile, antagonistic, a threat to international peace and order?

One way to approach an answer to this question is by reflecting on a more personal situation that may involve similar considerations. Assuming that it is possible to make the distinctions implicit in any objectivist moral system, it is clear that the best of human beings need on occasions to make decisions respecting how they would interact with or relate to people of low virtue. In the public domain, too, a possibly implacable legal system's enforcement agents would find themselves having to make decisions how to interact or relate to powerful criminals in the community. In neither of these cases would it be true that evil or criminal persons should always be related to in a hostile, aggressive, uncooperative manner. In either case certain greater values than moral ostracism or legal retaliation might need protection and preservation, so that consorting with bad characters or cooperating with criminals could be fully justified. Punitive action is not required as a matter of necessity, either in personal or in legal affairs. Cases are not difficult to imagine, although the value system in terms of which decisions would have to be made cannot be taken for granted here. Still, assuming that saving the life of a kidnapped child is of great value, legal authorities could justifiably seek out the assistance and cooperation of criminals who would under normal circumstances be in danger of retaliation from representatives of the legal system. In personal circumstances as well, a decent human being might on occasions engage in limited voluntary association with a morally corrupt individual, provided this individual holds out values that need to be secured and could not be secured without this association. Although the local pharmacist may be a cheat and a liar, a thoroughly detestable individual excepting his performance as a pharmacist, in time of medical emergency, with the other pharmacy closed, a decent person might find it imperative to trade with this otherwise-to-be-avoided individual.

In short, while we could acknowledge others' immorality or criminality, we are not morally or legally required (as decent or lawful individuals) to act punitively toward them.

A similar consideration would apply in international relations in case the thesis about lawfulness versus lawlessness suggested here were to be accepted and implemented to guide the conduct and policies of lawful regimes throughout the world. For example, ministers of lawless regimes should not always be rebuked and opposed directly. A proper conception of lawfulness can be rendered operative and influential in diplomacy without such ostentation. We can be clear about the lawlessness of legal systems and regimes (including the possible subtleties and complexities of partial lawlessness), and it is still a matter of independent choice just what the proper diplomatic approach should be in their face.

What I have claimed here, and tried to back with some reflections on our approach to immorality and criminality in familiar cases, may explain the underlying ethical and political framework for numerous diplomatic events in our times. It is equally possible that some of the points advanced might be fruitfully applied in such diplomatic endeavors to improve a familiar situation.

For example, it is a common complaint of some people that whereas the government of the United States freely condemns such regimes as the government of Rhodesia, it engages in elaborate diplomatic and numerous related and unrelated contacts with the Soviet Union. Admirers of Aleksandre Solzhenitsyn point up the paradox of this situation, given the established fact that the crimes of the government of the Soviet Union are far greater and more vicious than those of the admittedly objectionable Rhodesian regime. Moreover, the ambassador of the United States to South Africa could refuse to attend a segregated concert to which he was officially invited, but such a rebuke against, for example, the appearance of some state-sponsored Soviet ballet company sent to America by the Soviet government is virtually unthinkable.

On the one hand, the present thesis would render it proper for a lawful regime—which for present purposes I shall assume the U.S. government to be—to regard both the Soviet Union and Rhodesia as seriously flawed countries in the lawfulness of their respective regimes. On the other hand, the decisions as to *how to express* the recognition of and concern about this flaw cannot be made abstractly apart from the day-to-day diplomatic problems the lawful regime faces in the world. Clearly, the first consideration would help engender a more integrated, less arbitrary foreign policy for the lawful regime. Here also the precise directions cannot be foretold and a great deal must hinge on the personal integrity of those who are part of the lawful regime facing such problems in their diplomatic endeavors. The crucial point for present purposes is that a recognition of the objective distinction between bona fide and fraudulent claims to lawfulness would alter current thinking and, subsequently, action and policy concerning international developments. Thus it may be appropriate to make declarations of fundamental disapproval without, however, implying that any threatening international actions will be forthcoming vis-à-vis lawless regimes, for example, that must nevertheless be contended with as parties to certain advancements of a lawful regime's justified diplomatic purposes.

The point has been illustrated to some degree by the situation of the United States refusal to help Hungary in 1956, as well as by Great Britain's refusal to help Hungary in 1848. These are inadequate samples, of course, since neither the U.S. nor Great Britain of past can be called societies in full conformity with human rights. The practical import of this is that certain alternatives available to citizens in a free society, such as sending mercenaries to help the revolutionaries, were not in fact available under the existing system. For example, in 1956 the U.S. government prohibited a number of Americans with Hungarian ancestry from leaving for Hungary en masse in aid of the Hungarian revolutionaries against the Soviet Union. When such private efforts are forbidden by statute, the ethics of relating to the justified revolutionary activities of citizens of neighboring countries is complicated considerably. There are no general principles governing what should be done. As an example, for those with friends and relatives in the country under tyranny, the imperatives could be very different from what they are for those who have no such relationships. But even for the former group, it is not necessarily imperative to give aid, especially to risk imprisonment in their own country while attempting to aid citizens of another. The main concern must be whether the loyalty is justified—whether the individuals whom one might aid merit the help, whether one has previously assumed responsibilities that would be breached by lending aid. From the point of view of an egoistic ethics, it is such principled personal concerns that one must reflect on in deliberating about these sorts of issues. (Sometimes deliberation will not be needed, namely, when one has become acclimated to having to cope with such circumstances daily, as for instance in the French resistance movement during the Nazi occupation.)

Contrary, then, to certain widely held views, the fact of tyranny in one society does not necessarily justify aid from the governments, nor even from the private citizens, of other societies to the oppressed. I am, of course, speaking of physical assistance, involving persons and property. Ideological assistance is, of course, imperative, but would be virtually automatic in the case of any truly free society. Its existence stands in explicit condemnation of tyrannies. What is often forgotten is that the free society is not just suitable for some people—North Americans but not Africans, as some thinkers argue in their defense of African or Asian or Latin American dictatorships. It is a system with universal applicability, although the precise manifestation of freedom in different societies may not be the same. Technological, educational, cultural, and even climactic circumstances can make a difference in how freedom will be implemented and upheld. But the difference is not whether, but how it will be done. The mere fact that the capability of most human beings to protect and preserve their human rights has been limited by a lack of widespread support from their fellow human beings does not prove that no defense of such rights should have been forthcoming, anymore than the fact that someone is murdered shows that his right to life should not have been respected and protected.

From these general points, numerous particular implications can be drawn for purposes of both understanding the disasters and high points of human history and guiding future conduct on the personal and diplomatic fronts. This is all than can be done from the point of view of philosophical analysis and argument.

CONCLUSION

This has been a very long discussion of issues that would require even more extensive treatment to make each point fully warranted. In political theory we draw on virtually all human knowledge, since we are dealing with the most complicated being known to us, namely, man, and we are considering the principles of his community existence. My task has been to discuss human rights from a natural rights framework and indicate the implications of taking these rights very seriously for purposes of guiding conduct that aims at the domestic institution of a constitution of human rights and the rational treatment of foreign affairs in the light of such a basic framework.

In order to accomplish this task, I have provided a brief historical review of the major ideas on human rights up to the present. I have tried to indicate why the natural rights approach, first spelled out in some detail by John Locke, is still, with some amendments, the correct approach. Then I outlined the reasons why, when using this approach, we can learn that human rights exist and what they are. I have also indicated what bearing the existence of these human rights has for practical community affairs.

I then tried to indicate the most general ethical imperatives applicable to those living in societies, for example feudal or semifeudal, that should be transformed into communities with a constitution of human rights. I stressed the variability of the implications of these general principles for particular individuals striving to accomplish this transformation. And, finally, I tried to provide some clues, given the perspective of natural rights and what this implies about the nature of a legal system, its absence, and its partial approximation, about the proper approach to foreign affairs.

There is no question that much of this discussion will appear to be somewhat unrealistic for many readers. My reply to those who still doubt the value of taking human rights seriously and the overall normative approach within which this can be done, is to offer the observation of Andrei Sakharov:

You always need to make ideals clear to yourself . . . . You always have to be aware of them, even if there is no direct path to their realization. Were there no ideals, there would be no hope whatsoever. Then everything would be hopelessness, darkness—a blind alley.[74]

NOTES

1. Martin P. Golding, "Towards a Theory of Human Rights," *The Monist* 52 (1968):549.

2. Richard P. Claude, "The Classical Model of Human Rights Development," in *Comparative Human Rights* (Baltimore: Johns Hopkins University Press, 1976).

3. For a summary of evidence for this, *see* Joseph R. Peden, "Property Rights in Celtic Irish Law," *Journal of Libertarian Studies* 1 (1977): 81-95.

4. By "moral universe" I refer to that distinctive aspect of existence, concerning (to my knowledge only) human beings, that exhibits principles involving considerations about what should or should not be done as a matter of the agent's choice. The underlying metaphysical view, namely, that there exist different ontological domains, including one where we identify normative principles, cannot be worked out here. *See* my "Toward a Theory of Natural Human Rights" (unpublished).

5. The edition by J. Gough, *The Second Treatise of Government* (London: Basil Blackwell, 1966), argues that Locke did not actually embark upon a philosophical inquiry about political matters but produced, instead, an ideological tract so as to rationalize various political developments in England. *See* C. B. Macpherson, *Possessive Individualism* (Oxford: Clarendon Press, 1962).

6. Quoted in Martin P. Golding, "The Concept of Rights: A Historical Sketch," *Bioethics and Human Rights*, ed. E. B. Bandman (Boston: Little, Brown & Co., 1978), p. 48. The original reads: "Ius autem poli non est aliud quam potestas conformis rationi rectae absque pactione; ius fori est potestas ex pactione aliquando conformi rationi rectae, et aliquando discordanti." Ockham also defended the institution of private property somewhat like John Locke, based on the view that God gave mankind this institution, which meant, to him, "that the right to private property is a dictate of right reason." (As expressed by Heinrich A. Rommen, "The Genealogy of Natural Rights," *Thought* 29 (1954): 419.

7. Quoted in Fred D. Miller, Jr., "The State and the Community in Aristotle's *Politics*," *Reason Papers*, no. 1 (1974): 66.

8. In support of the view that Locke influenced the American tradition, *see* Bernard Bailyn, *The Origins of American Politics* (New York: Vintage Books, 1967); Harry V. Jaffa, *How to Think about the American Revolution* (Durham, N.C.: Carolina Academic Press, 1978); Frank M. Coleman, *Hobbes and America* (Toronto: University of Toronto Press, 1977). I am not suggesting that John Locke alone influenced the political system of the United States, nor do Bailyn and Jaffa advance such a thesis.

9. For a collection of studies on Locke, *see* Gordon J. Schochet, ed., *Life, Liberty, and Property* (Belmont, Calif.: Wadsworth Publishing Company, 1971). For one of the most provocative criticisms of the Lockean approach, *see* Leo Strauss, *Natural Right and History*, 2d ed. (Chicago: University of Chicago Press, 1970), pp. 202-51. The controversy about Locke is discussed, from the point of view Strauss, inspired by

Michael P. Zuckert, "The Recent Literature on Locke's Political Philosophy," *The Political Science Reviewer* 5 (1975): 271-304.

10. For a detailed discussion, *see* my *Human Rights and Human Liberties* (Chicago: Nelson-Hall, 1975), ch. 2.

11. E.g., Hugo Bedau, "The Right to Life," *The Monist* 52 (1968): 550-72; Gregory Vlastos, "Justice and Equality," in *Human Rights,* ed. A. I. Melden (Belmont, Calif.: Wadsworth Publishing Company, 1970), pp. 76-95; Alan Gewirth, *Reason and Morality* (Chicago: University of Chicago Press, 1978).

12. In criticism of this view, *see* Maurice Cranston, "Human Rights, Real and Supposed," in *Political Theory and the Rights of Man,* ed. D. D. Raphael (Bloomington: Indiana University Press, 1967), pp. 43-53; Tibor R. Machan, "Prima Facie versus Natural (Human) Rights," *The Journal of Value Inquiry* 10 (1976): 119-31; Ayn Rand, *The Virtue of Selfishness, A New Concept of Egoism* (New York: New American Library, 1964), pp. 101-06.

13. Ayn Rand, "Value and Rights," in *Readings in Introductory Philosophical Analysis,* ed. John Hospers (Englewood-Cliffs, N.J.: Prentice-Hall, 1968), p. 385.

14. Melden, *Human Rights,* pp. 143-49.

15. A. I. Melden, *Rights and Persons* (Berkely: University of California Press, 1977), p. 232.

16. Vladimir Kudryavtsev, "The Truth about Human Rights," *Human Rights* 5 (1976): 199.

17. Laszlo Versenyi, "Virtue as Self-directed Art," *The Personalist* 53 (1972): 282.

18. E. g., Robert W. Hanula and Peter Waverly Hill, "Using Metaright Theory to Ascribe Kantian Rights to Animals within Nozick's Minimal State," *Arizona Law Review* 19 (1977): 242-83. *See also,* Christopher D. Stone, *Should Trees Have Standing? Toward Legal Rights for Natural Objects* (Los Altos, Calif.: William Kaufmann, Inc. 1974).

19. John Locke, *An Essay Concerning Human Understanding,* vol. 1, ed. A. C. Fraser, (Oxford: Clarendon Press, 1894), bk. 2, chap. 31, sect. 6.

20. Jeremy Bentham, "Anarchical Fallacies," vol. 2, in *Works,* ed. John Bowring (1843). Selections printed in Melden, *Human Rights,* pp.28-39.

21. John Stuart Mill, *Utilitarianism,* ed. Oskar Priest (Indianapolis, Ind.: Bobbs-Merrill Co., 1957), p. 66. It is not that the defense of the natural rights of individuals would not probably lead to wealth, prosperity, and general welfare, but to argue for rights on grounds of what they might possibly produce to protect them is not a natural rights approach. It is also much easier to introduce exceptions and temporary suspensions, for example, on grounds that urgency requires not leaving matters to their natural evolution; experts can sometimes know better what will enhance the general welfare, even if generally the laissez-faire attitude is sound. It is very likely that the utilitarian defense of rights has helped usher in the systematic weakening of the integrity of even the American Bill of Rights. (With the help of pragmatism, the judiciary of the American government began to abandon a principled approach to the U. S. Constitution itself. *See* Grant Gilmore, *The Ages of American Law* [New Haven, Conn.: Yale University Press, 1977], pp. 46ff.)

22. Karl Marx, *Selected Writings,* ed. David McLellan (Oxford: Oxford University Press, 1977), p. 53.

23. Margaret Macdonald, "Natural Rights," in Melden, *Human Rights*, pp. 47-49.

24. Quoted in Macdonald, ibid., p. 49.

25. Ibid., pp. 54-55.

26. Ludwig Wittgenstein, *Philosophical Investigations*, ed. G. E. M. Anscombe (New York: Macmillan Company, 1953), p. 20e.

27. Ibid., p. 30e.

28. Quoted in Kenneth R. Minogue, "Natural Rights, Ideology and the Game of Life," *Human Rights*, eds. Eugene Kamenka and Alice Erh-Soon Tay (London: Edward Arnold, 1978), p. 34.

29. Ibid.

30. Sidney Hook, *Pragmatism and the Tragic Sense of Life* (New York: Basic Books, 1976), ch. 5, "Absolutism and Human Rights." Hook is carrying on the pragmatist argument concerning first principles in any realm of existence, metaphysics, or politics. In general, pragmatism, perhaps the only "home grown" American philosophical movement—nonetheless, with debts to utilitarianism and Kantianism—is hostile to individualism. John Dewey, for example, has flatly denied the efficacy of the mind for individual human beings, in *The Philosophy of John Dewey*, ed. John J. McDermott (New York: G. P. Putnam's Sons, 1973), p. 713, where we are told that "The stuff of belief and proposition is not originated in us. It comes from others, by education, tradition, and the suggestion of the environment." For Dewey's very influential attack on the firmness of moral principles, *see* James Gouinlock, ed., *The Moral Writings of John Dewey* (New York: Hafner Press, 1976), pp. 176-205. On further developments of the collectivist conception of thinking, especially in science, *see* Thomas S. Kuhn, *The Structure of Scientific Revolutions*, 2d ed. (Chicago: University of Chicago Press, 1970). *See* Tibor R. Machan, "On the Possibility of Objectivity and Moral Determinants in Scientific Change," *Determinants and Controls of Scientific Development*, ed. Karen Knorr et. al. (Dordrecht: D. Reidel, 1975). To appreciate the deep-seated difference between individualism and collectivism—of a point of view that affirms individual, natural human rights and one that denies them—consider Karl Marx's claim that "The phantoms formed in the human brain are, also, necessarily sublimates of their material life-process, which is empirically verifiable and bound to material premisses. Morality, religion, metaphysics, all the rest of ideology and their corresponding forms of consciousness, thus no longer retain the semblance of independence. . . . Life is not determined by consciousness, but consciousness by life." Marx, *Selected Writings*, p. 164.

31. For a more detailed treatment, *see* my *Human Rights and Human Liberties* and *The Pseudo-Science of B. F. Skinner* (New Rochelle, N. Y.: Arlington House, 1974). Although many scientists appear to be denying the reality of free will—that is, the real capacity of human individuals to cause (some of) their behavior, or purposive chosen conduct—there is no scientific reason to deny it, only some assumptions made about the objects of study of various fields of science extended (but not with conclusively good reasons and with much to contradict it from other sciences) to apply to human beings. For one recent scientific explanation of human consciousness that is compatible with modern science, yet incompatible with the denial of free will, *see* Roger W. Sperry, "Changing Concepts of Consciousness and Free Will," *Perspectives in Biology and Medicine* 20 (1976): 9-19. (Note 30 also pertains here.)

32. By no means do I mean that this form of discrimination is unjustified as a matter of practical effort; there is no way to live without such discrimination between various alternative possibilities. Various human rights organizations can be doing much good simply by focusing on certain areas of human rights violation. What is unjustified is to single these out as the only human rights violations, and the only ones against which defending oneself is justified.

33. Much is made of the idea that man does not live by bread alone, but neither does he live by word or political dissent alone, so his rights in other spheres of action need recognition, respect, and protection as well. I would suggest that here an antimaterialist prejudice is at work—only the conscious (spiritually significant or highlighted) is given free reign. But man is a conscious animal, both aspects being essential to his life. In both he must take responsibility. Without his rights recognized, he is denied his humanity, whether the rights pertain to freedom of thought or to freedom of action. For an interesting analysis, see Ayn Rand, "Censorship: Local and Express," *The Ayn Rand Letter* 2 (1973): 1-6, 1-4 (nos. 23, 24, 25). Here the debate rages between liberals and conservatives, roughly, as to what to control, body or mind. Rand argues that each wants to control what he regards as more important. And if one considers that the extreme left has been materialist while the extreme right has been idealist (even mystical from a theological perspective), one can perceive evidence for this. But the point cannot be considered here in detail.

34. But gray makes sense only with clear cases of black and white in mind. Borderline cases and undecided ones are not all there is. *See* more on this in my *Human Rights and Human Liberties*. My learning here comes from the works of Rand, Austin, C. I. Lewis, Barry Stroud, Gilbert Harman, and many others, but I do not wish to impute full agreement between me and these philosophers, nor any among them. The point is complicated. Suffice it to appreciate that essences need be neither rigid, nor purely nominal, conventional, or arbitrary. They can be objectively correct and open to warranted change.

35. The most recent Soviet Constitution states that "Legal action is taken in conformity with Soviet law in the case of individuals who engage in anti-Soviet propaganda and agitation, designed to undermine or weaken the established social and political system in our country, or who systematically spread deliberate falsifications vilifying the Soviet state or social system," *Pravda*, February 1977 (as reprinted in the Soviet publication *New Times*, February 1977). This utterly vague and broad prohibition of choice in the area of speech, of course, is matched thoroughly with other forms of conduct.

36. A human individual may value himself as a social being, but he may also place greater value on his own individuality. This is not because he is rudely self-centered, but because only his self can make value judgments and benefit or suffer. Society isn't the sort of being that can do such things—it exists by dependence upon the individual choices of individual human beings. For a most recent denial of this, *see* Lewis Thomas, *The Lives of a Cell* (New York: Bantam Books, 1975). For a full defense of the individualist stance, *see* David L. Norton, *Personal Destinies, A Philosophy of Ethical Individualism* (Princeton, N. J.: Princeton University Press, 1976). Norton considers the individualist viewpoint from various branches of philosophical perspective, metaphysical, epistemological, ethical, and political (although this last he plans to expand in a forthcoming volume).

37. Debate ensues as to whether the due process clause is purely formal, requiring that laws be administered with internal consistency, or substantive, requiring that law itself reflect a correct idea of justice. For the history of the concept, *see* Rodney L. Mott, *Due Process of Law* (Indianapolis, Ind.: Bobbs-Merrill, 1926). For a defense of substantive due process in connection with laws pertaining not merely to speech but also to commerce, *see* Robert G. McClosky, "Economic Due Process and the Supreme Court," in *The Supreme Court and the Constitution*, ed. P. B. Kurland (Chicago: University of Chicago Press, 1965), and William Letwin, "Economic Due Process in the American Constitution, and the Rule of Law," in *Law and Liberty, Essays on F. A. Hayek*, ed. R. L. Cunningham (College State: Texas A and M University Press, 1979).

38. For example, *see* Joan Kennedy Taylor, "Slavery: America's Fatal Compromise," *The Libertarian Alternative*, ed.T. R. Machan (Chicago: Nelson-Hall, 1974), pp. 235-44. On the general economic front, *see* Jonathan R. T. Hughes, *The Governmental Habit* (New York: Basic Books, 1977). Contrary to what *Pravda* charged me with (Georgii Ratiani, December 10, 1976), my theory is not a whitewash of the American system as it presently manifests itself, mainly because that system has been (a) thoroughly corrupted and (b) contained contradictions from the start. The supposition that all theories that are not supportive of the Soviet system are ipso facto expressions of class interest, usually accepted by Marxists or orthodox Marxists, is too general and thus false. True, under a certain interpretation even a sound theory expresses class interest, namely, the interest of those who wish to understand reality correctly and flourish through it.

39. I develop this, with the help of numerous theorists, in my *Human Rights and Human Liberties.*

40. For more on this, *see* Ayn Rand, *Capitalism: The Unknown Ideal* (New York: New American Library, 1967), p. 322.

41. *See* Murray N. Rothbard, *Man, Economy, and State* (Princeton, N. J.: Van Nostrand, 1962) and the general economic literature of free market analysis. For historical revision of the myth of robber barons rising from free market competition, *see* F. A. Hayek, ed., *Capitalism and the Historians* (Chicago: University of Chicago Press, 1954).

42. In essentials, John Rawls's *A Theory of Justice* (Cambridge, Mass.: Harvard University Press, 1971), introduces the "difference principle" in addition to the "freedom principle," so as to make allowances for those who find themselves in circumstances far below what they would like to be (put broadly but translated into mostly economic terms). The complaint that free markets are of great advantage to the wealthy and of little advantage to the poor is so widespread that it needs no documentation. One attempt to criticize natural rights theory directly from this perspective occurs in Samuel Scheffler, "Natural Rights, Equality, and the Minimal State," *Canadian Journal of Philosophy* 6 (1976): 59-76. *See* my reply, "Against Nonlibertarian Natural Rights," *Journal of Libertarian Studies* 2 (1978): 233-38. For extensive replies to criticisms of the free market, see my "Considerations of the Libertarian Alternative," *Harvard Journal of Law and Public Policy* (forthcoming). For various positions on the dispute, with none making a moral case for the free society, unfortunately, *see* Gerald Dworkin, Gordon Bermant, and Peter G. Brown, eds., *Markets and Morals* (New York: Halsted Press, 1977), and for extensive considerations of these

sorts of criticisms, *see* H. B. Acton, *The Morals of Markets* (New York: Humanities Press, 1971).

43. Among prominent thinkers in Western societies, it is mainly economists who have argued for the free society, primarily because they have concluded that such a society lends itself to economic prosperity (but not only for this reason). Those who have discussed social and political affairs from the point of view of normative inquiry—ethics, normative political science, aesthetics—have not been defenders of freedom. This is because they have thought that freedom permits too much divergence from virtue, be this the virtue of generosity, temperance, modesty, or continence, and from beauty, for example, through the preponderance of commerce in mediocre art.

44. Exceptions are Robert Nozick, *Anarchy, State and Utopia* (New York: Basic Books, 1974), but without the underpinnings here outlined: Murray N. Rothbard, *For a New Liberty* (New York: Macmillan Co., 1978), and Rand, *Capitalism: The Unknown Ideal.* Others have supported the free society—F. A. Hayek, Milton Friedman, William Simon—but not mainly from the point of view of natural rights theory.

45. That is, a sound system of criminal and civil law, the natural purpose of which, for members of a human community, is to secure (interpersonal) justice, not to right all wrongs or solve all problems.

46. This is the well-known dispute between those who believe that a legal system must be founded on principles of justice and those who believe that legal systems do not require such foundations. For supporters and opponents of the natural law position, *see*, Martin P. Golding, ed., *The Nature of Law* (New York: Random House, 1966). For my treatment of the dispute, *see* "Law, Justice and Natural Rights," *Western Ontario Law Review* 14, (1975): 119-30, and "Human Dignity and the Law," *DePaul Law Review* 26 (1977): 807-31.

47. For a good exploration of these issues, *see* Eugene F. Miller, "Positivism, Historicism, and Political Inquiry," *American Political Science Review* 66 (1972): 796-817. *See* also, Strauss, *Natural Right and History.*

48. A good example of the close combination between mechanistic and value-free views of human nature and social engineering exists in B. F. Skinner, *Beyond Freedom and Dignity* (New York: Bantam Books, 1971). For criticism of this tradition, especially in psychology, *see* Isidor Chein, *The Science of Behavior and the Image of Man* (New York: Basic Books, 1972).

49. *See* my *The Pseudo-Science of B. F. Skinner* for more on this.

50. *See* Strauss, *Natural Right and History.*

51. Eugene F. Miller, "Political Philosophy and Human Nature," *The Personalist* 53 (1972): 209-21. "The denial of human nature undercuts the possibility of reliable knowledge of the best way of life for man and society. It encourages the belief that 'values' are simply the arbitrary creations of individuals or societies. It renders doubtful any generalizations about the actions of men or institutions and their causes" (p. 218).

52. Under Mao Tse Tung the People's Republic of China was a feudal state, although this is not what it was called.

53. Robert Nisbet, *The Social Philosophers, Community and Conflict in Western*

Thought (New York: Thomas Y. Crowell Company, 1973), p. 45. *See also*, Marc Bloch, *Feudal Society*, trans. L. A. Manyon, 2 vols. (Chicago: University of Chicago Press, 1964).

54. Bloch, *Feudal Society*, p. 225: "The obligation was equally binding on the lord in his relation to his vassal and on the vassal in his relation to the lord." But this is true in the welfare state, for example, whereby the social worker must care for the welfare recipient, while the recipient must give account of himself to the social worker. It is the centralized direction, relative to size, that makes the difference appear to be major. Nisbet says that "feudalism [was] decentralized and localized in essence" (p. 125), yet so is much of the welfare state. The fact of federalism in many welfare states even makes this a legal requirement. It is likely that technology, more than the logical elements of the system, make the difference here.

55. *See* Erich Fromm, *Escape from Freedom* (New York: Rinehart, 1941), from the left, and Robert Beum, "Middle-Class Power and Its Critics," *University Bookman* 28 (1978): 75-78, from the right.

56. In the Communist Manifesto. *See* Marx, *Selected Writings*, pp. 222-26. The more hectic life of a free society, where security is not accepted as the highest human value, did not appeal to Marx.

57. Ernst Freund, *Standards of American Legislation* (Chicago: University of Chicago Press, 1965), p. 38.

58. *See* earlier sections of this chapter.

59. Plainly put, from the Ten Commandments to utilitarianism, hardly any moral code can be practiced consistently and fully by human beings. For example, surely some parents just cannot be honored, they are so evil. The greatest happiness of the greatest number, in turn, is impossible to pursue, since one cannot know what it is, surely most of the time if not always. But this doctrine of pursuing the impossible dream has often been justified on grounds that morally it is better if human beings aim for the impossible, since then at least they will reach something noble. Such a view, however, breeds cynicism, not nobility of character, since persistent failure of reaching what one should achieve leads to doubt and the view that there is something askew in the entire endeavor of morality.

60. That in ancient Egypt the concept of human rights might not have been developed does not mean that no one thought of the horrible treatment men received. Yet, it is one thing to observe what is wrong with one man's treatment of another (including oneself), and another to determine what one should do in light of this treatment.

61. Only those who hold to the view that everyone necessarily seeks his *vested* interest would deny this. Yet we have already seen that human affairs are misconceived along those lines.

62. I defend this in my *Human Rights and Human Liberties*, but the position was made clear to me first in Ayn Rand, *The Virtue of Selfishness, A New Concept of Egoism*. I believe a position very close to this was developed, in more philosophical detail, by David L. Norton, *Personal Destinies, A Philosophy of Ethical Individualism*. For why this view may properly be called egoism, despite the unfortunate usage the terms "selfish" and "egoistic" have acquired, *see* my "Recent Work in Ethical Egoism," *American Philosophical Quarterly* 16 (1979): 1-15.

63. A Marxian example should suffice here as an illustration. In Marxism it is for the future of a matured mankind—as distinct from the present prehuman beings—that we must support the revolution! *See* Marx, *Selected Writings,* pp. 89, 96, passim.

64. *See* Norton, *Personal Destinies.*

65. "One who voluntarily undergoes the penalty of death for refusing to renounce his Christian faith...." *The Compact Edition of the Oxford English Dictionary* (Oxford: Oxford University Press, 1971), p. 1733. The part about faith renders martyrdom as misguided, since there is a lack of rational conviction that the choice of death is necessary.

66. This idea is currently advocated by such impressive individuals as Aleksandre Solzhenitsyn, "A World Split Apart," *Imprimis* 7 (1978): 1-6, and Irving Kristol, *Two Cheers for Capitalism* (New York: Basic Books, 1978), pp. 55-72.

67. It is crucial to realize that partly because of the deterministic view of human nature, the idea that anyone neglects to make the effort to improve his lot has been all but completely rejected. This is clearly revealed in the predominance of rehabilitory theories of imprisonment, in contradistinction to the idea of the punitive view. If none can help what he or she is doing—if our genes or environment made it so—then holding individuals responsible and extacting atonement or penalty is nonsense.

68. Ethnicity built into a war cry has been the tragic flaw of Hungary's history. It has undermined the moral validity of its 1848 revolution and is still part of the outlook of many of its citizens.

69. Quoted in George H. Sabine, *A History of Political Theory* (New York: Henry Holt & Co., 1959), p. 215 (from Munroe Smith, *The Development of European Law* [New York: Columbia University Press, 1928] p. 165).

70. Sabine, *Political Theory,* p. 215.

71. Adam Smith, *The Wealth of Nations* (New York: Modern Library, 1937), p. 726.

72. Tibor R. Machan, "Escape from Tyranny," *World Research INK,"* February 1977, pp. 9-11.

73. That is to say, the capacity of each (not crucially incapacitated, nor severely abnormal) human being to activate the use of his mind. *See* note 31.

74. Quoted in Hendrick Smith, "The Intolerable Andrei Sakharov" *The New York Times Magazine,* Nov. 4, 1973, p. 71.

Further Readings in Human Rights

Adams, E. M. "Personhood and Human Rights." *Man and World*, 8, no. 1 (February 1975).

Adler, Mortimer. *The Idea of Freedom*. Garden City, N. Y.: Doubleday and Co., 1958.

Ashmore, Harry S., ed. *The William O. Douglas Inquiry into the State of Individual Freedom*. Boulder, Colo.: Westview Press, 1979.

Bandman, Bertram. "Are There Any Human Rights?" *Journal of Value Inquiry*, 12 (Fall 1978).

Bandman, Elsie, ed. *Bioethics and Human Rights*. Boston: Little, Brown and Co., 1978.

Barnhardt, J. E. "Human Rights as Absolute Claims and Reasonable Expectations." *American Philosophical Quarterly*, 6, no. 4 (October 1969).

Bassiouni, M. Cherif. *International Terrorism and Political Crimes*. Springfield, Ill.: Charles C Thomas, 1975.

Bay, Christian. "A Human Rights Approach to Transnational Politics." *Universal Human Rights*, 1, no. 1 (January-March 1979).

Bernal, J. D. *Science in History*, vols. 1-4. Cambridge: The M.I.T. Press, 1971.

Bronaugh, Richard, ed. *Philosophical Law*. Westport, Conn.: Greenwood Press, 1978.

Buergenthal, Thomas, ed. *Human Rights, International Law and the Helsinki Accord*. Montclair, N. J.: Allanheld, Osmun and Co., 1978.

Chomsky, Noam. "The United States Versus Human Rights in the Third World." *Monthly Review*, 29, no. 3 (July-August, 1977).

Claude, Richard, ed. *Comparative Human Rights*. Baltimore: The Johns Hopkins Press, 1977.

Dobrosielski, Marion. "Polish Approach to Human Rights." *Dialectics and Humanism*, 5 (Summer 1978).

Dunn, John. *Western Political Theory in the Face of the Future*. Cambridge: Cambridge University Press, 1979.

Emerson, Rupert. "The Fate of Human Rights in the Third World." *Western Politics*, 27, no. 2 (January 1975).

Farber, Marvin. *Naturalism and Subjectivism*. Springfield, Ill.: Charles C Thomas, 1959.

Feinberg, Joel. "The Nature and Value of Rights." *The Journal of Value Inquiry*, 4, no. 4 (Winter 1970).

Frankel, Charles. *Human Rights and Foreign Policy*. New York: Foreign Policy Association, 1978.

Glaser, Kurt, ed. *Victims of Politics: The State of Human Rights*. New York: Columbia University Press, 1979.

Golding, Martin P. "Towards a Theory of Human Rights." *The Monist*, 52, no. 4 (October 1968).

Goodpaster, K., ed. *Ethics and Problems of the Twenty-First Century*. Indiana: University of Notre Dame Press, 1979.

Grace, Edmond. "Strategy for Human Rights." *Month*, 12 (April 1979).

Handy, Rollo. *The Measurement of Values*. St. Louis: Warren H. Green, 1970.

Herbert, Gary. "Human Rights and Historicist Ontology." *Philosophical Forum*, 9 (Fall 1979).

Howe, Irving. "Socialism and Liberalism: Articles of Conciliation." *Dissent* (Winter 1977).

Jaspers, Karl. *The Question of German Guilt*. New York: Capricorn Books, 1961.

Kahn, M. Zafrulla. *Islam and Human Rights*. London: The London Mosque, 1976.

Kamenka, Eugene. *Human Rights*. New York: St. Martin's Press, 1978.

Kelman, Herbert. "The Conditions, Criteria, and Dialectics of Human Dignity." *International Studies Quarterly*, 21, no. 3 (September 1977).

Kent, E. A., ed. *Law and Philosophy*. New York: Appleton, Century and Crofts, 1970.

Kolnai, Aurel. *The War Against the West*. New York: The Viking Press, 1938.

Kuhn, James. "Conflicts between Rights; Substance and Sophistry." *Christianity and Crisis*, 38 (January 15, 1979).

Kutner, Luis, ed. *The Right to Individual Freedom: A Symposium on World Habeas Corpus*. Coral Gables: University of Miami Press, 1970.

Laqueur, Walter, ed. *Human Rights Reader*, Philadelphia: Temple University Press, 1979.

———. "Interpretations of Terrorism: Fact, Fiction and Political Science." *Journal of Contemporary History*, 12 (1977).

Leonhard, Wolfgang. *Three Faces of Marxism*. New York: Holt, Rinehart and Winston, 1974.

Loescher, Gil. *Human Rights: A Global Crisis*. New York: E. P. Dutton, 1979.

Lukacs, Georg. *Marxism and Human Liberation*. New York: Delta Books, 1973.

Lukes, Steven, *Individualism*. New York: Harper Torchbooks, 1973.

Lyons, David, ed. *Rights*. Belmont, Calif.: Wadsworth Publishing Co., 1979.

———. "Human Rights and the General Welfare." *Philosophy and Public Affairs*, 6, no. 2 (Winter 1977).

Machan, Tibor. "Are There Any Human Rights?" *The Personalist* (April 1978).

———. "Prima Facie Versus Natural (Human) Rights." *Journal of Value Inquiry*, 10, no. 2(Summer 1976).

———. *Human Rights and Human Liberties*. Chicago: Nelson-Hall, 1975.

Mackay, Donald. *Human Science and Human Dignity*. Downer's Grove, Ill.: Inter-Varsity Press, 1979.

McKeon, Richard. "The Philosophic Bases and Material Circumstances of the Rights of Man." *Ethics*, 58, no. 3 (April 1948).

Melden, A. I. *Rights and Persons*. Berkeley: University of California Press, 1977.

———, ed. *Human Rights*. Belmont, Calif.: Wadsworth Publishing Co., 1970.

Meltzer, Milton. *Human Rights Book*. New York: Farrar, Straus and Giroux, 1979.

Mower, A. Glenn, Jr. "Human Rights in Western Europe: Progress and Problems." *International Affairs*, 52, no. 2 (April 1976).

Muelder, Walter. "Socialism Revisited: A Personalistic Perspective." *Idealistic Studies*, 9 (January 1979).

Norton, David. *Personal Destinies, A Philosophy of Ethical Individualism*. Princeton, N. J.: Princeton University Press, 1976.

Oppenheim, Feliz. *Dimensions of Freedom*. New York: St. Martin's Press, 1961.

Owen, David. *Human Rights*. New York: W. W. Norton, 1978.

Peffer, Rodney. "A Defense of Rights to Well-Being." *Philosophy and Public Affairs*, 8, no. 1 (Fall 1978).

Perelman, Ch. "Liberty, Equality and Public Interest." *Archives for Philosophy of Law and Social Philosophy*, 10, Wiesbaden: F. S. Verlag, 1977.

———. "Equality and Justice." *Equality*, 5. Brussels: Bruylant, 1977.

Perry, Ralph B. *Puritanism and Democracy*. New York: Harper Torchbooks, 1944.

Peyraube, A. "New-found Freedom in China." *Tel Quel*, 80 (1979).

Pollis, A., ed. *Human Rights: Cultural and Ideological Perspectives*. New York: Praeger, 1979.

Powell, J. Enoch. "Human Rights." *Journal of Medical Ethics*, 3, no. 4 (1977).

Rader, Melvin. *Marx's Interpretation of History*. New York: Oxford University Press, 1979.

———. *Ethics and the Human Community*. New York: Holt, Rinehart and Winston, 1966.

Raphael, D. D., ed. *Political Theory and the Rights of Man*. Bloomington: Indiana University Press, 1967.

Rempel, Henry. "On Forcing People to Be Free." *Ethics*, 87, no. 1 (October 1976).

Rosenbaum, Alan S. "Socialism Versus Liberal Capitalism: Conflict or Compromise in the Works of J. S. Mill?" *Philosophy Research Activities*, forthcoming.

———. "Socialism, Liberalism and the So-called Mixed Economy." *Darshana International Journal of Philosophy*, 19, no. 2 (April 1979).

———. "The Idea of Liberalism and J. S. Mill." *Philosophy in Context*, 5 (May 1976).

Rubin, Barry M. *Human Rights and U.S. Foreign Policy*. Boulder, Colo.: Westview Press, 1979.

Said, Abdul A., ed. *Human Rights and World Order*. New York: Praeger, 1978.

Sapontzis, S. F. "The Value of Human Rights." *Journal of Value Inquiry*, 12 (Fall 1978).

Schaff, Adam. *Marxism and the Human Individual*. New York: McGraw-Hill Book Co., 1970.

Shibata, Shingo. "Fundamental Human Rights and Problems of Freedom." *Social Praxis*, 3, no. 4 (1975).

Shuchman, Philip, ed. *Cohen and Cohen's Readings in Jurisprudence and Legal Philosophy.* Boston: Little, Brown and Co., 1979.

Simpson, A. W. B., ed. *Oxford Essays in Jurisprudence.* Oxford: Clarendon Press, 1973.

Talmon, J. L. *The Origins of Totalitarian Democracy.* New York: W. W. Norton and Co., 1970.

Watson, David. "Welfare Rights and Human Rights." *Journal of Social Policy,* 6, pt. 1 (1977).

Wolfe, Alan. *The Limits of Legitimacy.* New York: The Free Press, 1977.

Name Index

Subject Index

About the Contributors

Leslie Armour is professor of philosophy at the University of Ottawa, Canada, and director of the Center for Canadian Philosophical Studies. His books include *The Rational and The Real* and *Logic and Reality*. He has published a wide range of papers in both interdisciplinary and professional philosophical journals.

D. P. Chattopadhyaya is a member of Parliament in India and professor of philosophy at Jadavpur University, Calcutta. His books include *What Is Real and What Is Dead in Indian Philosophy, Individuals and Worlds: Essays in Anthropological Rationalism*, and *History, Society, and Polity*.

R. S. Downie is professor of moral philosophy at Glasgow University, Scotland. Among his books are *Government Action and Morality, Respect for Persons*, and *Roles and Values*. He is a contributor to many philosophical journals: *Mind, Analysis, Aristotelian Society*, and *Political Studies*.

Robert J. Henle is currently (since 1976) McDonnell Professor of Justice in American Society at St. Louis University, Missouri. He taught philosophy for many years before he became president of Georgetown University (1969) in Washington, D.C. He is author of over 200 books and articles, and a recipient of many awards, including six honorary degrees.

Abraham Kaplan is Gruenblat Professor of Social Ethics and chairman of the Department of Philosophy at the University of Haifa, Israel. He is the author of *In Pursuit of Wisdom, The Conduct of Inquiry, American Ethics and Public Policy, The New World of Philosophy, Power and Society*, and many other writings.

Andrew Levine is associate professor of philosophy at the University of Wisconsin-Madison. His writings include *The Politics of Autonomy: A Kantian Reading of Rousseau's Social Contract* and numerous articles in international philosophical journals.

Tibor Machan is associate professor of philosophy at the State University College at Fredonia, New York, and educational programs director of the Reason Foundation, Santa Barbara, California. His books include *Human Rights and Human Liberties, The Pseudo-Science of B. F. Skinner*, and an edited volume entitled *The Libertarian Alternative*. His many articles have appeared in such journals as *Harvard Journal of*

Law and Public Policy, American Philosophical Quarterly, The Personalist, law reviews, and others.

Seyyed H. Nasr, currently professor of religion at Temple University, was former director of the Iranian Academy of Philosophy. He is a distinguished authority on Islamic philosophy and religion. His most well-known books in the English language include *Islam and the Plight of Modern Man, Science and Civilization in Islam, Ideals and Realities of Islam.* Also, his numerous articles have appeared in professional philosophical journals.

Ch. Perelman is director of the Free University of Brussels, Belgium. His many books include *The Idea of Justice and the Problem of Argument, New Rhetoric: A Treatise on Argumentation, Justice,* and *An Historical Introduction to Philosophical Thinking.* He is a frequent contributor to scholarly international publications in the fields of philosophy and law.

Ishwar Sharma is a visiting professor and lecturer at American universities. He is a former chairman of the Philosophy Department and dean of students at Udaipur University, India. His most prominent publications include *Ethical Philosophies of India, India's Democracy and the Communist Challenge,* and *Essentials of Ethics: East and West,* and many articles in philosophical journals.

Efraim Shmueli is currently professor emeritus and head of the Society for Phenomenology and Existentialism in Israel. His many publications in both English and Hebrew include *Studies in Phenomenology, Max Weber: Politics as a Vocation,* and *History of the Jewish People in Modern Times* (seven volumes). He is a frequent contributor to professional journals in the philosophical disciplines of metaphysics, history of philosophy, and phenomenology.

Peter K. Y. Woo is professor of philosophy at the National Taiwan University and editor-in-chief of *Universitas* and of *Column of Western Philosophers.* He is a leading authority on Chinese and Western philosophies. His writings include over 250 books and articles which have appeared in Chinese, German, and English publications.

About the Editor

ALAN S. ROSENBAUM is Assistant Professor of Philosophy at Cleveland State University. His articles have appeared in *Darshana International Journal of Philosophy*, *Philosophy Research Archives*, and *Philosophy in Context*.